THE GREAT Chicken COOKBOOK

Thai chicken stir-fry, *page 203*

THE GREAT
Chicken
COOKBOOK

A feast of simple, delicious recipes for every occasion

Reader's Digest

The world's most popular meal

A generation or so ago, chicken was a rare treat: a special meal that was eagerly anticipated and greatly relished. Today chicken is so abundantly available we almost take it for granted, so it's time to give this beautiful-tasting bird the appreciation it deserves. Chicken has so many virtues: it's very economical, highly nutritious and amazingly adaptable, suited to roasting, poaching, sautéing or stir-frying. Whether you have time to cook a leisurely dinner or just minutes to get a meal on the table, here you'll find a whole host of wonderful chicken dishes from which to choose. From appetising starters, delicious salads and perfect picnic treats to all manner of tempting mains, you can rest assured a tasty meal awaits.

THE EDITORS

Chicken tikka, page 114

Chicken cacciatore with spaghetti, *page 182*

Contents

Chicken basics: All you need to know

Besides its beautiful flavour and texture, versatility and budget-friendly price, there are two other great reasons why chicken is a top choice for home cooks: many cuts cook quickly, and it is low in fat if you use portions trimmed of skin and fat.

In this book we have labelled recipes 'Quick' and 'Low Fat'—to help you choose recipes at a glance.

If you're in a hurry, you'll appreciate the recipes labelled 'Quick', as these can be prepared and cooked in 30 minutes or less, from start to finish. If you're watching your weight or fat intake, look for recipes labelled 'Low Fat'—these contain a maximum of 30 g fat per serve, with no more than 8 g of saturated fat. Some recipes are both quick and low fat!

For easy reference, you'll find the Low Fat and Quick recipes indexed separately on page 319.

Rotisserie chickens are a convenient option when a recipe calls for pre-cooked chicken

Buying chicken

Chicken comes in so many different forms—whole, cut into various parts and portions (as shown in the chart on the opposite page), pre-seasoned and ready-to-cook, already roasted or rotisserie-cooked, and as cold cuts and sausages.

Serving chicken does not always mean turning on the oven or stove: you can pick up a cooked chicken on your way home and combine it with your choice of fresh ingredients to make a quick, satisfying meal.

Here's a basic rundown of some of the main chicken choices available.

Tenderloins (tenders)

These delicate morsels are cut from the chicken breast—the narrow strips at the side that can be separated from the rest of the breast meat. When you buy chicken tenderloins you pay a premium for the labour involved in preparing them.

Minced (ground) chicken

The variety sold at the supermarket is often made from thigh meat and skin. For a lower-fat version, it's easy to make your own: buy boneless chicken breasts, cut them into chunks and chop them in a food processor, using an on/off pulse action.

Chicken nuggets

These are small pieces of chicken breast that have been crumbed and deep-fried, fast-food style. They can be reheated in the oven or microwave. Children love chicken nuggets, but remember that their fat content is quite high.

Pre-seasoned (uncooked) chicken

For a fresh hot meal with minimal preparation, you can buy pre-seasoned chicken, either whole or presented in parts such as boneless breasts, breast strips for stir-fries, chunks for skewering, or wings for baking. The chicken has already been seasoned with a spice rub or a marinade—all you need to do is take it home and cook it.

Fresh chicken portions

This table shows the most popular cuts of chicken—the varieties you'll find stocked in most supermarkets. These cuts are also available frozen.

CHICKEN PART	SOLD AS	HOW MUCH PER SERVE?
Whole and half chickens	• Available in various sizes, from 1.2 kg (2½ lb) to 2.5 kg (5 lb), and are sometimes just referred to as small, regular or large chickens, or by a size number • Small chickens can also be sold split in half lengthwise	Allow 250 g (8 oz) per person
Quarters	• Breast quarters consist of a split breast with the wing and back portion still attached—all white meat • Leg quarters consist of a drumstick, thigh and back portion—all dark meat	Allow 250 g (8 oz) per person
Breasts	• Whole breasts have the breastbone and both sets of ribs • Split breasts, or breast halves, are just one side of the rib cage; they are sold bone-in, with skin, as well as skinned and boned	1 bone-in breast half, or 1 large or 2 small boneless, skinless halves, per person
Legs	• Legs consist of the drumstick with the thigh attached; sometimes referred to as chicken marylands • Thighs are the meaty portion above the knee joint, either bone-in with skin on, or skinned and boned • Drumsticks are the lower portion of the leg	1 leg, 2 thighs or 2 drumsticks per person; 2 drumettes as a starter
Wings	• Whole wings consist of the little drumstick, the two-boned mid-joint, and the short wing tip • Drumettes are the meaty part of the chicken wing, with the wing tip discarded	As a starter, 1 whole wing
Livers	• Sold in tubs or trays; or save up (and freeze) the single livers that come with the giblets of a whole chicken (store them in the freezer)	375 g (¾ lb) for 8 servings

Rotisserie chicken

The popularity of rotisserie chicken—whole chickens cooked on a turning spit—has skyrocketed in recent years. Many supermarkets feature rotisseries that turn out juicy, crisp-skinned roasted birds all day long. Follow your nose to the deli department to find these, and be sure to choose one that's plump and not dried out.

Roasted or barbecued chicken

These are widely available from supermarkets, delicatessens and restaurants. Choose from whole or half chickens, legs or breasts; reheat the chicken in a conventional oven or microwave, or enjoy it cold.

Chicken sausages

Many of the same types of sausages traditionally made with beef, veal or pork are now made with chicken—such as Italian-style sausages and chorizo-style sausages. Both fresh and fully cooked sausages are available. If you can't find them at your supermarket, check at a gourmet grocer, butcher or chicken shop.

Chicken franks are similar to hotdog sausages, except they are made from chicken. They may be slightly lower in fat than their beef or pork counterparts, depending on whether skin and dark meat have been included. Like all processed meats, they are high in sodium, so if this is an issue, always check the label.

Getting the most for your money

In terms of cost, there are several factors to consider when shopping for chicken. The more chicken is processed (boned, skinned, cut up), the higher the price. Whole chickens are almost always cheaper than chicken parts, but of course you'll have to do the work yourself if you want individual serving portions. Cutting up a whole chicken into serving portions really isn't difficult to do; see the step-by-step photos on pages 14 and 15.

Supermarkets regularly offer sales on various chicken parts and whole birds; stock up on your favourites when they're well priced and freeze them for later use (see pages 12 and 13).

Boneless, skinless chicken vs bone-in chicken with skin

There are good reasons for buying both types of cuts. With boneless, skinless cuts there is virtually no waste—you get exactly what you pay for. If you're watching your fat intake, you won't want the skin anyway. Boneless parts also cook more quickly.

On the other hand, bone-in cuts with skin cost less, and it's not too tricky to bone them yourself (see the step-by-step photos, right). Bone-in parts also hold their shape better, and meat is more flavourful when cooked on the bone. Furthermore, the skin keeps the chicken moist while it's cooking.

Recipes in this book will specify whether to use chicken with or without the skin and bones, so always follow the recipe, as it will be using the cut most appropriate to that particular dish.

Whole breasts vs breast halves

Chicken breasts are usually sold split, with each half-breast intended as a portion. However, you can also buy whole, bone-in chicken breasts and split them yourself (see the step-by-step photos, right).

Ultimately, let the price—and how much time you have—guide you in your choice.

SKINNING & BONING A THIGH

1 Grasp the skin at the edge of the thigh and pull the skin off. Remove any loose pieces of fat.

2 Place the thigh skinned-side down. With a sharp paring knife, cut along the bone, from end to end, on the thinner side of the thigh. Cut around one end of the bone to free it.

3 Grasp the free end of the bone and scrape the flesh away from it. Finally, cut around the opposite end of the bone and pull it free.

SKINNING & BONING A BREAST HALF

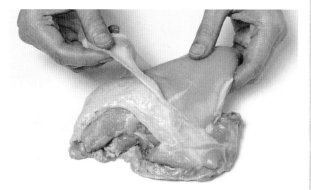

1 Grasp the skin at the edge of the breast and pull the skin off. Remove any loose pieces of fat.

2 With the chicken skinned-side down, start at the thicker side of the breast and work a boning knife between the flesh and the rib bones. Keep the knife pressed against the bones to remove the flesh as cleanly as possible.

3 Continue cutting along the bones with a slicing motion to free the breast meat in a single piece.

HALVING A WHOLE BREAST

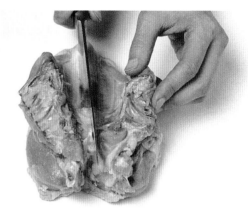

1 Begin by scoring (but not cutting through) the bony side of the breast with a chef's knife. (This helps when you pop the breastbone out; see below.)

2 Holding the breast skin-side down, bend the two sides back until the breastbone pops up.

3 Pull out the breastbone. If you want single-serving breast halves, place the breast skin-side down and cut through it lengthwise.

Safe handling

As with all meats and seafood, bacteria may be present in raw or undercooked chicken, and the organism most associated with chicken is salmonella. You can't tell by looking at a chicken whether these bacteria are present, so to avoid any contamination problems, follow these simple guidelines.

- **Refrigerate or freeze chicken** as soon as you bring it home. Remove the wrapping and rewrap it in a zip-seal plastic bag. If freezing, remove the air from the bag. Your refrigerator should be at 4°C (40°F) or lower, and your freezer at −17°C (0°F)—check with a freezer thermometer. Keep the chicken refrigerated until you're ready to prepare and cook it. Thaw frozen chicken in the fridge or in cold water, not on the benchtop.
- **Store uncooked raw chicken** on the bottom shelf of the fridge, and be careful not to let its juices touch other foods. If salmonella is present, it can cross-contaminate other foods. The greatest danger from cross-contamination is to foods that will be eaten uncooked, such as fruit and vegetables.
- **Keep a separate cutting board** for raw meat, poultry and fish. The best materials are dense ones—either sturdy plastic or a hardwood. After use, scrub the board with hot soapy water or, if it's not a wooden board, wash it in the dishwasher. (Although a plastic or hardwood cutting board is preferable for safety, we have photographed all our step-by-step photos on a white laminated surface for clarity.)
- **Use a separate sponge** for wiping benchtops (not the one used for washing dishes). Wash the sponge frequently, preferably in the dishwasher. Replace it often so it doesn't harbour bacteria.
- **Don't prepare chicken** at the same time as you are handling foods that will be eaten raw, such as salad greens.
- **Wash all utensils,** your hands and the benchtop with hot soapy water after preparing raw chicken.
- **Discard the marinade** after marinating chicken, unless you are using it for basting, in which case it will get hot enough to be safe. If you want to use the marinade as a sauce, bring it to a full boil and allow to boil for 1 minute to kill off bacteria.
- **Remove all the stuffing** from a stuffed bird while you're carving. Refrigerate any leftovers separately.

- **Don't place cooked food** on a plate that has held raw chicken. For instance, if you bring raw chicken outside for barbecuing, bring a second platter to hold the cooked chicken.
- **Cook chicken** to an internal temperature of at least 71°C (160°F)—see page 20 for more detail on this.
- **Refrigerate leftovers promptly,** and in hot weather immediately—shortly after cooking, chicken becomes an ideal medium for bacterial growth.

Thawing frozen chicken

- **Never thaw chicken at room temperature,** because of the danger of bacteria multiplying.
- **If time allows,** let chicken thaw in the refrigerator in its original wrapping, allowing 5 hours per 500 g (1 lb). A very large roasting bird may take several days to thaw.
- **For speedier thawing,** place the wrapped chicken in a sealable plastic bag and set it in a basin of cold water. Change the water every half hour. A whole chicken will thaw in 2–3 hours and a package of boneless breasts will thaw in under an hour.
- **You can use a microwave** to thaw frozen chicken. Follow the manufacturer's directions carefully, and be sure to cook the chicken immediately after thawing.

Prepare chicken separately to foods that will be eaten raw, such as salad greens

Selection and storage

- **Shop for chicken in a reputable, clean store** that has a rapid turnover. The contents of the meat cabinet should look clean and feel cold, and there should be no unpleasant odours.

- **Any wrapping should be well sealed,** and not torn or punctured. If the chicken is visible through clear packaging, it should look plump and clean. There should not be an excessive amount of liquid in the packet.

- **Look for the 'use-by' or 'sell-by' date** on packaged chicken and chicken products. The 'sell-by' date is the last day on which you should buy the product; you can confidently serve the chicken within 2 days after the 'sell-by' date. The 'use-by' date is the last date on which you should consume the product for optimal quality. Buy the package with the latest possible date, and if you can't use the chicken immediately, freeze it. Don't rely totally on the dates marked on the package: take a good look at what you're buying, and trust your nose.

- **Skin colour** doesn't indicate the freshness of chicken. Depending on the feed used, chicken skin can vary between shades of white and yellow. However, chicken skin should never look discoloured, and the flesh should look pink, not grey.

- **Chicken should always smell fresh**—it should either have no aroma at all, or a pleasant 'chicken smell'. As soon as you get home, unwrap the chicken and sniff. If it smells 'off', return it to the store.

Storing chicken

Wrap or cover fresh or cooked chicken before refrigerating. When freezing chicken, overwrap with plastic or foil, then label and date the package.

PRODUCT	REFRIGERATED AT 4°C (40°F)	FROZEN AT −17°C (0°F)
Fresh whole chicken, raw	1–2 days	9 months
Fresh chicken parts, raw	1–2 days	9 months
Minced (ground) chicken, raw, and fresh chicken sausages	1–2 days	3–4 months
Liver and giblets	1–2 days	3–4 months
Roast, baked, grilled (broiled) or barbecued chicken, leftover home-cooked	3–4 days	4 months
Cooked chicken in soup or gravy, leftover home-cooked	1–2 days	6 months
Cooked minced (ground) chicken (burgers or meatloaf)	3–4 days	2–3 months
Chicken casseroles or soups	3–4 days	4–6 months
Chicken stock or gravy, homemade	1–2 days	6 months
Store-bought roast, barbecued or rotisserie chicken	3–4 days	4 months
Packaged cooked chicken, unopened	5–7 days	3–6 months
Packaged cooked chicken, after opening	1–3 days	4 months
Chicken cold cuts, unopened	2 weeks	1–2 months
Chicken cold cuts, after opening	3–5 days	1–2 months
Cooked chicken sausages	3–4 days	9 months
Chicken salad	3–4 days	not recommended

Preparing chicken

Here are some basic techniques for preparing and seasoning chicken before cooking.

Cutting a chicken into serving pieces

You can buy a chicken already cut up for cooking, or chop up the bird yourself. To get fairly equal servings from a whole bird, see the step-by-step photos featured here. For the recipes in this book, we call for chicken to be cut into 8 serving pieces and occasionally into 10 pieces. The 8 serving pieces are: 2 drumsticks, 2 thighs and 4 breast quarters. The 10 pieces include the wings (although, because they're largely skin, bone and fat, wings are not really equivalent to leaner, meatier portions of the bird).

Marinating chicken

Letting chicken soak in a marinade is a wonderful way to add subtle flavour. There is often an acidic element in the marinade, such as wine, vinegar or citrus juice. Acidic ingredients will penetrate the surface of the chicken slightly. Most marinades also contain some oil, but this is not an essential component. The other ingredients are flavourings, such as herbs, spices, chillies, citrus zest and ginger.

When a recipe says the chicken can be marinated overnight, it's usually fine to let it sit for up to 24 hours. If the marinade is acidic, however, it can start to break down the chicken and make it mushy, so marinate the bird for no longer than the indicated time.

Always place the chicken and marinade in a non-reactive container, such as a glass, ceramic or stainless steel bowl or baking dish. A heavy-duty sealable plastic bag also works very well, and makes it easy to turn the chicken periodically to coat it with marinade. Place the bag in a dish just in case of leaks; if you're not using a bag, cover the dish.

Always marinate chicken in the refrigerator.

Using seasoning rubs

Rubbing a mixture of spices, herbs or other dry flavourings onto chicken skin (or skinless chicken) before cooking serves as the dry equivalent of a marinade. If you're cooking the chicken with the skin on, be sure to rub some of the flavouring mixture under the skin as well. That way, if you remove the skin before eating, the flavour will remain.

CUTTING UP A WHOLE CHICKEN

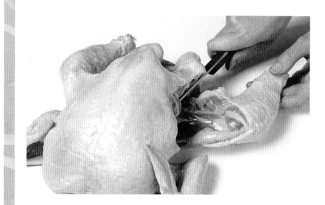

1 Pull the leg away from the body and cut through the skin and flesh with a cook's knife. Bend the thigh back until the joint pops apart, then cut through it.

2 Start to cut into the flesh at the joint between the leg and thigh. Bend the two sections together to help you locate the joint. Cut through the joint.

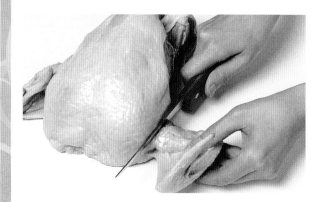

3 Pull the wing out from the body; cut through the skin. Bend the wing back until the joint breaks; cut through the joint. Cut off wing tips and save for stock.

4 Starting at the tail end, use poultry shears to cut through the rib bones along each side of the backbone to separate the breast from the back.

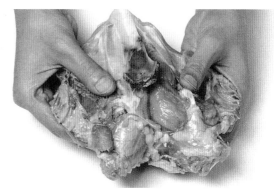

7 Holding the breast skin-side down, bend the two sides back until the breastbone pops up. Pull out the breastbone.

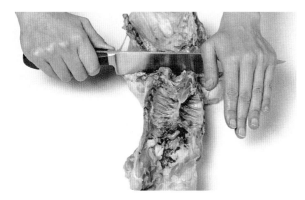

5 Open up the two pieces to expose the joints at the neck end, and cut through the joints with a cook's knife. Discard the back or save for stock.

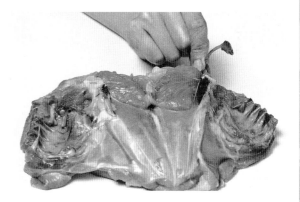

8 Check the flesh at the top of the breast for the wishbone and pull it out. With poultry shears or a cook's knife, cut the breast lengthwise into 2 halves.

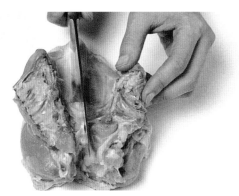

6 Begin by scoring (but not cutting through) the bony side of the breast with a cook's knife. (This helps when you pop the breastbone out; see step 7.)

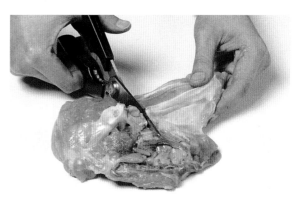

9 Using a pair of poultry shears, cut crosswise through each breast half, giving you a total of 4 breast pieces.

Making chicken cutlets

Chicken cutlets (also known as escalopes or scallops, and sometimes sold as schnitzels) are the quickest-cooking portions for sautéing; they can also be rolled around fillings for an elegant presentation.

Cutlets are made by pounding boneless, skinless chicken breasts with a meat pounder (or a rolling pin or wooden mallet) until the meat is of an even thickness—usually 5 mm to 1 cm (¼ or ½ inch), depending on the recipe (see step-by-step photos, above). Be gentle when pounding the chicken: if you're used to pounding veal for scaloppine, you'll find that chicken is much softer.

Cutting chicken breast for stir-fries

Cutting ingredients into uniform pieces is the secret to a successful stir-fry. Because boneless chicken breasts are tapered in shape, simply cutting across the breast will produce pieces of unequal size. To avoid this problem, cut the chicken following our step-by-step photos, above. Firstly separate the tenderloin (tender) and set aside, then cut the narrow end of the breast crosswise into strips about 1 cm (½ inch) wide, until the portion that remains is roughly rectangular. Cut that piece in half lengthwise, then cut each piece crosswise into strips. Finally, cut the tenderloin crosswise into strips.

MAKING A CHICKEN CUTLET

1 Place a boneless, skinless chicken breast half on a sheet of plastic wrap. Cover with a second sheet of plastic wrap and pound with the flat side of a meat pounder or a rolling pin.

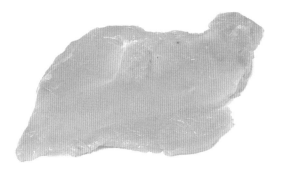

2 Concentrate on the thicker portion of the chicken breast so that the cutlet is of an even thickness. If the escalope is to be sautéed, it is usually pounded 1 cm (½ inch) thick. If it is to be stuffed and rolled up, it should be pounded 5 mm (¼ inch) thick (as shown above).

CUTTING CHICKEN FOR STIR-FRIES

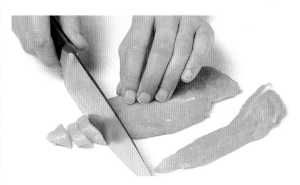

1 Cut off the tenderloin (tender). With a sharp knife, cut the narrow end of the chicken breast crosswise into strips 1 cm (½ inch) wide. Stop cutting as soon as the breast has been squared off.

2 Cut the square section of chicken breast lengthwise into 2 pieces; the idea is to cut all pieces uniformly, approximately the width of the chicken tenderloin (tender). Then cut each piece crosswise into strips 1 cm (½ inch) wide. Cut the chicken tenderloin crosswise also.

Stuffing flavourings under the skin

Quite a different process from filling a bird with a starchy stuffing, this creates a savoury layer between the skin and flesh. Even if you remove the skin before you eat the chicken, the flavourful coating will remain.

The stuffing can be fresh herbs, lemon slices, or a smooth, creamy mixture that you can spread onto the chicken without tearing the skin.

If using a whole chicken, place it on a board, breast-side up, with the neck facing away from you. Use your fingers to gently separate the skin from the flesh of the drumsticks and breast, being careful not to tear the skin. Gently slip in some herbs or flavoured butter and pat the skin back into place.

If using a chicken breast, gently loosen the skin from the edge of a bone-in breast half. Slip your fingers under the skin to make a pocket, then place flavourings (such as lemon slices) under the skin. Take care to leave the skin attached in as many spots as possible so the flavouring does not fall out.

Crumbing and flouring

Coating chicken with crumbs or flour before it is fried, sautéed or baked creates a tasty crust that may be coarse and crunchy, or fine and delicate.

These coatings need something to help them adhere to the chicken, such as beaten eggs or eggwhites, milk or another liquid.

After moistening the chicken in the liquid, roll it in the coating so that all sides are evenly covered, then gently tap off any excess coating.

If you have time, refrigerate the coated chicken pieces for at least 1 hour: this allows the coating to set, so it is less likely to come off while the chicken is being cooked.

Trussing chicken

A whole chicken that is destined for roasting is commonly 'trussed', which means that its legs are tied together. This helps to keep the bird more compact when it is baking in the oven. Not only does trussing lend a nicer presentation to the bird, it also helps to keep the stuffing inside from drying out.

Forget about the traditional needle-and-thread technique: trussing is really very easy. After placing any stuffing or aromatics inside the chicken cavity, all you need to do is firmly hold the ends of the drumsticks together and tie them up with a long piece of kitchen string.

To further enhance the shape of the roast chicken (and to keep the wing tips from scorching), twist the wings slightly and tuck their tips behind the 'shoulders' of the chicken. Just before carving the chicken, snip the string with scissors to release it.

TRUSSING CHICKEN

1 Bring the 'ankles' of the drumsticks together and secure them with a long piece of kitchen string. Tie the string in a double knot.

2 Twist the wings and tuck the wing tips behind the shoulders of the chicken. This helps stop the wing tips burning and also keeps the chicken in a nicer shape as it roasts.

Cooking chicken

Cooking techniques are usually divided into 'moist heat' methods (stewing, braising, poaching) and 'dry heat' methods (roasting, baking, barbecuing and grilling/broiling). Stir-frying and sautéing fall somewhere in between the two.

In general, leaner cuts of chicken (breast meat, especially skinless) fare better when cooked by moist heat, while juicier, fattier meats (dark meat, such as drumsticks and thighs, especially with the skin on) will still be moist and juicy after cooking by dry heat. The chart on the opposite page shows you which cuts are best suited for which methods.

Stewing
Chicken and vegetables are slow-cooked in a deep pot of stock or other liquid until all the ingredients are tender and the flavours well blended. Some ingredients, such as onions, may be browned first to bring out their flavour, but some recipes omit this step, resulting in a stew with a creamy, delicate colour and texture.

Braising
In this two-stage process, chicken and other ingredients are browned, then a small amount of liquid is added to the pan. The pan is tightly covered; the mixture is then simmered on the stove or in the oven until the food is tender and the liquid has formed a delicious sauce.

Sautéing and frying
Sauté means 'jump'. When you sauté, you continually shake the pan so that the food 'jumps' as it cooks. This constant motion prevents sticking, even when a very small amount of oil is used. More oil is used for frying and the chicken may be coated with flour or breadcrumbs.

Stir-frying
This technique is fast, fun and invites creativity in combining ingredients. You don't need a wok to cook up a stir-fry—in fact, on a standard gas or electric stove, a heavy-based frying pan or skillet will often do a better job. The key is to have the wok or pan sizzling hot before adding the oil, and to cut all your ingredients into small, uniformly sized pieces (see 'Cutting chicken breast for stir-fries,' page 16). Stir and toss the food vigorously until it is only just cooked through. Serve stir-fries immediately, while they're steaming hot.

POACHING CHICKEN BREASTS

1 Poach chicken breasts for about 15 minutes in enough water to cover by at least 1 cm (½ inch). The water—which can include simple seasonings such as bay leaves or peppercorns—should be at a simmer, not a rolling boil.

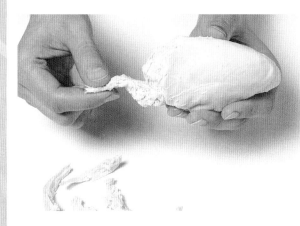

2 As soon as the chicken is cooked through, remove it from the poaching liquid to cool. You can then slice it, or shred it—as shown here—by pulling off pieces with your fingers. The shreds will follow the natural grain of the meat.

Poaching
A technique most often used for skinless breasts, poaching is the gentlest way to cook chicken. The breasts are placed in a shallow pan of simmering liquid (water, broth or even fruit juice), to which simple seasonings are usually added. The pan is covered and the chicken cooked at a bare simmer until tender (see the step-by-step photos above).

Grilling (broiling)

Here food is cooked under an open flame or electrical heating element. Grilling quickly cooks the flesh of the chicken, and if it's not protected—by its skin, a crumb coating or a thick, clinging sauce—it will be tough and dry. Our recipes direct you to position the oven rack so the food is 15–20 cm (6–8 inches) below the heat source. If your grill does not allow this, bake the chicken at a high temperature (230°C/450°F/Gas 8) in the upper third of the oven for roughly the same amount of time, checking often to ensure it is not overcooking.

Barbecuing

Cooking chicken portions and burgers over the coals of a barbecue grill adds a delicious smoky flavour. Like grilling, barbecuing employs a fierce heat that can dry out lean chicken if it isn't sauced or basted. Another precaution about barbecuing: fatty drippings falling onto the coals can create harmful substances called HCAs, or heterocyclic amines, which are then deposited on the food as the smoke rises. To avoid this, don't place the chicken directly over the coals. Instead, push the coals to the side, leaving a clear space for drippings to land.

Baking

The term 'baking' is generally used for poultry portions that are cooked in the oven in a shallow pan, either covered or uncovered. To help keep the chicken moist, it is often baked with vegetables, or in a sauce.

Roasting

For this dry-heat method, in which the food is cooked by the circulating hot air in the oven, the chicken should be elevated above the bottom of the roasting pan on a rack (see page 21). Rubbing the chicken skin with fat before roasting helps it brown nicely; basting helps too, but it doesn't keep the chicken moist, because the basting liquid rolls right off the chicken skin.

It's important to let a roast chicken stand for at least 5 minutes before carving: this allows the juices to redistribute themselves throughout the meat so that it's juicy all the way through.

Which cooking method for which cut of chicken?

Although chicken is very versatile, some cuts are more suitable for certain cooking methods than others.

PART	SUITABLE COOKING METHODS
Whole	Roast, barbecue (on a spit)
Halves	Roast, bake, grill (broil), barbecue, braise, stew
Quarters	Bake, grill (broil), barbecue, braise, stew, fry
Breast halves, bone-in	Bake, sauté, grill (broil), barbecue, braise, poach, fry
Breasts, boneless	Sauté, poach, grill (broil), barbecue (whole or on skewers), bake; cook in foil packets; slice for stir-fry; pound for cutlets to sauté or stuff; chop for minced (ground) chicken
Legs	Roast, bake, grill (broil), barbecue, braise, stew, fry
Thighs, bone-in	Bake, grill (broil), barbecue, braise, stew
Thighs, boneless	Bake, grill (broil), barbecue, braise, stew, sauté, stir-fry; chop for minced (ground) chicken
Drumsticks	Roast, bake, grill (broil), barbecue, oven-fry, braise, stew, fry
Wings	Bake, grill (broil), barbecue, braise, fry
Minced (ground) chicken	Grill (broil), barbecue (burgers); bake (meatloaf); simmer (pasta sauce and chilli mixes)
Liver	Sauté, grill (broil), barbecue
Neck and giblets (gizzard, heart)	Sauté and use in stuffing; use for making stock

When is it cooked?

- **Chicken must always** be completely cooked through. Rare poultry is neither palatable nor safe to eat. Chicken should be cooked to an internal temperature of at least 71°C (160°F), and the best way to test this is with an instant-read thermometer (see page 21). However, even when cooked to this temperature, chicken may not be 'done' in terms of appetising taste and texture. The meat may still be pink, and the juices may appear cloudy when the flesh is pierced. If so, keep cooking the chicken until the juices run clear, and when, on a whole chicken, the leg joint will wiggle easily in its socket. At this point, the thermometer will read about 77°C (170°F).

- **'Done' does not mean overdone.** Chicken— especially when cooked by dry-heat methods—can quickly change from perfectly cooked to dry and tough. Check for doneness promptly, and remember that retained heat in roasted and baked chicken will continue to cook the bird a little after it comes out of the oven.

- **Breast meat, being leaner, cooks more quickly** than the dark meat of the legs and thighs. If you want perfectly done chicken when cooking a cut-up bird, check the breast portions first and remove them when they're done, leaving the dark-meat parts to finish cooking. Keep the breast portions warm until serving time by covering them with foil.

Nutrition facts

- **Chicken is high-quality protein.** Substituting chicken for some of the red meat in your diet is an excellent way to get your share of high-quality protein. Chicken is also a rich source of B vitamins and the minerals iron and phosphorus.

- **The cholesterol content** is the same as most meats and other poultry at 20–25 mg cholesterol per 25 g (1 oz). Cholesterol is not actually found in the skin, but in the lean muscle of animal protein. So chicken—even skinless chicken—does not contain markedly less cholesterol than beef or other meats. However, saturated fat intake also affects our blood cholesterol levels, and skinless chicken is lower in saturated fat than any cut of beef, pork or lamb.

- **To reduce the fat,** follow the special recipe tips such as suggestions for simple ingredient substitutions and alternative cooking techniques. You'll find these tips in the recipes under the heading, 'To Reduce the Fat'. See also our tips in the box on the opposite page.

- **Watch the kilojoule (calorie) content.** Some dishes may appear to have a high calorie content, but they are almost always one-dish meals, where accompaniments that would add extra calories are not necessary. Some recipes in the 'Casseroles, Stews & One-Dish Meals' chapter fall into this category, as they include vegetables and a starch (such as potatoes, pasta or grains) as part of the meal.

How to check if your chicken is done

The 'doneness' tests suggested below are useful indicators, but for safety's sake, test chicken with a thermometer.

CUT	COOK TO	DONENESS TEST
Whole chicken	82°C (180°F)	A drumstick wiggles easily in its socket; the juices run clear when the chicken is pierced
Whole stuffed chicken	82°C (180°F) (chicken) 74°C (165°F) (stuffing)	Chicken: as above Stuffing: must be checked with a thermometer
Legs, breasts, thighs, drumsticks or wings, bone-in	77°C (170°F)	The juices run clear; when cut, the flesh appears opaque, not translucent
Breasts or thighs, boneless	71°C (160°F)	The flesh is opaque when cut
Minced (ground) chicken	74°C (165°F)	The meat appears opaque and is firm to the touch; the juices run clear
Combination dishes made with cooked chicken	74°C (165°F)	Check with a thermometer
Leftovers, reheated	74°C (165°F)	Check with a thermometer

Great kitchen gadgets

Boning knife

A boning knife for chicken should have a blade that is sharp enough to scrape flesh from bones, but also flexible enough to follow the contours of rib bones.

Bulb baster

Easier to use than a spoon, a bulb baster sucks up juices from the pan so that you can squeeze them over the chicken, over particular parts of the bird if necessary.

Instant-read thermometer

An invaluable pocket-size device, about the size of a fountain pen. The shaft of the thermometer is briefly inserted into the roasting meat, registering the internal temperature in 5–10 seconds.

Meat pounder (mallet)

Although you can use a wooden mallet to pound chicken, a metal pounder is easier to keep clean. Most pounders have both a flat face and a faceted face (for tenderising meat); always use the flat side on chicken.

Poultry shears

These are stainless steel scissors with short, sharp blades and the strength to cut through bones.

Roasting pan

A big, deep roasting pan (27 x 38 cm/11 x 15 inches) can handle a big stuffed chicken plus vegetables, and has many other kitchen uses, too. Smaller birds can be roasted in a 23 x 33 cm (9 x 13 inch) pan. Avoid disposable foil pans, which are dangerously flimsy and can buckle as you take them out of the oven.

V-rack

This simple accessory elevates a roasting bird out of the fatty juices in the roasting pan, helping it to brown and crisp. It also holds the chicken securely.

Tips for reducing fat

- Removing the skin from chicken lowers the fat content of chicken dramatically. However, studies have shown that if you're cooking by a dry-heat method (roasting, baking, barbecuing or grilling/broiling), very little of the fat will be absorbed by the meat during cooking. So you can leave the skin on while the chicken cooks, then remove it before eating.

- Cooking chicken with the skin on keeps it moist and flavourful, and in most cases the bird looks much more appetising if brought to the table with its skin on. Note, however, that if you roast or bake skin-on chicken with vegetables, the vegetables—especially starchy ones such as potatoes—will absorb some of the fat.

- When you sauté skin-on chicken, the fat will end up in the pan; you then have the option of pouring it off before continuing with the recipe.

- When you braise or stew skin-on chicken, however, the fat melts into the cooking liquid and becomes an integral part of the dish. It's best to remove the skin from chicken parts used in such dishes. Occasionally, in some old-fashioned stews, we have left the skin on, but if you'd prefer, you can remove the skin before cooking.

- Pan drippings from roast chicken make delicious sauces and gravies, but these are very fatty. Either chill the drippings and skim off the congealed fat, or pour them into a gravy separator (pictured), which will separate the clear juices, leaving the fat behind.

Snacks & starters

Designed to stimulate the appetite, the tasty bites in this chapter include sit-down starters as well as festive finger foods. Here's where fun foods such as drumettes and dumplings take centre stage, alongside more sophisticated offerings such as quiche and chicken liver pâté.

Inspired by the cuisine of South-East Asia, chicken is poached in a ginger broth, then shredded and tossed with slivered vegetables in a soy-vinegar dressing. The salad is then rolled up in soft lettuce leaves with mint and roasted peanuts and served with a sweet-and-sour dipping sauce.

Little chicken salad rolls

DIPPING SAUCE

¼ cup (60 ml) salt-reduced soy sauce

1 tablespoon rice vinegar

1 teaspoon sugar

1 cup (250 ml) salt-reduced chicken stock (page 49)

2 slices fresh ginger, each about 5 mm (¼ inch) thick

375 g (¾ lb) boneless, skinless chicken breasts or thighs

¼ cup (60 ml) rice vinegar

1 tablespoon soy sauce

1 carrot, shredded

1 red capsicum (bell pepper), cut into thin matchsticks

16 soft lettuce leaves (such as butter lettuce or Boston lettuce)

16 fresh mint leaves

¼ cup (40 g) finely chopped dry-roasted peanuts

LOW FAT

PREPARATION 40 minutes

COOKING 15 minutes

MAKES 8 servings

PER SERVING 501 kJ, 120 kcal, 13 g protein, 5 g fat (1 g saturated fat), 3 g carbohydrate (3 g sugars), 570 mg sodium, 2 g fibre

1 In a small saucepan, combine dipping sauce ingredients. Stir over low heat until sugar has dissolved; set aside to cool.

2 In a saucepan, bring stock and ginger to a boil over medium heat. Add chicken, reduce to a simmer, then cover and cook for 12 minutes, or until chicken is cooked through, turning chicken over halfway during cooking. Remove chicken from stock, discarding the stock. Leave chicken until cool enough to handle, then shred.

3 In a bowl, stir together vinegar and soy sauce. Add shredded chicken, carrot and capsicum and toss to combine.

4 Place lettuce leaves, hollow-side up, on a work surface. Place a mint leaf in each. Dividing evenly, spoon chicken mixture into the lettuce leaves and sprinkle peanuts on top. Roll leaves up and serve with the dipping sauce.

IN A HURRY?

Use 1¾ cups (¾ lb) shredded leftover roast chicken and omit step 2. In step 3, add 1 teaspoon finely grated fresh ginger to the chicken mixture.

Quiche has made a bit of a comeback in recent times. Tasty warm or cold, slender wedges of this mouthwatering savoury pie make appealing starters. For a light meal, serve a larger portion with a vinaigrette-dressed salad on the side.

Chicken & broccoli quiche

1 ready-made 23 cm (9 inch diameter), shortcrust (pie) pastry sheet, thawed if frozen

1½ cups (80 g) broccoli florets

½ cup (125 ml) milk

¾ cup (180 ml) pouring (light) cream

4 large eggs

½ teaspoon salt

¼ teaspoon cayenne pepper

1 cup (125 g) grated sharp cheddar

1 cup (150 g) shredded cooked chicken breasts or thighs—leftover or poached (see Basics)

PREPARATION 15 minutes
COOKING 1 hour 10 minutes, plus 30 minutes cooling
MAKES 6 servings

PER SERVING 1890 kJ, 451 kcal, 21 g protein, 35 g fat (20 g saturated fat), 15 g carbohydrate (3 g sugars), 550 mg sodium, 1 g fibre

1 Preheat the oven to 190°C (375°F/Gas 5). Line a 23 cm (9 inch) pie dish with the pastry; trim any overhang and crimp the edges decoratively if desired. Using a fork, prick pastry base several times. Line pastry shell with foil and fill with pie weights, uncooked rice or dried beans. Bake for 15 minutes. Remove foil and pie weights; bake for another 10 minutes, or until crust is cooked through. Remove from oven, but leave the oven on.

2 Meanwhile, bring a saucepan of water to a boil. Add broccoli, cover and cook for 5 minutes, or until tender. (Alternatively, steam broccoli for 5 minutes.) Drain well and set aside.

3 In a bowl, whisk together milk, cream, eggs, salt and cayenne pepper, then stir in cheese.

4 Arrange broccoli and chicken in baked pastry shell. Transfer to a baking tray and pour in egg mixture. Bake for 35 to 40 minutes, until filling has set. Cool for 30 minutes before cutting into wedges.

VARIATION *Chicken & asparagus quiche*
Substitute 1 cup (125 g) chopped asparagus for the broccoli, and use gruyère instead of cheddar. In step 3, add 3 thinly sliced spring onions (scallions) and 4 tablespoons finely chopped fresh dill to the egg mixture.

Chicken wings are perfect for nibbling on. These ones are flavoured with soy, ginger and honey—always a popular combination. If you like food on the spicy side, a chopped red chilli in the marinade wouldn't go amiss.

Honey-soy chicken wings

12 chicken wings, about 1 kg (2 lb) in total

½ cup (125 ml) salt-reduced soy sauce

juice of 1 lemon

2 tablespoons tomato sauce (ketchup)

1 small piece fresh ginger, peeled and thinly sliced

¼ cup (90 g) honey

LOW FAT

PREPARATION 20 minutes, plus overnight marinating
COOKING 40 minutes
MAKES 12 chicken wings

PER SERVING 591 kJ, 141 kcal, 18 g protein, 4 g fat (1 g saturated fat), 8 g carbohydrate (7 g sugars), 485 mg sodium, <1 g fibre

1 Cut wing tips off chicken wings and discard. Place chicken wings in an airtight container.

2 In a bowl, mix together soy sauce, lemon juice, tomato sauce and ginger, then pour over chicken wings. Toss well to coat. Cover and marinate in the refrigerator overnight.

3 Preheat the oven to 180°C (350°C/Gas 4). Lightly grease a baking tray and line with a sheet of baking (parchment) paper. Drain chicken wings, reserving ¼ cup (60 ml) of the marinade. In a small saucepan, mix the reserved marinade and honey; heat for 1 to 2 minutes, or until well combined.

4 Place chicken wings on the baking tray. Brush warm honey mixture over both sides of chicken. Bake for 30 to 40 minutes, until wings are cooked through. Serve warm or cold.

Buffalo chicken wings

½ cup (125 ml) hot pepper sauce, such as Tabasco

2 tablespoons olive oil

¾ teaspoon salt

1 teaspoon freshly ground black pepper

16 chicken wings (about 1.5 kg/3 lb), wing tips removed, or 32 drumettes

6 stalks celery, cut into long matchsticks

LOW FAT
PREPARATION 10 minutes
COOKING 40 minutes
MAKES 8 servings

PER SERVING 1207 kJ, 288 kcal, 40 g protein, 14 g fat (4 g saturated fat), <1 g carbohydrate (<1 g sugars), 498 mg sodium, <1 g fibre

1 Preheat the oven to 230°C (450°F/Gas 8). In a large bowl, whisk together hot pepper sauce, oil, salt and pepper to make a marinade.

2 Cut each chicken wing in half at the joint. Add to marinade and toss well to coat. Place in a deep-sided baking tray and pour any remaining marinade over. Bake for 35 to 40 minutes, turning the wings occasionally, until skin is browned and lightly crisp.

3 Serve chicken wings hot, with celery sticks.

VARIATION *Blue cheese dipping sauce*
Here's a delicious accompaniment for the spicy wings. In a bowl, mix together 1 cup (250 g) reduced-fat sour cream, ¼ cup (60 g) reduced-fat mayonnaise and 1 teaspoon worcestershire sauce. Stir in 125 g (4 oz) crumbled blue cheese and 2 finely chopped spring onions (scallions); cover and refrigerate until serving time.

These filo-wrapped turnovers are reminiscent of samosas—little Indian snacks filled with vegetables or meat. Though small in size, they are big on flavour, spiced with curry powder, ground ginger and mango chutney. Serve hot, with extra chutney for dipping.

Curried chicken turnovers

2 teaspoons olive oil

1 small onion, finely chopped

2 cloves garlic, crushed

1½ teaspoons curry powder

¾ teaspoon ground ginger

1 all-purpose potato, about 125 g (4 oz), peeled and cut into small dice

½ cup (125 ml) salt-reduced chicken stock (page 49)

½ teaspoon salt

2 cups (300 g) diced cooked chicken breasts or thighs—leftover or poached (see Basics)

¼ cup (70 g) mango chutney, finely chopped

10 sheets filo pastry, each about 28 x 43 cm (11 x 17 inches)

½ cup (125 ml) melted butter

LOW FAT
PREPARATION 45 minutes
COOKING 30 minutes
MAKES 40 turnovers

PER SERVING 221 kJ, 53 kcal, 2 g protein, 3 g fat (2 g saturated fat), 3 g carbohydrate (1 g sugars), 111 mg sodium, <1 g fibre

1 In a large non-stick frying pan, heat oil over medium heat. Add onion and garlic and cook, stirring frequently, for 7 minutes, or until onion is soft. Stir in curry powder and ginger and cook until fragrant, about 1 minute.

2 Stir in potato, stock, salt and ¼ cup (60 ml) water and bring to a boil. Reduce to a simmer, cover and cook for 7 minutes, or until potato is tender. Transfer mixture to a bowl and stir in chicken and chutney. Allow filling to cool to room temperature.

3 Preheat the oven to 200°C (400°F/Gas 6). Work with 2 sheets of pastry at a time and keep the rest covered with plastic wrap. Lay 1 sheet on a work surface, with the long side facing you. Brush with some melted butter. Place the second sheet on top and brush with more butter. Cut crosswise into 8 strips.

4 Place a generous teaspoon of filling onto the top corner of each strip. Fold the short end diagonally over filling, so it meets the long side. Flip the triangle downward. Flip the triangle downward again, this time along the diagonal. Continue folding in this fashion (like folding a flag) until you reach the end of the pastry strip. Repeat with remaining filling and pastry sheets.

5 Place turnovers on a lightly greased baking tray and brush tops with butter. Repeat with the remaining dough and filling.

6 Bake turnovers for 10 minutes. Flip them over and bake for another 5 minutes, or until golden brown. Serve hot.

Chicken satay

2 cm (¾ inch) piece fresh ginger,
  peeled and finely chopped

2 tablespoons salt-reduced soy sauce

juice of ½ lime

1 tablespoon sunflower oil

350 g (12 oz) boneless, skinless chicken
  breasts, cut into large chunks

1 lime, cut into 8 wedges

8 cherry tomatoes

1 yellow capsicum (bell pepper),
  cut into chunks

1 zucchini (courgette), about 150 g
  (5 oz), thickly sliced

fresh coriander (cilantro) sprigs,
  to garnish

SATAY SAUCE

2 teaspoons sunflower oil

1 small onion, finely chopped

⅓ cup (50 g) unsalted peanuts,
  finely chopped

1 clove garlic, chopped

1 teaspoon Thai green curry paste

1 tablespoon salt-reduced soy sauce

½ teaspoon caster (superfine) sugar

⅔ cup (150 ml) coconut milk

PREPARATION 35 minutes, plus at least
  2 hours marinating
COOKING 30 minutes
MAKES 4 servings

PER SERVING 1517 kJ, 362 kcal, 25 g protein,
26 g fat (10 g saturated fat), 9 g carbohydrate
(6 g sugars), 659 mg sodium, 4 g fibre

1 In a bowl, mix together ginger, soy sauce, lime juice and oil. Add chicken and toss to coat. Cover and marinate in the refrigerator for at least 2 hours, turning once or twice.

2 Before cooking, soak 8 wooden skewers in cold water for at least 30 minutes, to prevent scorching.

3 To make satay sauce, heat oil in a small saucepan over medium heat. Add onion and cook, stirring, for 3 minutes. Add peanuts and cook for 3 to 5 minutes, until nuts and onion are lightly browned, stirring occasionally. Add garlic, curry paste, soy sauce, sugar and coconut milk and bring to a boil. Reduce to a simmer and cook for 5 minutes, or until sauce has thickened, stirring occasionally. Transfer to a blender or food processor and purée sauce to a thick cream. Return to saucepan and set aside.

4 Preheat the grill (broiler) to high. Remove chicken from marinade, reserving marinade. Alternately thread the chicken pieces, a lime wedge, a cherry tomato and the capsicum and zucchini onto each skewer. Arrange skewers on the grill rack and brush with marinade. Place under grill, close to the heat. Cook skewers for 10 to 15 minutes, turning once or twice, until vegetables are browned and chicken is cooked through.

5 While skewers are cooking, reheat satay sauce. Arrange hot skewers on serving plates, garnish with coriander sprigs and serve with satay sauce.

VARIATIONS
- Replace half the chicken with 250 g (8 oz) firm tofu. Drain tofu well, cut into large dice and marinate with the chicken.
- For a vegetarian dish, replace the chicken with 500 g (1 lb) tofu.
- For a main dish, use 500 g (1 lb) chicken and serve on a bed of steamed white rice with a cucumber salad.

Coriander, also known as cilantro or Chinese parsley, is often sold with the roots still attached. If you buy it this way, don't chop off the roots as these are a signature ingredient in Thai cooking. Rinse the roots thoroughly and keep them intact in this recipe for an authentic Thai flavour.

Thai drumettes

¾ cup (25 g) coriander (cilantro) sprigs, with roots if possible

2 cloves garlic, crushed

1 tablespoon chopped fresh ginger

¼ cup (60 ml) lime juice (about 3 limes)

1 tablespoon olive oil

1 small green chilli, roughly chopped

½ teaspoon salt

24 chicken drumettes, about 1 kg (2 lb), skin removed

LOW FAT
PREPARATION 15 minutes
COOKING 30 minutes
MAKES 24 pieces

PER PIECE 157 kJ, 38 kcal, 4 g protein, 2 g fat (<1 g saturated fat), <1 g carbohydrate (<1 g sugars), 74 mg sodium, <1 g fibre

1 Preheat the oven to 220°C (425°F/Gas 7). In a food processor or blender, process coriander, garlic, ginger, lime juice, oil, chilli and salt until combined. Add ¼ cup (60 ml) water and process to a smooth paste. Transfer to a shallow glass baking dish.

2 Add chicken drumettes to the baking dish and rub the coriander mixture into them.

3 Bake for 30 minutes, or until skin is golden brown and chicken is cooked through.

Chicken & ham-stuffed mushrooms

24 large cap mushrooms,
    about 1.25 kg (2½ lb)

¼ cup (60 ml) olive oil

1 small onion, finely chopped

2 cloves garlic, crushed

250 g (8 oz) minced (ground) chicken

125 g (4 oz) ham, finely chopped

3 tablespoons chopped fresh parsley

2 tablespoons dijon mustard

½ teaspoon salt

½ teaspoon dried marjoram or oregano

PREPARATION 30 minutes
COOKING 50 minutes
MAKES 24 mushrooms

PER MUSHROOM 218 kJ, 52 kcal, 3 g protein,
34 g fat (<1 g saturated fat), 3 g carbohydrate
(<1 g sugars), 135 mg sodium, <1 g fibre

1 Separate mushroom caps and stems. Trim the very ends of 12 stems and roughly chop; discard remaining stems.

2 In a large frying pan, heat 1 tablespoon oil over low heat. Add onion and garlic and cook for 5 minutes. Add chopped mushroom stems and cook, stirring frequently, for 15 minutes, or until stems are tender and liquid has evaporated. Transfer to a large bowl; allow to cool to room temperature. Add chicken, ham, parsley, mustard, salt and marjoram and mix well.

3 Meanwhile, preheat the oven to 220°C (425°F/Gas 7). In a large bowl, toss mushroom caps with remaining oil.

4 Place mushroom caps on a baking tray, gill side down. Bake for 12 minutes, or until firm-tender, but not collapsed. Remove from oven, turn gill side up and cool to room temperature; leave oven on.

5 Fill each cap with chicken mixture. Bake for another 15 minutes, or until chicken is cooked through. Serve hot.

Imagine how impressed your guests will be when you serve this Chinese-restaurant specialty at home! The dumplings are easy to assemble using won ton wrappers, which are sold in larger supermarkets and in Asian grocery stores.

Chicken dumplings

250 g (8 oz) minced (ground) chicken

¼ cup (30 g) thinly sliced spring onions (scallions)

¼ cup (45 g) finely chopped canned water chestnuts

3 tablespoons chopped fresh coriander (cilantro)

1 tablespoon salt-reduced soy sauce

½ teaspoon ground ginger

½ teaspoon salt

¼ teaspoon freshly ground black pepper

24 won ton wrappers (7.5 cm/3 inch square)

SESAME DIPPING SAUCE

¼ cup (60 ml) salt-reduced soy sauce

1 tablespoon sesame oil

2 teaspoons rice vinegar

½ teaspoon sugar

¼ cup (30 g) thinly sliced spring onions (scallions)

LOW FAT
PREPARATION 30 minutes
COOKING 15 minutes
MAKES 24 dumplings

PER DUMPLING 190 kJ, 45 kcal, 3 g protein, 2 g fat (<1 g saturated fat), 4 g carbohydrate (<1 g sugars), 200 mg sodium, <1 g fibre

1 In a bowl, combine chicken, spring onions, water chestnuts, coriander, soy sauce, ginger, salt and pepper. Mix well.

2 Work with several won ton wrappers at a time and keep the rest loosely covered with a clean, dampened cloth. With the point of a wrapper facing you, place a generous teaspoon of filling on the bottom half of the wrapper. With a moistened finger or pastry brush, moisten 2 adjoining edges. Fold the 2 moistened sides over filling; press dough together to seal and form a triangle, working in from pastry edges all the way to the filling; this helps ensure dumplings will not fall apart when boiled. Repeat with remaining won ton wrappers and filling.

3 In a small bowl, whisk together dipping sauce ingredients.

4 Bring a large pot of water to a boil. Add dumplings in batches and cook for 4 minutes, or until they float to surface and chicken is cooked through (the filling will be firm to the touch). Drain.

5 Serve dumplings warm, with dipping sauce.

VARIATION *Won ton soup*
Prepare dumplings as directed. In a saucepan, bring 3 cups (750 ml) salt-reduced chicken stock (page 49) and 3 cups (750 ml) water to a boil over medium heat. Add dumplings and cook as directed. Stir the sesame dipping sauce ingredients directly into the soup. Makes 6 servings.

Crunchy coconut nuggets

Crunchy coconut nuggets

2½ teaspoons ground cumin

1½ teaspoons ground coriander

½ teaspoon salt

1 teaspoon curry powder

½ teaspoon freshly ground black pepper

1 kg (2 lb) chicken tenderloins (tenders), or boneless, skinless chicken breasts or thighs cut into large chunks

1½ cups (85 g) flaked coconut

1 cup (160 g) peanuts, finely chopped

2 eggwhites

YOGURT DIPPING SAUCE

1 cup (250 g) low-fat natural (plain) yogurt

¼ cup (70 g) mango chutney, finely chopped

1 tablespoon lemon juice

1 Preheat the oven to 220°C (425°F/Gas 7). In a large bowl, stir together cumin, coriander, salt, curry powder and pepper. Set aside 2 teaspoons of the spice mixture for the dipping sauce; add chicken to remaining spice mixture and toss to coat.

2 In a shallow dish, combine coconut and peanuts. In another shallow dish, beat eggwhites with 1 tablespoon water. Dip chicken pieces in the eggwhites, then the coconut mixture, pressing coating on well. Place chicken in a greased, deep-sided baking tray and bake for 15 minutes, or until cooked through.

3 Meanwhile, in a bowl, mix yogurt dipping sauce ingredients with reserved spice mixture. Serve with the hot nuggets.

PREPARATION 20 minutes
COOKING 15 minutes
MAKES 6 servings

PER SERVING 2149 kJ, 513 kcal, 47 g protein, 31 g fat (13 g saturated fat), 12 g carbohydrate (10 g sugars), 431 mg sodium, 5 g fibre

Honey-mustard chicken

½ cup (125 g) dijon, wholegrain or spicy brown mustard

1 tablespoon honey

1½ teaspoons dried tarragon

½ teaspoon cayenne pepper

1 kg (2 lb) chicken tenderloins (tenders)

6 slices firm-textured white bread

¼ cup (60 ml) olive oil

LOW FAT, QUICK
PREPARATION 5 minutes
COOKING 15 minutes
MAKES 6 servings

PER SERVING 1861 kJ, 445 kcal, 40 g protein, 21 g fat (4 g saturated fat), 25 g carbohydrate (6 g sugars), 711 mg sodium, 1 g fibre

1 Preheat the oven to 220°C (425°F/Gas 7). In a large bowl, whisk together mustard, honey, tarragon, salt and cayenne pepper. Add chicken, tossing to coat.

2 In a food processor, process bread slices to fine crumbs, then tip onto a plate or sheet of baking (parchment) paper. Dip chicken in crumbs, pressing to coat. Transfer to a lightly greased baking tray and drizzle with the oil. Bake for 15 minutes, or until crust is set and golden brown and chicken is cooked through. Serve hot.

VARIATION
Chicken tenderloins (tenders) are choice morsels, but are also among the most expensive cuts. You can substitute 2.5 cm (1 inch) chunks of boneless, skinless chicken breasts or thighs here.

A splash of brandy makes this light, smooth pâté special enough for a dinner party first course. Poaching the chicken livers with vegetables and herbs, instead of frying them, infuses them with flavour, while fromage frais adds the richness that would traditionally be added by butter, without the saturated fat.

Chicken liver pâté

250 g (8 oz) chicken livers, well trimmed

1 onion, finely chopped

1 clove garlic, crushed

2⅓ cups (600 ml) salt-reduced vegetable stock or water, approximately

3 sprigs fresh parsley

3 sprigs fresh thyme

1 bay leaf

1–1½ tablespoons fromage frais, quark or sour cream

2 teaspoons garlic vinegar or white wine vinegar

2 teaspoons brandy or Calvados, or to taste

¼ teaspoon salt

½ teaspoon freshly ground black pepper

1 tablespoon pink or green peppercorns in brine, drained and patted dry

2 tablespoons finely chopped fresh parsley

toasted slices of country-style bread or baguette, to serve

LOW FAT
PREPARATION 10 minutes, plus at least 4 hours chilling
COOKING 15 minutes
MAKES 4 servings

PER SERVING 492 kJ, 118 kcal, 13 g protein, 3 g fat (1 g saturated fat), 8 g carbohydrate (5 g sugars), 878 mg sodium, <1 g fibre

1 In a saucepan, combine chicken livers, onion and garlic and add enough stock to cover. Tie parsley, thyme and bay leaf into a bouquet garni and add to saucepan. Slowly bring to a boil, skimming off any foam that rises to the surface, then reduce to a gentle simmer. Cook for 5 to 8 minutes, until livers are cooked through but still slightly pink in the centre when you cut into one. Drain, discarding bouquet garni.

2 Transfer livers, onions and garlic to a food processor. Add 1 tablespoon fromage frais, the vinegar, brandy, salt and pepper. Process until smooth, adding remaining fromage frais if necessary for a lighter texture. Stir in peppercorns. (Alternatively, transfer livers, onion and garlic into a bowl and mash to a slightly coarse paste with a fork. Add fromage frais, vinegar and brandy, salt and pepper and mix well, then stir in peppercorns.)

3 Spoon pâté into a serving bowl, or individual ramekins, and smooth the top. Sprinkle with parsley. Cover with plastic wrap and refrigerate for at least 4 hours, or preferably overnight.

4 Bring pâté to room temperature and serve with toasted bread.

VARIATION *Chicken liver pâté with orange and capers*
Replace brandy with orange juice and add the finely grated zest of ½ orange. Replace the pink or green peppercorns with finely chopped drained capers. You can also vary the herbs—try chopped fresh chives, tarragon, sage or mint.

COOK'S TIP
To make a smooth pâté without a food processor, omit onion, and push the cooked livers and garlic through a sieve. Add 2 finely chopped spring onions (scallions) with the peppercorns.

SNACKS & STARTERS **41**

Look for ready-to-bake pizza dough in the freezer or refrigerator cabinet of large supermarkets. You'll need to thaw frozen dough for a few hours at room temperature before using. Some pizzerias may also sell you a portion of their own fresh pizza dough, but you can also use four ready-made 18 cm (7 inch) pizza bases.

Individual chicken-sausage pizzas

1 tablespoon olive oil

2 cloves garlic, crushed

500 g (1 lb) mushrooms, thinly sliced

625 g (1¼ lb) ready-made thin-crust pizza or bread dough

1 cup (250 ml) bottled pizza or pasta sauce

1½ cups (225 g) shredded reduced-fat mozzarella

375 g (¾ lb) cooked chicken sausages, thinly sliced

1 small red onion, halved and thinly sliced

PREPARATION 20 minutes
COOKING 25 minutes
MAKES 4 servings

PER SERVING 3899 kJ, 932 kcal, 55 g protein, 36 g fat (13 g saturated fat), 94 g carbohydrate (10 g sugars), 887 mg sodium, 12 g fibre

1 Preheat the oven to 230°C (450°F/Gas 8). In a large frying pan, heat oil over low heat. Add garlic and cook for 1 minute. Add mushrooms, sprinkle with the salt and cook, stirring frequently, for 5 minutes, or until tender. Drain off mushroom liquid.

2 Divide pizza dough into 4 pieces. On a lightly floured work surface, roll each out to an 18 cm (7 inch) round and place on 2 lightly greased baking trays. Roll the sides of dough up slightly to form raised edges. Spread pizza sauce over dough rounds. Sprinkle with mozzarella, then the mushrooms, sausages and onion.

3 Bake for 15 minutes, or until pizza bases are crusty and the cheese is bubbling, swapping baking trays around halfway during baking so the pizzas brown evenly.

VARIATION *Chicken, olive & artichoke pizzas*
Omit mushrooms, sausages and onion. In step 1, sauté garlic with 500 g (1 lb) boneless, skinless chicken breasts, cut into large chunks, for 4 minutes, or until chicken is almost cooked through. Shape dough and top with pizza sauce, then mozzarella, then 1 cup (150 g) pitted and chopped kalamata olives, 2 jars (175 g/6 oz each) drained marinated artichoke hearts, then chicken. Bake for 25 minutes, or until bases are crusty and cheese is bubbling.

Indian-style grilled chicken breasts

4 boneless, skinless chicken breasts,
    about 150 g (5 oz) each

lemon or lime wedges, to serve

fresh coriander (cilantro) sprigs, to garnish

YOGURT MARINADE

1 clove garlic, crushed

1 tablespoon finely chopped fresh ginger

1½ teaspoons tomato passata
    (tomato purée)

1½ teaspoons garam masala

1½ teaspoons ground coriander

1½ teaspoons ground cumin

¼ teaspoon turmeric

pinch of cayenne pepper, or to taste

½ cup (100 g) natural (plain) yogurt

RAITA

1½ cups (350 g) natural (plain) yogurt

1 cucumber, about 300 g (10 oz), cut into
    quarters lengthwise and seeded

½ cup (100 g) very finely chopped tomato

½ teaspoon ground coriander

½ teaspoon ground cumin

pinch of cayenne pepper

pinch of salt

LOW FAT, QUICK
PREPARATION 15 minutes
COOKING 15 minutes
MAKES 4 servings

PER SERVING 1283 kJ, 306 kcal, 39 g protein,
13 g fat (5 g saturated fat), 10 g carbohydrate
(7 g sugars), 175 mg sodium, 1 g fibre

1 Preheat a chargrill pan or barbecue to high. In a large bowl, whisk together yogurt marinade ingredients (or process in a blender or food processor until well combined). Transfer to a bowl large enough to hold all the chicken breasts, reserving about ½ cup (125 g) to use as a baste.

2 Score 2 slits on each side of each chicken breast. Place in the marinade, turning to coat and rubbing marinade into slits.

3 Brush the chargrill or barbecue with oil. Cook chicken breasts for 12 to 15 minutes, turning and basting with reserved marinade, until juices run clear when the chicken is pierced with a knife, and marinade looks slightly charred.

4 Meanwhile, make the raita. Place yogurt in a bowl. Coarsely grate the cucumber, then squeeze to remove as much moisture as possible. Add cucumber to the yogurt with remaining raita ingredients and mix well. Spoon into a serving bowl.

5 Transfer chicken breasts to a serving plate. Add lemon wedges and garnish with coriander sprigs. Serve the raita on the side.

VARIATIONS

Indian-style skewers
Dice the chicken breasts before adding to marinade. While preheating the chargrill pan or barbecue, soak 8 bamboo skewers in water. Thread chicken onto the soaked skewers, alternating with chunks of zucchini (courgette) and red and yellow capsicum (bell pepper). Grill, basting with marinade and turning skewers several times, for 12 to 15 minutes, until chicken juices run clear.

Onion & herb raita
In a bowl, stir together 1 cup (150 g) very finely chopped sweet onion or spring onions (scallions), 4–6 tablespoons finely chopped fresh mint, 2 tablespoons finely chopped fresh coriander (cilantro), 1 finely chopped fresh green chilli (or to taste) and 1½ cups (350 g) natural (plain) yogurt. In a dry frying pan over high heat, fry 2 teaspoons cumin seeds, stirring constantly until fragrant; immediately tip over the raita and serve.

Soups

The healing powers of chicken soup are nothing short of legendary. From Mexico to Greece to West Africa and South-East Asia, cooks the world over have perfected their own versions of the ultimate chicken soup. Here are some of our all-time favourites for you to try yourself.

In this recipe, instead of a whole chicken, you could use 1.5 kg (3 lb) chicken pieces. Many recipes in this chapter call for chicken stock. For the best flavour, make your own—see our recipe opposite. Although stock needs a few hours to simmer, it requires minimal effort and can be frozen in convenient quantities for later use.

Chicken noodle soup

1 whole chicken, about 1.75 kg (3½ lb), neck and giblets reserved, liver discarded

1 large onion, halved

2 cloves garlic, peeled

1 bay leaf

2 teaspoons salt

½ teaspoon dried rosemary

¼ teaspoon freshly ground black pepper

2 tablespoons olive oil

3 carrots, cut into matchsticks

2 stalks celery, thinly sliced

2 leeks, white part only, halved and thinly sliced

1 red capsicum (bell pepper), thinly sliced

1 parsnip, peeled and cut into matchsticks

1 white turnip, peeled and cut into matchsticks

180 g (6 oz) linguine

⅔ cup (40 g) chopped fresh dill

LOW FAT

PREPARATION 20 minutes

COOKING 1 hour 40 minutes

MAKES 8 servings

PER SERVING 1207 kJ, 288 kcal, 22 g protein, 13 g fat (3 g saturated fat), 21 g carbohydrate (4 g sugars), 714 mg sodium, 4 g fibre

1 In a large heavy-based saucepan, combine chicken, chicken neck and giblets (excluding liver). Add enough water (about 11 cups/ 2.75 litres) to cover chicken by 2.5 cm (1 inch). Bring mixture to a boil; skim off any foam that rises to the surface. Add onion, garlic, bay leaf, 1 teaspoon salt, the rosemary and black pepper and return to a boil. Reduce to a simmer and cook for 1 hour, or until chicken is cooked through. Discard giblets and neck. Leave chicken in the stock until cool enough to handle, then remove chicken, reserving the stock. Pull off and discard the chicken skin, then remove meat from bones, discarding bones. Shred chicken meat and set aside.

2 Strain stock and discard solids. Rinse saucepan and return strained stock to the pan.

3 In a large heavy-based frying pan or saucepan, heat oil over medium heat. Add carrots, celery, leeks, capsicum, parsnip and turnip, then stir to coat with the oil. Cover and cook, stirring occasionally, for 20 minutes, or until vegetables are crisp-tender. Remove lid and cook for another 10 minutes, or until vegetables are tender and lightly browned.

4 Meanwhile, cover the stock and bring to a boil. When vegetables are 10 minutes from being cooked, add linguine to stock and cook for 10 minutes, or until al dente.

5 Add sautéed vegetables, chicken, remaining salt and dill to the stock. Return to a boil to heat through; serve immediately.

Chicken noodle soup

Homemade chicken stock

1 whole chicken, about 1.75 kg (3½ lb),
    cut into pieces, liver discarded

2 carrots, cut into large chunks

1 large onion, skin on, quartered

1 stalk celery, cut into large chunks

1 tomato, halved

2 cloves garlic, unpeeled

¼ teaspoon salt

¼ teaspoon dried rosemary

¼ teaspoon dried thyme

LOW FAT
PREPARATION 10 minutes
COOKING 2 hours 30 minutes
MAKES 9 cups (2.25 litres)

PER CUP (250 ML) 147 kJ, 35 kcal, 7 g protein,
<1 g fat (<1 g saturated fat), 1 g carbohydrate
(<1 g sugars), 132 mg sodium, 1 g fibre

1 Place chicken pieces in a large heavy-based saucepan and add enough water (about 10 cups/2.5 litres) to cover by 5 cm (2 inches). Bring to a boil over high heat; skim off any foam that rises to the surface.

2 Add remaining ingredients and return to a boil. Reduce to a simmer and cook for 2½ hours, or until stock is rich and flavourful.

3 Remove chicken and reserve meaty portions for recipes requiring shredded cooked chicken. Strain stock, discarding solids. Allow to cool, then skim off fat. Refrigerate in a sealed container for up to 3 days, or freeze in 1 cup (250 ml) portions for later use.

Fresh coriander, green chillies and lime juice bring an authentic Mexican flavour to this warming soup, which is perfect for a chilly evening. The sautéed tortilla strips float like crunchy 'noodles' atop each bowl.

Mexican chicken soup

¼ cup (60 ml) olive oil

6 corn tortillas (15 cm/6 inches in diameter), halved, then cut crosswise into strips 1 cm (½ inch) wide

1 small onion, finely chopped

2 cloves garlic, crushed

1 cup (250 g) canned chopped tomatoes

3 mild green chillies, or to taste, chopped

1 pickled jalapeño chilli, finely chopped

1½ cups (375 ml) salt-reduced chicken stock (page 49)

½ teaspoon chilli powder

½ teaspoon salt

625 g (1 lb 4 oz) boneless, skinless chicken thighs, diced

4 tablespoons chopped fresh coriander (cilantro) leaves

¼ cup (60 ml) lime juice (about 2 limes)

LOW FAT
PREPARATION 20 minutes
COOKING 25 minutes
MAKES 4 servings

PER SERVING 1826 kJ, 436 kcal, 33 g protein, 26 g fat (5 g saturated fat), 18 g carbohydrate (5 g sugars), 773 mg sodium, 4 g fibre

1 In a heavy-based saucepan, heat 1 tablespoon oil over medium heat. Add half the tortilla strips and sauté for 3 minutes, or until lightly crisped. Remove with a slotted spoon and drain on paper towel. Repeat with 1 tablespoon oil and remaining tortilla strips.

2 Add remaining oil, onion and garlic to the pan and cook for 5 minutes, or until onion has softened. Add tomatoes, chillies, jalapeño, stock, chilli powder, salt and 1½ cups (375 ml) water; bring to a boil. Reduce to a simmer, cover and cook for 5 minutes.

3 Add chicken, then cover and simmer for 5 minutes, or until chicken is cooked through. Stir in coriander and lime juice. Ladle into serving bowls and garnish with tortilla strips.

TO REDUCE THE FAT
Omit the oil in step 1; instead spray the tortilla strips with olive oil cooking spray and toast in a preheated 180°C (350°F/Gas 4) oven for 5 minutes, or until slightly crisped. Substitute boneless, skinless chicken breasts for thighs.

Here's a real 'pantry shelf' soup—one you can make from ingredients you have on hand. If there's no cream in the fridge, you can use evaporated milk (you'll save calories, too—see tip below).

Quick chicken & corn chowder

2 tablespoons olive oil

4 spring onions (scallions), thinly sliced

1 green capsicum (bell pepper), diced

250 g (8 oz) red-skinned potatoes, such as desiree or pontiac, unpeeled and finely diced

¼ cup (35 g) plain (all-purpose) flour

1 cup (250 ml) salt-reduced chicken stock (page 49)

½ teaspoon salt

¼ teaspoon cayenne pepper

¼ teaspoon dried thyme

1⅔ cups (420 g) canned creamed corn

1½ cups (225 g) diced cooked chicken breasts or thighs—leftover or poached (see Basics)

½ cup (125 ml) thick (heavy/double) cream

LOW FAT, QUICK
PREPARATION 15 minutes
COOKING 15 minutes
MAKES 4 to 6 servings

PER SERVING 1549 kJ, 370 kcal, 18 g protein, 21 g fat (8 g saturated fat), 28 g carbohydrate (7 g sugars), 806 mg sodium, 5 g fibre

1 In a large saucepan, heat oil over medium heat. Add spring onions, capsicum and potatoes and cook for 5 minutes, or until capsicum is crisp-tender. Add flour, stirring to coat.

2 Stir in stock, salt, cayenne pepper, thyme and 1 cup (250 ml) water; bring to a boil. Reduce to a simmer, cover and cook for 5 minutes, or until potatoes are tender. Stir in corn, chicken and cream. Return to a boil to heat through; serve immediately.

TO REDUCE THE FAT
In step 1, reduce the oil to 1 tablespoon and use a non-stick saucepan. In step 2, use evaporated milk in place of cream.

Simple to prepare, this soup is fragrant with lemongrass, coconut, ginger and chilli. The addition of thin rice noodles rounds out the soup, adding a slippery texture and extra body for an easy meal in a bowl.

Thai-style chicken noodle soup

6 cups (1.5 litres) salt-reduced chicken stock (page 49)

2 lemongrass stems, white part only, finely chopped

2 teaspoons finely chopped fresh ginger

1 red chilli, seeded and finely chopped

2 garlic cloves, finely chopped

400 g (14 oz) boneless, skinless chicken breasts

150 g (5 oz) instant thin rice noodles (rice vermicelli)

1 cup (175 g) fresh or canned baby corn, sliced on the diagonal

1⅔ cups (150 g) thinly sliced small button mushrooms

1 tablespoon salt-reduced soy sauce

400 ml (14 fl oz) can light coconut milk

grated zest and juice of 1 lime

225 g (8 oz) bok choy, sliced

3 spring onions (scallions), thinly sliced on the diagonal

3 tablespoons chopped fresh coriander (cilantro) leaves

PREPARATION 20 minutes

COOKING 25 minutes

MAKES 4 servings

PER SERVING 2090 kJ, 499 kcal, 34 g protein, 18 g fat (12 g saturated fat), 48 g carbohydrate (8 g sugars), 1293 mg sodium, 4 g fibre

1 In a large saucepan, bring stock, lemongrass, ginger, chilli and garlic to a boil over high heat. Add chicken, reduce heat to a simmer and cook for 15 minutes, or until chicken is cooked through, turning chicken over halfway during cooking.

2 Remove chicken from stock and set aside to cool. Leave the pan of stock on the heat.

3 Break or cut the noodles into the hot stock; add baby corn, mushrooms, soy sauce and coconut milk. Return to a simmer, then cook for 3 minutes.

4 Meanwhile, shred the chicken. Stir chicken into soup with the lime zest, lime juice and bok choy and simmer gently for 2 minutes, or until bok choy has wilted.

5 Ladle into serving bowls and scatter with spring onions and coriander. Provide a spoon and fork for ease of eating.

VARIATION *Quick Chinese chicken noodle soup*
In a large saucepan, bring 2 cups (500 ml) salt-reduced chicken stock, 3 cups (750 ml) water, 2 teaspoons soy sauce, 1 teaspoon sesame oil and 1 tablespoon rice vinegar to a boil. Add 225 g (8 oz) sliced boneless, skinless chicken breast and cook for 2 minutes. Add 200 g (7 oz) thin rice noodles (rice vermicelli) or fresh egg noodles, the bok choy and 1 chopped spring onion (scallion). Cook for another 2 minutes, or until noodles are tender. Serve immediately.

Smoked paprika, so beloved of Spanish cooks, adds an enticing warmth and smoky depth to this hearty soup. Instead of the chickpeas, you can also used canned white beans, such as cannellini beans.

Chicken & chickpea soup

375 g (¾ lb) bone-in chicken thighs, skin removed

1 tablespoon olive oil

1 small onion, finely chopped

3 cloves garlic, crushed

2 carrots, halved lengthwise and thinly sliced crosswise

1 red capsicum (bell pepper), thinly sliced

1 green capsicum (bell pepper), thinly sliced

1⅓ cups (125 g) thinly sliced mushrooms

3 teaspoons smoked paprika

2 cups (400 g) canned chickpeas, drained and rinsed

2 tablespoons tomato paste (concentrated purée)

½ teaspoon salt

½ teaspoon dried rosemary

LOW FAT
PREPARATION 20 minutes
COOKING 45 minutes
MAKES 4 servings

PER SERVING 1134 kJ, 271 kcal, 24 g protein, 13 g fat (3 g saturated fat), 15 g carbohydrate (5 g sugars), 630 mg sodium, 7 g fibre

1 In a saucepan, bring chicken and 4 cups (1 litre) water to a boil over medium heat. Reduce to a simmer, then partially cover and cook for 30 minutes, or until chicken is tender. Remove chicken; strain and reserve stock. Leave chicken until cool enough to handle, then remove meat from bones. Discard bones, and cut meat into bite-sized pieces.

2 Meanwhile, in a large saucepan, heat oil over low heat. Add onion and garlic and cook for 7 minutes, or until onion is tender. Add carrots and cook for 2 minutes. Add capsicums and cook, stirring frequently, for 7 minutes, or until crisp-tender. Add mushrooms and paprika and cook for another 5 minutes, or until mushrooms are tender.

3 Pour in reserved chicken stock. Stir in chickpeas, tomato paste, salt and rosemary and bring to a boil. Reduce to a simmer, cover and cook for 10 minutes to develop the flavours. Stir in chicken and cook another 2 minutes, or until heated through. Ladle into serving bowls and serve.

COOK'S TIP
You can cook the chicken ahead of time, then refrigerate the chicken and strained stock separately. When you're ready to continue cooking, skim off any fat from the stock, then add stock as directed in step 3, along with the chicken to give it time to reheat.

This dish is based on a traditional West African stew that is made with a cut-up chicken; our version uses chicken thighs. There's no need for chicken stock here as the chicken thighs are slowly simmered with ginger and garlic, creating all the stock you need.

West African chicken soup

375 g (¾ lb) bone-in chicken thighs, skin removed

1 tablespoon ground ginger

2 cloves garlic, crushed

2 teaspoons olive oil

1 small onion, finely chopped

½ cup (125 g) canned chopped tomatoes

2 tablespoons tomato paste (concentrated purée)

½ cup (125 g) smooth peanut butter

½ teaspoon salt

¼ teaspoon cayenne pepper

4 tablespoons chopped fresh coriander (cilantro) leaves

LOW FAT
PREPARATION 15 minutes
COOKING 40 minutes
MAKES 4 servings

PER SERVING 1532 kJ, 366 kcal, 25 g protein, 26 g fat (5 g saturated fat), 8 g carbohydrate (5 g sugars), 677 mg sodium, 1 g fibre

1 In a saucepan, combine chicken, ginger and garlic. Add enough water (about 4 cups/1 litre) to cover chicken by 2.5 cm (1 inch). Bring to a boil over medium heat. Reduce to a simmer, partially cover and cook for 30 minutes, or until chicken is cooked through. Remove chicken from stock; strain and reserve stock. Leave chicken until cool enough to handle, then shred.

2 Meanwhile, in a large saucepan, heat oil over low heat. Add onion and cook, stirring occasionally, for 5 minutes, or until softened. Stir in tomatoes and tomato paste, then cook until slightly thickened, about 5 minutes.

3 Whisk in peanut butter, salt, cayenne pepper and 3 cups (750 ml) of the reserved chicken stock. Bring to a boil, then reduce to a simmer and add chicken. Simmer for 5 minutes to blend the flavours. Stir in coriander and serve.

IN A HURRY?
Substitute 1½ cups (225 g) shredded cooked chicken breasts or thighs for uncooked chicken. In step 1, combine 3 cups (750 ml) salt-reduced chicken stock (page 49) with ginger and garlic, then simmer, covered, for 15 minutes. Strain stock and use as directed in step 3. Add cooked chicken to soup in step 3.

Creamy curried chicken soup

1 tablespoon olive oil

3 spring onions (scallions), thinly sliced

1 clove garlic, crushed

2 teaspoons mild curry powder

¾ teaspoon ground ginger

2 tablespoons plain (all-purpose) flour

1½ cups (375 ml) salt-reduced chicken
    stock (page 49)

1 cup (250 ml) milk

½ teaspoon salt

1 cup (150 g) diced cooked chicken
    breast or thighs—leftover or poached
    (see Basics)

½ cup (80 g) frozen peas

4 tablespoons chopped fresh coriander
    (cilantro) leaves, optional

1 In a saucepan, heat oil over low heat. Add spring onions and garlic and cook, stirring frequently, for 2 minutes, or until spring onions have wilted. Stir in curry powder and ginger, then cook for 1 minute. Stir in flour until smooth.

2 Add stock and 1½ cups (375 ml) water, then whisk over medium heat until mixture comes to a boil. Stir in milk and salt. Add chicken and peas and cook for 3 minutes, or until peas are tender and chicken is heated through. Stir in coriander, if using, and serve.

LOW FAT, QUICK
PREPARATION 10 minutes
COOKING 10 minutes
MAKES 4 servings

PER SERVING 839 kJ, 200 kcal, 16 g protein, 10 g fat (3 g saturated fat), 10 g carbohydrate (5 g sugars), 606 mg sodium, 1 g fibre

Avgolemono is a smooth, tangy and surprisingly delicious Greek egg and lemon soup. This variation is fortified with little chicken meatballs for a heartier dish. It also contains orzo, a pasta shaped like long grains of rice. Once the egg and lemon mixture is added, do not let the soup boil or it will curdle.

Avgolemono with meatballs

250 g (8 oz) minced (ground) chicken

3 large eggs

3 slices firm-textured white bread,
  about 85 g (3 oz), crumbled

2 cloves garlic, crushed

4 tablespoons finely chopped fresh mint

½ cup (30 g) snipped fresh dill

½ teaspoon salt

½ teaspoon grated lemon zest

2½ cups (625 ml) salt-reduced chicken
  stock (page 49)

½ cup (110 g) orzo or risoni

¼ cup (60 ml) lemon juice (about 2 lemons)

LOW FAT
PREPARATION 25 minutes
COOKING 15 minutes
MAKES 4 servings

PER SERVING 1392 kJ, 333 kcal, 24 g protein,
11 g fat (3 g saturated fat), 34 g carbohydrate
(3 g sugars), 926 mg sodium, 2 g fibre

1 In a bowl, combine chicken, 1 egg, bread, garlic, mint, 3 tablespoons dill, ½ teaspoon salt and the lemon zest. Mix until well combined, then shape into 24 meatballs.

2 In a heavy-based saucepan, bring stock, remaining salt and 2½ cups (625 ml) water to a boil over medium heat. Add orzo and cook for 7 minutes.

3 Reduce stock to a simmer. Gently drop the meatballs into the stock and cook for 5 minutes, or until meatballs are cooked through and orzo is tender.

4 In a small bowl, whisk the lemon juice and remaining 2 eggs to combine. Slowly stir some hot soup stock into the egg mixture. Stir the egg mixture back into the soup, simmer for 30 seconds only, then remove from the heat. Stir in the remaining dill. Serve immediately; do not reheat.

*With its vibrant colour and harmonious blend of
Indian spices, this soup is a panacea for all manner
of ills. Extra vegetables can be added for a chunkier
soup. Instead of chickpeas, you can use canned
cannellini or red kidney beans, or even green lentils.*

Spicy chicken soup

2 tablespoons vegetable oil

2 onions, finely chopped

2 large garlic cloves, crushed

1 teaspoon ground coriander

1 teaspoon ground cumin

¼ teaspoon cayenne pepper, or to taste,
    plus extra to sprinkle

¼ teaspoon ground cloves

¼ teaspoon ground ginger

¼ teaspoon ground turmeric

4 cups (1 litre) salt-reduced chicken stock
    (page 49) or vegetable stock

1⅔ cups (14 oz) canned chopped tomatoes

500 g (1 lb) boneless, skinless chicken
    breasts, thinly sliced

250 g (8 oz) green beans, trimmed
    and chopped

2 cups (400 g) canned chickpeas, drained
    and rinsed

2 tablespoons chopped fresh coriander
    (cilantro) leaves, plus extra sprigs
    to garnish

½ teaspoon salt

½ teaspoon freshly ground black pepper

⅓ cup (85 g) natural (plain) yogurt

chapatti or naan bread, to serve

1 In a large heavy-based saucepan, heat oil over medium heat. Add onions and cook, stirring occasionally, for 3 minutes. Add garlic and continue stirring for 2 minutes, or until onions are soft, but not brown.

2 Reduce heat slightly and stir in spices. Continue stirring over a gentle heat for a few minutes so the spices release their aroma. Take care not to let the mixture burn.

3 Stir in stock and tomatoes with their juice. Bring to a boil, then reduce to a simmer.

4 Add chicken, beans and chickpeas and return to a boil. Reduce to a gentle simmer, then cover and cook for 10 minutes, or until chicken is cooked through and beans are just tender. Stir in chopped coriander, salt and pepper.

5 Ladle into serving bowls; add a dollop of yogurt to each one. Sprinkle with extra cayenne pepper and garnish with extra coriander sprigs. Serve with chapatti or naan bread.

LOW FAT
PREPARATION 15 minutes
COOKING 25 minutes
MAKES 4 servings

PER SERVING 1694 kJ, 405 kcal, 38 g protein,
19 g fat (4 g saturated fat), 20 g carbohydrate
(10 g sugars), 1251 mg sodium, 7 g fibre

In this nourishing fireside soup, chunks of smoked chicken stand in for the cured sausage often used to flavour such dishes. Serve with thick slices of buttered sourdough or rustic, crusty bread. Instead of smoked chicken, you can use shredded leftover turkey here.

Smoked chicken & barley soup

1 tablespoon olive oil

1 large onion, finely chopped

3 cloves garlic, crushed

2 carrots, thinly sliced

225 g (8 oz) mushrooms, thickly sliced

¼ cup (55 g) pearl barley

½ cup (125 g) canned chopped tomatoes

375 g (¾ lb) boneless, skinless chicken
    thighs

1¼ teaspoons salt

¾ teaspoon freshly ground black pepper

85 g (3 oz) smoked chicken, diced

2 tablespoons finely chopped fresh parsley

LOW FAT
PREPARATION 15 minutes
COOKING 1 hour
MAKES 8 servings

PER SERVING 606 kJ, 145 kcal, 14 g protein,
7 g fat (2 g saturated fat), 7 g carbohydrate
(2 g sugars), 451 mg sodium, 3 g fibre

1 In a large saucepan, heat oil over medium heat. Add onion and garlic and cook, stirring frequently, for 7 minutes, or until onion is tender. Add carrots and cook for 2 minutes. Add mushrooms and cook for 2 to 3 minutes. Stir in barley.

2 Add tomatoes, chicken thighs, salt, pepper and 5 cups (1.25 litres) water. Bring to a boil, reduce to a simmer, then cover and cook for 40 minutes, or until barley is tender and chicken is cooked through.

3 Remove chicken and set aside to cool. Skim off any fat from the soup. When chicken is cool enough to handle, shred and return to soup along with smoked chicken. Cook for 2 minutes, or until heated through. Serve sprinkled with parsley.

This dish captures the exciting spicy and sour flavours of South-East Asia. Frozen peas can be added to the soup, and you can also replace the green beans with asparagus tips—add them with the zucchini in step 2.

Chicken lemongrass soup

1 small red birdseye (Thai) chilli,
  split open lengthwise but left whole
1 garlic clove, cut in half
1 cm (½ inch) piece fresh ginger, peeled
  and cut into 4 slices
2 stems lemongrass, bruised and cut in half
400 ml (14 fl oz) can light coconut milk
4 bone-in chicken breasts or thighs,
  about 175 g (6 oz) each, skinned
1 shallot (eschalot), finely chopped
250 g (8 oz) green beans, trimmed
  and chopped
1 zucchini (courgette), sliced lengthwise
  with a vegetable peeler into thin strips
finely grated zest and juice of 1 lime
1 teaspoon salt
¼ teaspoon freshly ground black pepper
2 tablespoons chopped fresh coriander
  (cilantro) leaves

PREPARATION 25 minutes,
  plus 30 minutes infusing
COOKING 20 minutes
MAKES 4 servings

PER SERVING 1640 kJ, 392 kcal, 40 g protein,
22 g fat (14 g saturated fat), 9 g carbohydrate
(2 g sugars), 723 mg sodium, <1 g fibre

1 Spear the chilli, garlic and ginger slices on a wooden cocktail stick (this makes them easy to remove later). Place in a saucepan with the lemongrass. Add 4 cups (1 litre) water and bring to a boil over high heat. Boil for 1 minute, remove from heat, cover and set aside to infuse for 30 minutes.

2 Return liquid to a boil, then stir in coconut milk and reduce heat to low. Add chicken, shallot and beans and gently poach for 12 minutes. Add zucchini and cook for 2 minutes, or until chicken is cooked through.

3 Remove chicken from soup. Remove meat from bones, discarding bones. Shred meat roughly, return to the soup and reheat briefly. Stir in lime zest, lime juice, salt and pepper.

4 Divide chicken and vegetables among serving bowls. Spoon the liquid over, discarding the lemongrass and spice stick. Sprinkle with coriander and serve.

COOK'S TIP
Tiny red birdseye (Thai) chillies are fiery-hot. To reduce the heat in this soup, seed the chilli, or remove the chilli after the liquid infuses, or replace it with a milder red or green chilli.

This popular South-East Asian noodle soup is very versatile; you can make it using chicken, tofu, mixed seafood or a combination of all three, if you desire! Laksa paste is sold in jars in specialist grocery stores, larger supermarkets and online—it can vary a little in heat, so adjust the quantity to suit your taste.

Quick chicken laksa

150 g (5 oz) packet rice vermicelli noodles

1 tablespoon peanut oil

3 tablespoons ready-made laksa paste

3 cups (750 ml) salt-reduced chicken stock (page 49)

400 ml (14 fl oz) can coconut milk

500 g (1 lb) boneless, skinless chicken breasts, thinly sliced

½ teaspoon salt

1 heaped cup (100 g) bean sprouts, tails trimmed

3 tablespoons chopped fresh Vietnamese mint or regular mint

⅔ cup (20 g) fresh coriander (cilantro) leaves

1 small red chilli, seeded and sliced

lime wedges, to serve

QUICK
PREPARATION 10 minutes
COOKING 10 minutes
MAKES 4 servings

PER SERVING 2549 kJ, 609 kcal, 34 g protein, 34 g fat (21 g saturated fat), 41 g carbohydrate (9 g sugars), 950 mg sodium, 4 g fibre

1 Place noodles in a heatproof bowl and pour enough boiling water over to cover. Leave to soak for 5 minutes, or according to packet instructions.

2 Meanwhile, in a wok or large heavy-based saucepan, heat oil over medium heat. Add laksa paste and fry until fragrant, about 1 minute. Stir in stock and bring to a boil. Add coconut milk and simmer for 2 to 3 minutes. Add chicken and simmer for 5 minutes, or until chicken is just cooked through. Stir in the salt.

3 Drain noodles and divide among serving bowls. Top each with bean sprouts, Vietnamese mint and coriander. Ladle soup over the noodles, dividing chicken evenly. Garnish with chilli and serve immediately, with lime wedges.

COOK'S TIP
To make your own laksa paste, chop 1 red onion, 4 cloves garlic, 3 red birdseye (Thai) chillies, 1 bunch (150 g) washed coriander (cilantro) roots and stems, 2 lemongrass stems (white part only) and a 2.5 cm (1 inch) piece of peeled fresh ginger or galangal. Place in a food processor with 1 teaspoon ground turmeric, 1 teaspoon ground cumin, ½ teaspoon shrimp or anchovy paste, 5 chopped macadamia nuts and 3 tablespoons chopped fresh Vietnamese mint or regular mint. Blend to a smooth paste, adding some mild vegetable oil if needed to loosen the mixture. Transfer any unused paste to a clean airtight container, cover with a thin layer of mild vegetable oil and refrigerate for up to 3 days, or freeze for up to 3 months.

Salads

Bursting with colour, texture and vitality, a health-giving salad is the perfect way to start a meal or add interest to a plate. Adding tender, cooked chicken to a simple salad makes it much more sustaining: a meal in a bowl when it's too hot—or you're just too tired!—to cook.

Potato salad may be a staple side order, but adding poached chicken breast and blanched green beans transforms it into an appealing warm-weather main dish. The chicken and vegetables are tossed with a basil and garlic dressing and served up on a bed of baby spinach; other salad leaves are also good.

Chicken potato salad

225 g (8 oz) green beans, trimmed

500 g (1 lb) all-purpose potatoes, peeled and cut into large chunks

1 cup (250 ml) chicken stock (page 49)

3 cloves garlic, peeled

750 g (1½ lb) boneless, skinless chicken breasts

1 cup (50 g) firmly packed fresh basil

2 tablespoons mayonnaise

½ teaspoon grated lemon zest

1 tablespoon lemon juice

½ teaspoon salt

125 g (4 oz) baby spinach leaves, rinsed and dried

LOW FAT
PREPARATION 25 minutes
COOKING 20 minutes
MAKES 4 servings

PER SERVING 1674 kJ, 400 kcal, 46 g protein, 14 g fat (4 g saturated fat), 21.g carbohydrate (4 g sugars), sodium 532 mg, 5 g fibre

1 In a large pot of boiling salted water, cook beans for 4 minutes, or until crisp-tender. With a slotted spoon, transfer beans to a large bowl. Add potatoes to boiling water, reduce to a gentle boil and cook for 15 minutes, or until tender. Drain and add to the beans.

2 Meanwhile, in a large frying pan, combine stock, garlic and 1 cup (250 ml) water. Bring to a boil and add chicken. Reduce to a simmer, cover and cook for 15 minutes, or until chicken is cooked through, turning chicken over halfway during cooking.

3 Remove chicken and garlic from stock and set aside. Measure out ⅓ cup (80 ml) stock and set aside (reserve remaining stock for use in other recipes). When chicken is cool enough to handle, dice it and add to the beans and potatoes.

4 In a food processor or blender, combine reserved garlic and stock, the basil, mayonnaise, lemon zest, lemon juice and salt. Purée until smooth, then pour over chicken mixture and toss well to coat. Serve on a bed of spinach leaves.

IN A HURRY?
Instead of uncooked chicken breasts, use 3 cups (450 g) diced leftover roast or cooked chicken. In step 2, place garlic in a small saucepan with ½ cup (125 ml) chicken stock, omitting the water. Cook for 3 minutes, then complete recipe as directed.

Cobb salad

125 g (4 oz) rindless (regular) bacon (about 6 slices)

½ large iceberg lettuce, shredded

2 cups (300 g) shredded cooked chicken breasts or thighs—leftover or poached (see Basics)

1 large tomato, diced

125 g (4 oz) blue cheese, crumbled

2 hard-boiled eggs, roughly chopped

1 avocado, diced

⅓ cup (80 ml) olive oil

¼ cup (60 ml) red wine vinegar

½ teaspoon salt

1 In a large frying pan, cook bacon over medium–low heat for 7 minutes, or until crisp and cooked through. Drain on paper towel, then crumble.

2 Place lettuce, chicken, tomato, cheese, eggs, avocado and crumbled bacon in a large bowl.

3 In a small bowl, whisk together oil, vinegar and salt. Pour dressing over salad ingredients, toss together gently and serve.

PREPARATION 25 minutes
COOKING 10 minutes
MAKES 6 servings

PER SERVING 1801 kJ, 430 kcal, 26 g protein, 36 g fat (10 g saturated fat), 1 g carbohydrate (1 g sugars), sodium 812 mg, 2 g fibre

Enjoy the sunny taste of summer in midwinter when you serve this colourful salad brightened with orange and grapefruit segments. Red onion and piquant Greek olives provide the perfect counterpoint to the citrus.

Chicken, orange & grapefruit salad

3 navel oranges

2 ruby red or pink grapefruit

¼ cup (60 ml) olive oil

1 tablespoon balsamic vinegar

2 teaspoons dijon mustard

½ teaspoon salt

2 cups (300 g) shredded cooked chicken breasts or thighs—leftover or poached (see Basics)

½ cup (80 g) kalamata olives, pitted and sliced

½ red onion, finely sliced

125 g (4 oz) rocket (arugula), tough stems trimmed

LOW FAT, QUICK
PREPARATION **30 minutes**
MAKES **4 servings**

PER SERVING 1633 kJ, 390 kcal, 24 g protein, 24 g fat (4 g saturated fat), 18 g carbohydrate (15 g sugars), sodium 702 mg, 3 g fibre

1 Using a paring knife, cut off and discard the outer skin, white pith and outer membrane of the oranges and grapefruit. Working over a bowl to catch juices, remove the orange and grapefruit segments from their membranes. To do this, use the paring knife to cut along both sides of each dividing membrane to release the segments, then place in a smaller bowl. Squeeze any juice left in membranes into the bowl. Measure out ¼ cup (60 ml) citrus juice and pour into a large salad bowl (reserve any extra juice for another use).

2 Whisk oil, vinegar, mustard and salt into the citrus juice in the salad bowl. Add chicken, olives, onion, rocket and orange and grapefruit segments. Toss well and serve.

TO REDUCE THE FAT
Substitute ½ cup (125 ml) non-fat or low-fat ready-made balsamic vinaigrette for the citrus dressing and stir in 2 teaspoons dijon mustard until well combined.

Caribbean chicken salad

5 cm (2 inch) piece fresh ginger, peeled

½ cup (125 ml) tomato sauce (ketchup)

¼ cup (60 ml) lime juice (about 2 limes)

1 tablespoon plus 1 teaspoon honey

1 teaspoon hot chilli (pepper) sauce

½ teaspoon salt

1 small red onion, halved and thinly sliced

1 large tomato, cut into 16 wedges

3 cups (450 g) shredded cooked chicken
   breasts or thighs—leftover or poached
   (see Basics)

1 large mango, cut into large chunks

1 large papaya (425 g/15 oz), peeled
   and cut into large chunks

1 Grate ginger over a bowl. With your fingers, squeeze ginger to extract as much juice as possible. Measure out 1 tablespoon ginger juice and transfer to a large bowl.

2 Whisk tomato sauce, lime juice, honey, hot chilli sauce and salt into ginger juice until well mixed. Add onion and tomato and toss.

3 Add chicken, mango and papaya and toss gently to combine. Serve salad immediately. If not serving immediately, toss all ingredients except papaya together and refrigerate; only add the papaya just before serving, or chicken will turn mushy.

LOW FAT, QUICK
PREPARATION 25 minutes
MAKES 4 servings

PER SERVING 1514 kJ, 362 kcal, 34 g protein,
9 g fat (3 g saturated fat), 37 g carbohydrate
(30 g sugars), sodium 740 mg, 4 g fibre

This salad is a taco turned inside-out—a bed of iceberg lettuce topped with crunchy tortilla chips, salsa-sauced chicken and beans, grated cheese and diced avocado.

Chicken taco salad

4 corn tortillas (15 cm/6 inch diameter), each cut into 8 wedges

¼ cup (60 ml) lime juice (about 2 limes)

½ teaspoon salt

½ teaspoon chilli powder

1½ cups (375 g) mild or medium-hot bottled tomato salsa

4 tablespoons chopped fresh coriander (cilantro) leaves

2 cups (300 g) shredded cooked chicken breasts or thighs—leftover or poached (see Basics)

1½ cups (300 g) canned pinto or red kidney beans, drained and rinsed

½ shredded iceberg lettuce

⅓ cup (40 g) grated mild white cheddar (or Monterey Jack cheese)

1 avocado, diced

LOW FAT, QUICK
PREPARATION 10 minutes
COOKING 10 minutes
MAKES 4 servings

PER SERVING 1809 kJ, 432 kcal, 31 g protein, 24 g fat (7 g saturated fat), 23 g carbohydrate (8 g sugars), sodium 1124 mg, 8 g fibre

1 Preheat the oven to 220°C (425°F/Gas 7). Place tortilla wedges on a baking tray. Spray with olive oil cooking spray, then sprinkle with 2 tablespoons lime juice. Sprinkle with the salt and chilli powder and bake for 7 minutes, or until crisp.

2 In a large bowl, toss together salsa, coriander and remaining lime juice. Add chicken and beans and toss to combine.

3 Line serving plates with shredded lettuce. Top with the tortilla chips, chicken mixture, cheddar and avocado and serve.

VARIATION *Chicken gazpacho salad*
Omit tortillas, lime juice, salt and chilli powder. Cut chicken into bite-sized pieces and toss with the salsa and coriander (cilantro). Add 1 large peeled, seeded and diced cucumber, 1 diced green capsicum (bell pepper) and ½ red onion finely chopped. Spoon chicken mixture over lettuce. Omit cheese and top with avocado as directed.

Chicken & orzo salad

500 g (1 lb) orzo or risoni

1 tablespoon grated lemon zest

⅔ cup (160 ml) lemon juice
(about 6 lemons)

½ cup (125 ml) olive oil

2 teaspoons salt

4 cups (600 g) shredded cooked chicken
breasts or thighs—leftover or poached
(see Basics)

2 red capsicums (bell peppers), finely diced

3 cups (600 g) canned chickpeas, drained
and rinsed

500 g (1 lb) cherry tomatoes, halved

4 tablespoons snipped fresh dill

6 spring onions (scallions), thinly sliced

1 In a large pot of boiling water, cook orzo according to packet instructions until al dente. Drain.

2 Meanwhile, in a large bowl, whisk together lemon zest, lemon juice, oil and salt. Add hot orzo and toss to combine.

3 Add remaining ingredients and toss to combine. Serve immediately, or chilled.

LOW FAT, QUICK
PREPARATION 15 minutes
COOKING 15 minutes
MAKES 8 servings

PER SERVING 1779 kJ, 425 kcal, 29 g protein,
7 g fat (2 g saturated fat), 59 g carbohydrate
(4 g sugars), sodium 796 mg, 4 g fibre

Caesar salad with chicken

1 tablespoon mild chilli powder

¾ teaspoon ground cumin

¼ teaspoon salt

½ teaspoon sugar

1 small baguette, cut into small cubes

2 tablespoons olive oil

750 g (1½ lb) boneless, skinless chicken
breasts

½ cup (125 g) low-fat mayonnaise

½ cup (50 g) grated parmesan

2 tablespoons lemon juice

1 tablespoon drained capers

½ teaspoon anchovy paste

2 baby cos (romaine) lettuces, torn

LOW FAT, QUICK
PREPARATION 15 minutes
COOKING 15 minutes
MAKES 4 servings

1 Preheat the oven to 200°C (400°F/Gas 6). In a small bowl, mix together chilli powder, cumin, salt and sugar. Transfer 1 tablespoon of the spice mixture to a large bowl. Add bread cubes and 1 tablespoon oil and toss to coat. Transfer bread to a baking tray and bake for 10 minutes, or until crisp and golden, tossing croutons halfway during baking.

2 Meanwhile, rub remaining spice mixture onto both sides of each chicken breast. In a non-stick frying pan, heat remaining oil over medium heat. Add chicken and cook, turning occasionally, for 15 minutes, or until cooked through. Remove chicken from pan, reserving any pan juices. When cool enough to handle, slice chicken on diagonal.

3 In a large bowl, whisk together mayonnaise, parmesan, lemon juice, capers, anchovy paste and any pan juices. Add lettuce and croutons and toss well. Divide salad among serving plates, top with sliced chicken and serve.

PER SERVING 2257 kJ, 539 kcal, 48 g protein, 29 g fat (8 g saturated fat),
21 g carbohydrate (7 g sugars), 866 mg sodium, 2 g fibre

Chicken & orzo salad

Penne, chicken & asparagus salad

2 cloves garlic, peeled

225 g (8 oz) penne or other tube pasta

500 g (1 lb) asparagus, trimmed and
    cut in half on the diagonal

½ cup (125 g) dijon mustard

¼ cup (60 ml) olive oil

¼ cup (60 ml) rice vinegar

¼ teaspoon salt

3 cups (450 g) diced cooked chicken
    breasts or thighs—leftover or poached
    (see Basics)

2 orange or red capsicums (bell peppers),
    thinly sliced

150 g (5 oz) salad greens

1 In a large pot of boiling water, blanch garlic cloves for 1 minute; remove with a slotted spoon and reserve. Add pasta to boiling water and cook according to packet instructions until al dente; 3 minutes before pasta is ready, add asparagus to cooking water. Drain pasta and asparagus well and allow to cool to room temperature.

2 Meanwhile, in a large bowl, whisk together mustard, oil, vinegar and salt. Finely chop the blanched garlic and add to dressing with chicken and capsicums. Add pasta and asparagus and toss well. Serve on a bed of salad greens.

LOW FAT
PREPARATION 15 minutes
COOKING 15 minutes
MAKES 4 servings

PER SERVING 2565 kJ, 613 kcal, 44 g protein,
25 g fat (4 g saturated fat), 49 g carbohydrate
(7 g sugars), sodium 879 mg, 5 g fibre

To save time, microwave rather than bake the sweet potatoes. Leave the skins on, pierce them in several spots with a sharp knife, then cook according to your microwave's instructions—usually about 12 minutes for 4 sweet potatoes.

Chicken, apple & sweet potato salad

750 g (1½ lb) bone-in chicken thighs, skin removed

½ teaspoon salt

500 g (1 lb) orange sweet potatoes, unpeeled

¼ cup (60 g) mayonnaise

¼ cup (60 ml) cider vinegar

½ teaspoon chilli powder

½ teaspoon ground cumin

½ teaspoon sugar

2 crisp red apples, diced

1 granny smith apple, diced

1 stalk celery, thinly sliced

LOW FAT
PREPARATION 20 minutes
COOKING 50 minutes
MAKES 4 servings

PER SERVING 1365 kJ, 326 kcal, 20 g protein, 12 g fat (3 g saturated fat), 35 g carbohydrate (22 g sugars), sodium 530 mg, 5 g fibre

1 Preheat the oven to 220°C (425°F/Gas 7). Place chicken thighs in a baking dish and sprinkle with ½ teaspoon salt; place sweet potatoes in a separate baking dish. Place both dishes in oven. Bake chicken for 30 minutes, or until cooked through; remove chicken from oven and leave to cool. Bake sweet potatoes for 50 minutes, or until tender but not falling apart (the actual timing will vary depending on their size).

2 In a large bowl, whisk together mayonnaise, vinegar, chilli powder, cumin, sugar and remaining salt. Add apples and celery and toss well to combine.

3 When chicken is cool enough to handle, remove meat from the bones and dice it. When sweet potatoes are cool enough to handle, peel and cut into large chunks.

4 Add chicken and sweet potatoes to salad and toss gently to combine. Serve immediately, or chilled.

TO REDUCE THE FAT
Use chicken breasts instead of thighs, and use reduced-fat mayonnaise instead of the regular version.

Jasmine rice is named for the faintly flowery fragrance it releases as it cooks. Native to Thailand, this soft, delicate rice is similar in flavour to Indian basmati rice, but considerably less expensive. For extra colour in this salad, use a mix of red and green grapes.

Rice salad with chicken & grapes

⅓ cup (80 ml) olive oil

2 onions, finely chopped

I teaspoon sugar

2 cups (400 g) jasmine rice (Thai fragrant rice) or basmati rice

1½ cups (375 ml) salt-reduced chicken stock (page 49)

1½ teaspoons salt

½ cup (125 ml) rice vinegar

4 cups (600 g) shredded cooked chicken breasts—leftover or poached (see Basics)

2 cups (350 g) seedless grapes

4 tablespoons chopped fresh coriander (cilantro)

½ cup (80 g) pine nuts, toasted

LOW FAT
PREPARATION 15 minutes
COOKING 25 minutes
MAKES 8 servings

PER SERVING 2178 kJ, 520 kcal, 28 g protein, 22 g fat (4 g saturated fat), 48 g carbohydrate (9 g sugars), sodium 771 mg, 1 g fibre

1 In a large saucepan, heat 2 tablespoons of the oil over medium–low heat. Add onions and sugar and cook, stirring frequently, for 7 minutes, or until onions are tender. Stir in rice, stock, ½ teaspoon salt and 1½ cups (375 ml) water. Bring to a boil, reduce to a simmer, then cover and cook for 17 minutes, or until rice is tender. Drain off any excess liquid.

2 In a large bowl, whisk together vinegar and remaining oil and remaining salt. Add rice mixture to bowl and toss with a fork to combine.

3 Add chicken, grapes, coriander and pine nuts and toss with a fork. Serve immediately, or chilled.

*With its robust, chewy texture and nutty flavour,
wild rice is great in a salad. Here, the rice is cooked
'pilaf' style by sautéing it, then simmering it in stock.
Wild rice takes much longer to cook than regular white
or brown rice—almost an hour.*

Wild rice salad with chicken & pecans

2 tablespoons olive oil

3 spring onions (scallions), thinly sliced

2 cloves garlic, finely chopped

1 cup (190 g) wild rice

2 cups (500 ml) salt-reduced chicken
    stock (page 49)

1 teaspoon grated lemon zest

½ teaspoon salt

⅓ cup (80 ml) lemon juice (about 3 lemons)

1 red capsicum (bell pepper), finely diced

⅓ cup (50 g) kalamata olives, pitted
    and halved

¼ cup pecans (25 g) or pine nuts (40 g),
    toasted

3 cups (450 g) shredded cooked chicken
    breasts or thighs—leftover or poached
    (see Basics)

LOW FAT
PREPARATION 25 minutes
COOKING 1 hour
MAKES 4 servings

PER SERVING 2256 kJ, 539 kcal, 45 g protein,
21 g fat (3 g saturated fat), 41 g carbohydrate
(5 g sugars), sodium 871 mg, 4 g fibre

1 In a large saucepan, heat 1 teaspoon oil over low heat. Add spring onions and garlic and cook, stirring frequently, for 1 minute, or until spring onions are soft. Add wild rice and stir to coat. Add stock, lemon zest, salt and 1 cup (250 ml) water and bring to a boil. Reduce to a simmer, then cover and cook for 55 minutes, or until rice is tender.

2 Meanwhile, in a large bowl, whisk together lemon juice and remaining oil.

3 When rice has cooked, drain off any remaining liquid. Spoon the hot rice into the lemon dressing and toss gently.

4 Add capsicum, olives, pecans and chicken and toss well. Serve immediately, or chilled.

Thai chicken salad

2 boneless, skinless chicken breasts, poached salt-reduced stock (see Basics)

⅓ cup (80 ml) lime juice (about 3 limes)

1 tablespoon Thai sweet chilli sauce

1 tablespoon fish sauce

1 clove garlic, crushed

2 lemongrass stems, white part only, finely chopped

1 small red onion, thinly sliced

1 small cucumber, seeded and cut into long strips

3 tablespoons chopped fresh mint

3 tablespoons chopped fresh coriander (cilantro)

salad leaves, to serve

1 Shred chicken into strips. Place in a large non-metallic bowl and pour in lime juice, chilli sauce and fish sauce. Add garlic and lemongrass and toss to combine well. Cover and marinate in the refrigerator for 30 minutes.

2 Add onion, cucumber, mint and coriander to chicken mixture. Gently toss until well combined.

3 Arrange salad leaves on serving plates. Spoon chicken mixture over salad leaves and serve.

LOW FAT
PREPARATION 15 minutes, plus
    30 minutes marinating
COOKING 30 minutes (for poaching chicken)
MAKES 4 serves

PER SERVING 591 kJ, 141 kcal, 18 g protein, 4 g fat (1 g saturated fat), 8 g carbohydrate (4 g sugars), sodium 744 mg, 1 g fibre

Sesame chicken salad

2 cloves garlic, peeled

225 g (8 oz) snow peas (mangetout)

1 red capsicum (bell pepper), cut into long matchsticks

5 cm (2 inch) piece fresh ginger, peeled and thickly sliced

¼ cup (60 ml) sesame oil

¼ cup (60 ml) salt-reduced soy sauce

2½ teaspoons sugar

2½ teaspoons rice vinegar

¼ teaspoon dried red chilli flakes

1 cucumber, peeled, halved lengthwise, seeded and cut into long matchsticks

2 cups (300 g) shredded cooked chicken breasts or thighs—leftover or poached (see Basics)

1 In a large pot of boiling water, blanch garlic cloves for 1 minute; remove with a slotted spoon and reserve. Add snow peas and capsicum to the pot and blanch for 15 seconds; drain well.

2 In a food processor, purée the blanched garlic, ginger, sesame oil, soy sauce, sugar, vinegar and chilli flakes until smooth.

3 Transfer dressing to a large bowl. Add blanched snow peas and capsicum, cucumber and chicken and toss to combine. Serve immediately, or chilled.

LOW FAT, QUICK
PREPARATION 20 minutes
COOKING 2 minutes
MAKES 4 servings

PER SERVING 1334 kJ, 319 kcal, 25 g protein, 20 g fat (4 g saturated fat), 10 g carbohydrate (7 g sugars), sodium 630 mg, 2 g fibre

Sesame chicken salad

Basic tabouleh is a mix of fresh parsley and mint, tomatoes and a type of cracked wheat called burghul, dressed with lemon juice and olive oil. The addition of shredded chicken turns it into a meal, and serving it on salad leaves extends it further. Look for burghul in health food or Middle Eastern grocery stores.

Chicken tabouleh salad

1⅓ cups (235 g) burghul (bulgur)

3 green capsicums (bell peppers), seeded and cut lengthwise into large, flat pieces

1¼ cups (310 ml) lemon juice (about 10 lemons)

⅔ cup (160 ml) olive oil

1½ teaspoons salt

½ teaspoon freshly ground black pepper

1½ cups (90 g) chopped fresh parsley

½ cup (25 g) chopped fresh mint

2 large tomatoes, diced

1 large cucumber, peeled, halved lengthwise, seeded and thinly sliced

4 cups (600 g) shredded cooked chicken breasts or thighs—leftover or poached (see Basics)

300 g (10 oz) mixed salad leaves (optional)

LOW FAT

PREPARATION 25 minutes, plus 30 minutes soaking and 1 hour chilling

COOKING 10 minutes

MAKES 8 servings

PER SERVING 1769 kJ, 423 kcal, 26 g protein, 25 g fat (4 g saturated fat), 22 g carbohydrate (5 g sugars), sodium 547 mg, 7 g fibre

1 In a large heatproof bowl, combine burghul and 3 cups (750 ml) hot water; leave to soak for 30 minutes. Drain burghul in a colander, then transfer to a clean cloth and press to remove excess liquid.

2 Meanwhile, preheat the grill (broiler) to high. Place capsicum pieces on a grill tray, skin side up, 10 cm (4 inches) from heat. Grill for 10 minutes, or until skins are blackened. When cool enough to handle, peel off the skins and dice the flesh.

3 In a large bowl, whisk together lemon juice, oil, salt and pepper. Add burghul and toss well. Add parsley, mint, tomatoes, cucumber, chicken and grilled capsicums and toss well.

4 Cover and refrigerate for at least 1 hour, to allow flavours to blend. Serve on a bed of salad leaves if desired.

Casseroles, stews & one-dish meals

What a comfort it is to have a dish gently simmering in the oven or bubbling away on the stove. Here's a great round-up of mouthwatering recipes from all around the globe.

Cold-weather appetites call for sustaining meals made with hearty ingredients, such as winter vegetables. Here, potatoes, brussels sprouts and carrots are oven-braised with juicy chicken.

Winter chicken stew

2 tablespoons olive oil

1 whole chicken, about 1.75 kg (3½ lb),
    cut into 8 serving pieces (see Basics)

¼ cup (35 g) plain (all-purpose) flour

3 carrots, cut into long chunks

8 cloves garlic, peeled and quartered

500 g (1 lb) small red-skinned potatoes,
    such as desiree or pontiac, quartered

300 g (10 oz) brussels sprouts, fresh
    or frozen

1 cup (250 ml) salt-reduced chicken stock
    (page 49)

½ teaspoon salt

½ teaspoon dried sage

PREPARATION 25 minutes
COOKING 1 hour 15 minutes
MAKES 4 servings

PER SERVING 3310 kJ, 791 kcal, 55 g protein,
53 g fat (15 g saturated fat), 19 g carbohydrate
(4 g sugars), 454 mg sodium, 5 g fibre

1 In a large flameproof casserole dish or Dutch oven, heat oil over medium heat. Dredge chicken in the flour; reserve excess flour. Add chicken to dish in batches and fry for 4 minutes per side, or until golden brown. Transfer chicken to a plate.

2 Preheat the oven to 180°C (350°F/Gas 4). Add carrots and garlic to dish and sauté for 5 minutes, or until carrots are lightly coloured. Add potatoes, brussels sprouts, stock, salt and sage and bring to a boil. Return chicken to pan and return to a boil. Cover, place in oven and bake for 45 minutes, or until chicken is cooked through and potatoes are tender.

3 Remove dish from oven. With a slotted spoon, transfer chicken to a platter. In a small bowl, blend reserved flour with ½ cup (125 ml) cooking liquid from the casserole dish. Stir flour mixture into the stew. On the stovetop, bring stew to a boil and cook for 1 minute, or until sauce is slightly thickened. Spoon over the chicken.

TO REDUCE THE FAT
Remove the skin from the chicken before cooking it in the stew.

VARIATION *Chicken stew with spring vegetables*
Substitute 4 boneless, skinless chicken breast halves (about 750 g/1½ lb) for the whole chicken. In step 1, use a non-stick casserole dish or Dutch oven and reduce oil to 1 tablespoon. In step 2, along with garlic and carrots, sauté 6 spring onions (scallions) cut into 2.5 cm (1 inch) lengths; omit brussels sprouts, decrease stock to ¾ cup (180 ml), substitute rosemary for sage, and add 1 cup (155 g) frozen peas. Complete as directed.

At its best in autumn, fennel should have a white, shiny bulb with pale green stalks and feathery, bright green tendrils. The firmness of these 'leaves' indicates the bulb's freshness. If fennel isn't available, substitute sliced celery stalks with a pinch of crushed fennel seeds.

Chicken with beans & fennel

225 g (8 oz) green beans, trimmed and cut into 5 cm (2 inch) lengths

2 tablespoons olive oil

1 whole chicken, about 1.75 kg (3½ lb), cut into 8 serving pieces (see Basics)

¼ cup (35 g) plain (all-purpose) flour

1 large bulb fennel, trimmed and sliced lengthwise into strips 1 cm (½ inch) wide

4 cloves garlic, thinly sliced

1 cup (250 ml) salt-reduced chicken stock (page 49)

2 tablespoons lemon juice

½ teaspoon salt

¼ teaspoon dried rosemary

¼ teaspoon dried thyme

¼ teaspoon freshly ground black pepper

400 g (14 oz) can cannellini beans, rinsed and drained

PREPARATION 20 minutes
COOKING 1 hour 15 minutes
MAKES 4 servings

PER SERVING 4765 kJ, 1138 kcal, 82 g protein, 80 g fat (23 g saturated fat), 17 g carbohydrate (5 g sugars), 648 mg sodium, 8 g fibre

1 Preheat the oven to 180°C (350°F/Gas 4). In a pot of boiling water, blanch green beans for 3 minutes; drain and set aside.

2 Meanwhile, in a large flameproof casserole dish or Dutch oven, heat oil over medium–high heat. Dredge chicken in the flour, shaking off excess. Add chicken to dish in batches and fry for 4 minutes per side, or until golden brown. Transfer chicken to a plate.

3 Add fennel to the dish, reduce heat to medium and cook, stirring frequently, for 7 minutes, or until lightly golden. Add garlic and cook for 1 minute. Add stock, lemon juice, salt, rosemary, thyme and pepper and return to a boil. Return chicken to the dish and bring to a boil. Cover, place in oven and bake for 35 minutes, or until chicken is cooked through.

4 Stir in cannellini beans and blanched green beans. Return to the oven and cook for 5 minutes, or until heated through.

TO REDUCE THE FAT
Remove the skin from the chicken before cooking it in the stew.

Topped with golden, flaky puff pastry, this popular one-pot dish takes classic comfort food and gives it a healthy modern twist: it contains a higher ratio of vegetables to poultry.

Chicken pot pie

2 tablespoons olive oil

3 leeks, white and pale green parts only, roughly chopped

2 stalks celery, roughly chopped

2 large carrots, thickly sliced

1 large red-skinned potato, such as desiree or pontiac, unpeeled and cut into bite-sized chunks

1 cup (75 g) thickly sliced button mushrooms

¼ cup (35 g) plain (all-purpose) flour

½ teaspoon dried thyme

¼ teaspoon salt

400 ml (14 fl oz) salt-reduced chicken stock (page 49)

1⅔ cups (250 g) diced cooked chicken breast or thighs—leftover or poached (see Basics)

1 cup (155 g) peas, fresh or frozen

1 sheet frozen puff pastry (large enough to cover a 23 cm/9 inch pie dish), thawed

1 large egg

1 tablespoon milk

LOW FAT
PREPARATION 25 minutes
COOKING 45 minutes, plus 10 minutes standing
MAKES 6 servings

PER SERVING 1397 kJ, 334 kcal, 19 g protein, 17 g fat (6 g saturated fat), 25 g carbohydrate (5 g sugars), 652 mg sodium, 4 g fibre

1 Heat oil in a large saucepan over medium heat. Add leeks, celery, carrots and potato. Cook, stirring occasionally, for 5 minutes. Add mushrooms and cook, stirring occasionally, for 5 minutes. Stir in flour, thyme and salt until blended, then stir in stock. Increase heat to medium–high and cook, stirring, for 2 minutes. Stir in chicken and peas. Transfer pie filling to a deep, 23 cm (9 inch) pie dish. Allow to cool to room temperature.

2 Meanwhile, preheat the oven to 200°C (400°C/Gas 6). Place pastry sheet on a flat surface. Whisk together egg and milk and brush over pastry. Place pastry, glazed side down, over filling in pie dish. Trim the edge of the pastry; crimp or mark decoratively with a fork if desired. Brush top with remaining egg mixture. Cut four 2.5 cm (1 inch) slits in the centre of pastry to allow steam to escape.

3 Place in oven and bake for 25 to 30 minutes, or until filling is bubbling and pastry is golden brown. Remove from oven and allow to stand at least 10 minutes before serving.

There's an old-world feeling to this dish, made with apples, cabbage and potatoes. It is especially good in autumn, served with crusty bread. Instead of apple cider, you can also use apple juice.

Chicken stew with cider & apples

2 tablespoons unsalted butter

1 whole chicken, about 1.75 kg (3½ lb), cut into 8 serving pieces (see Basics)

¼ cup (35 g) plain (all-purpose) flour

1 small onion, finely chopped

750 g (1½ lb) all-purpose potatoes, peeled and thickly sliced

1 small green cabbage, about 500 g (1 lb), halved and cut into thick wedges

2 granny smith apples, diced

½ cup (125 ml) apple cider

¾ teaspoon salt

½ teaspoon freshly ground black pepper

PREPARATION 25 minutes
COOKING 1 hour 30 minutes
MAKES 4 servings

PER SERVING 2938 kJ, 702 kcal, 40 g protein, 38 g fat (14 g saturated fat), 47 g carbohydrate (16 g sugars), 487 mg sodium, 9 g fibre

1 Preheat oven to 180°C (350°F/Gas 4). In a large flameproof casserole dish or Dutch oven, melt butter over medium heat. Dredge chicken in the flour, shaking off excess. Add chicken to dish in batches and fry for 4 minutes per side, or until golden brown. Transfer chicken to a plate.

2 Add onion to dish, reduce heat to low and cook, stirring frequently, for 5 minutes, or until softened. Add potatoes, cabbage and apples. Cover and cook, stirring occasionally, for 10 minutes, or until cabbage has wilted. Add cider, salt and pepper; increase heat to high and cook for 2 minutes, or until liquid is slightly reduced.

3 Return chicken to dish and bring to a boil. Cover, place in oven and bake for 50 minutes, or until chicken is cooked through.

TO REDUCE THE FAT
Remove the skin from the chicken before cooking it in the stew.

VARIATION *Chicken stew with baby onions & pears*
Brown chicken as directed in step 1. In step 2, use 300 g (10 oz) baby onions instead of the onion; sprinkle with 1 tablespoon sugar and sauté for 5 minutes, or until onions are golden brown. Omit potatoes and cabbage. Substitute 2 firm, ripe pears, peeled and sliced, for the apples; sauté for 5 minutes, or until pears are crisp-tender. Omit cider; add ¾ cup (180 ml) salt-reduced chicken stock (page 49), ¼ cup (60 ml) balsamic vinegar, ½ teaspoon salt, ½ teaspoon freshly ground black pepper and ½ teaspoon dried tarragon and bring to a boil. Cover and bake for 50 minutes, or until chicken is cooked through. On the stovetop, add ¼ cup (60 ml) pouring (light) cream to the stew and cook over high heat until cream is slightly reduced. Stir in 3 tablespoons chopped fresh parsley and serve.

Chicken with orange sauce

1 cup (125 g) sultanas (golden raisins)

¼ cup (60 ml) olive oil

1.5 kg (3 lb) skinless chicken breast halves

⅓ cup (50 g) plain (all-purpose) flour

3 shallots (eschalots), finely chopped

2 tablespoons sugar

⅓ cup (80 ml) red wine vinegar

3 tablespoons finely grated orange zest

1 cup (250 ml) orange juice

1 tablespoon dijon mustard

½ teaspoon salt

LOW FAT

PREPARATION 20 minutes

COOKING 45 minutes

MAKES 8 servings

PER SERVING 1899 kJ, 454 kcal, 42 g protein,
21 g fat (7 g saturated fat), 24 g carbohydrate
(19 g sugars), 363 mg sodium, 1 g fibre

1 In a small bowl, soak sultanas in ½ cup (125 ml) hot water for 20 minutes, or until softened; drain.

2 Meanwhile, in a large heavy-based saucepan, heat half the oil over medium heat. Dredge chicken in the flour, shaking off excess. Add half the chicken to the pan and fry for 4 minutes per side, or until golden. Transfer chicken to a plate. Add remaining oil to pan and fry remaining chicken; transfer to a plate.

3 Add shallots to the pan, reduce heat to low and cook for 4 minutes, or until tender. Sprinkle sugar over shallots, increase heat to medium–high and cook for 2 minutes, or until shallots have caramelised. Add vinegar and cook for 1 minute. Add orange zest, orange juice, mustard, salt and sultanas; bring to a boil and cook for 5 minutes.

4 Return chicken to pan and bring to a boil. Reduce to a simmer, cover and cook for 15 minutes, or until chicken is cooked through.

5 Transfer chicken to serving plates. Return sauce to a boil and cook for 2 minutes, or until slightly reduced. Remove sauce from heat and swirl in butter. Spoon over chicken and serve.

To cut up the butternut pumpkin, you'll need a large, sturdy chef's knife. To make the procedure easier, first cut off the 'neck' of the pumpkin, then halve the thicker bottom part.

Chicken, pumpkin & lentil stew

2 tablespoons olive oil

1 onion, finely chopped

3 cloves garlic, crushed

½ cup (95 g) lentils, rinsed and picked over

1 small (625 g/1¼ lb) butternut pumpkin (squash), peeled and diced

1 cup (250 g) canned chopped tomatoes

2 teaspoons chilli powder

1 teaspoon ground coriander

½ teaspoon salt

tiny pinch of ground cloves

750 g (1½ lb) boneless, skinless chicken thighs, cut into large chunks

LOW FAT
PREPARATION 15 minutes
COOKING 55 minutes
MAKES 4 servings

PER SERVING 2082 kJ, 497 kcal, 43 g protein, 24 g fat (6 g saturated fat), 31 g carbohydrate (7 g sugars), 529 mg sodium, 8 g fibre

1 Preheat the oven to 180°C (350°F/Gas 4). In a large flameproof casserole dish or Dutch oven, heat oil over medium heat. Add onion and garlic and sauté for 7 minutes, or until onion is soft.

2 Stir in lentils, pumpkin, tomatoes, chilli powder, coriander, salt, cloves and ½ cup (125 ml) water; bring to a boil. Add chicken. Cover, place in oven and bake for 45 minutes, or until chicken is cooked through and pumpkin and lentils are tender.

VARIATION
Use 3 cups (525 g) shredded cooked chicken thighs instead of uncooked chicken. Stir chicken into stew for last 15 minutes of cooking.

Fragrant hoisin sauce enhances chicken without overpowering it. Made from soybeans, garlic and chillies and other seasonings, its slightly sweet and spicy taste adds depth and richness.

Spicy braised chicken with capsicum

3 spring onions (scallions), thinly sliced

3 cloves garlic, crushed

3 slices fresh ginger, each about 5 mm
   (¼ inch) thick

2 tablespoons salt-reduced soy sauce

2 tablespoons hoisin sauce

¼ cup (60 ml) salt-reduced chicken stock
   (page 49)

1 tablespoon sesame oil

1 teaspoon dried red chilli flakes

1 teaspoon sugar

8 chicken drumsticks, about 1.25 kg
   (2½ lb) in total, skin removed

500 g (1 lb) button mushrooms, quartered

1 large green capsicum (bell pepper), cut
   into chunks

1½ teaspoons cornflour (cornstarch)

1 cup (200 g) long-grain white rice

LOW FAT

PREPARATION 15 minutes

COOKING 40 minutes

MAKES 8 servings

PER SERVING 1463 kJ, 350 kcal, 34 g protein,
13 g fat (3 g saturated fat), 24 g carbohydrate
(3 g sugars), 601 mg sodium, 3 g fibre

1 In a large heavy-based saucepan, combine spring onions, garlic, ginger, soy sauce, hoisin sauce, stock, sesame oil, chilli flakes and sugar. Add chicken, mushrooms and capsicum.

2 Bring to a boil over medium heat. Reduce heat to a simmer, then cover and cook for 35 minutes, or until chicken is cooked through and vegetables are tender. Mix cornflour with 1 tablespoon water to make a smooth paste; add to the pan and cook, stirring constantly, for 1 minute, or until sauce is slightly thickened.

3 Meanwhile, in a covered saucepan, bring 2¼ cups (560 ml) water to a boil. Add rice and reduce heat to a simmer. Cover and cook for 17 minutes, or until rice is tender.

4 Spoon rice onto serving plates and top with the chicken mixture. Drizzle with sauce from the pan and serve.

Mexican food is easy to make at home and its fresh taste makes the effort worthwhile. For this casual main dish, corn tortillas are filled with chicken and mild cheese and baked in a salsa. If you have more filling than you need—or if some falls out during baking— just spoon it over the enchiladas as you serve them.

Chicken-cheese enchiladas with salsa

¼ cup (60 ml) olive oil

1 small onion, finely chopped

2 cloves garlic, crushed

2 cups (300 g) shredded cooked chicken breasts or thighs—leftover or poached (see Basics)

2 mild green chillies, or to taste, chopped

4 tablespoons chopped fresh coriander (cilantro)

1 pickled jalapeño chilli, finely chopped with seeds

1 cup (250 g) thick mild-to-hot tomato salsa or tomatillo-based salsa verde

⅓ cup (80 ml) pouring (light) cream

8 corn tortillas (15 cm/6 inch diameter)

1½ cups (185 g) shredded mild white cheddar (or Monterey Jack cheese)

PREPARATION 15 minutes
COOKING 35 minutes
MAKES 4 servings

PER SERVING 2632 kJ, 628 kcal, 35 g protein, 45 g fat (19 g saturated fat), 21 g carbohydrate (6 g sugars), 815 mg sodium, 4 g fibre

1 In a frying pan, heat 1 tablespoon oil over low heat. Add onion and garlic and cook, stirring frequently, for 7 minutes, or until onion is soft. Stir in chicken, chillies, coriander and jalapeño until combined.

2 Preheat the oven to 180°C (350°F/Gas 4). In a bowl, combine salsa and cream.

3 In a large frying pan, heat remaining oil. Gently heat each tortilla in the oil for 5 seconds; drain on paper towels. Spread some salsa mixture over each tortilla, reserving remainder for topping. Dividing evenly, spoon chicken mixture down middle of each tortilla. Top each with 1 tablespoon cheddar and roll enchiladas up.

4 Spread ⅓ cup (80 g) of the salsa mixture over the bottom of an 18 x 28 cm (7 x 11 inch) glass baking dish. Place enchiladas in dish, seam side down. Pour remaining salsa over the top. Cover with foil and bake for 20 minutes, or until piping hot.

5 Remove foil, sprinkle with remaining cheddar and bake for another 5 minutes, or until cheese has melted.

COOK'S TIPS
• In Mexican cooking, salsa verde is usually a cooking sauce and condiment made from tomatillos (a type of small, tomato-like fruit used when it is still green and hard). The other ingredients in a basic salsa verde are green chillies and coriander. Look for bottled salsa verde in the Mexican foods section of major supermarkets and specialist grocery stores.
• A dollop of sour cream and a coriander sprig make an appealing garnish for these enchiladas.

Greek-style stuffed capsicums

4 capsicums (bell peppers)

1 tablespoon olive oil

1 large onion, finely chopped

1 cup (200 g) orzo or risoni

3 tablespoons snipped fresh dill

2 tablespoons finely chopped fresh mint

1 teaspoon grated lemon zest

2 cups (300 g) shredded cooked chicken

1¼ cups (185 g) crumbled fetta

1 cup (250 g) canned chopped tomatoes

¼ cup (60 ml) salt-reduced chicken stock

½ teaspoon dried oregano

PREPARATION 20 minutes
COOKING 55 minutes
MAKES 4 servings

PER SERVING 2166 kJ, 517 kcal, 33 g protein,
21 g fat (9 g saturated fat), 48 g carbohydrate
(7 g sugars), 618 mg sodium, 3 g fibre

1 Cut a thin slice from the bottom of each capsicum so it stands flat. Cut off and reserve tops; remove and discard seeds and membranes. In a large pot of boiling water, blanch capsicums and tops for 4 minutes. Drain on paper towels, cut side down.

2 In a frying pan, heat oil over medium heat. Add onion and cook, stirring frequently, for 10 minutes, or until soft and golden.

3 Meanwhile, in a large saucepan of boiling water, cook orzo for 8 minutes, or until tender; drain.

4 Preheat the oven to 190°C (375°F/Gas 5). In a large bowl, combine sautéed onion, drained orzo, dill, mint and lemon zest. Stir in chicken and fetta.

5 In a 23 cm (9 inch) square glass baking dish, stir together tomatoes, stock and oregano. Stand capsicums in the dish and spoon chicken mixture into them. Place tops on capsicums.

6 Place a 'tent' of foil over the dish. Transfer to the oven and bake for 40 minutes, or until capsicums are very tender and filling is piping hot. To serve, spoon sauce from the baking dish over capsicums.

This simple to make two-step Moroccan stew is highly satisfying, with chicken pieces, legumes and beans coated in a richly spiced sauce.

Moroccan chicken casserole

2 tablespoons butter

1 teaspoon ground cinnamon

½ teaspoon ground ginger

½ teaspoon ground turmeric

½ teaspoon paprika

½ teaspoon freshly ground black pepper

1 kg (2 lb) chicken legs, cut into drumsticks and thighs (see Basics), skin removed

1 onion, finely chopped

4 tablespoons chopped coriander (cilantro)

1 cup (250 ml) no-added-salt tomato sauce (ketchup)

2 x 300 g (10 oz) cans chickpeas, rinsed and drained

300 g (10 oz) can butterbeans (lima beans), rinsed and drained

PREPARATION 15 minutes
COOKING 45 minutes
MAKES 4 servings

PER SERVING 2477 kJ, 592 kcal, 56 g protein, 27 g fat (11 g saturated fat), 33 g carbohydrate (15 g sugars), 739 mg sodium, 8 g fibre

1 Preheat the oven to 180°C (350°F/Gas 4). In a large flameproof casserole dish or Dutch oven, melt butter over low heat. Add cinnamon, ginger, turmeric, paprika and pepper and cook for 30 seconds. Add chicken pieces, onion and coriander, then cover and cook for 7 minutes, or until onion is tender.

2 Stir in tomato sauce, chickpeas, butterbeans and ⅓ cup (80 ml) water; bring to a boil. Cover, place in oven and bake for 35 minutes, or until chicken is cooked through. Serve hot.

A medley of mushrooms—deeply flavourful Japanese shiitake, handsome Swiss browns and the classic white button—elevate this garlicky, tender chicken braise into gourmet territory. We're serving it with rice to soak up the savoury juices, but creamy mashed potato would be equally good.

Chicken braised with mushrooms

2 tablespoons olive oil

8 bone-in chicken thighs, about 1 kg (2 lb) in total

2 tablespoons plain (all-purpose) flour

1 green capsicum (bell pepper), cut into chunks

10 cloves garlic, finely sliced

500 g (1 lb) all-purpose potatoes, peeled and diced

300 g (10 oz) button mushrooms, thickly sliced

225 g (8 oz) shiitake mushrooms, stems trimmed and caps thickly sliced

225 g (8 oz) Swiss brown or porcini mushrooms, thickly sliced

¾ cup (180 ml) salt-reduced chicken stock (page 49)

400 g (14 oz) canned artichoke hearts, drained (or use frozen)

½ teaspoon salt

½ teaspoon dried tarragon

1 cup (200 g) long-grain white rice

1 tablespoon lemon juice

PREPARATION 35 minutes
COOKING 1 hour
MAKES 4 servings

PER SERVING 3888 kJ, 929 kcal, 57 g protein, 46 g fat (13 g saturated fat), 68 g carbohydrate (5 g sugars), 727 mg sodium, 8 g fibre

1 Preheat the oven to 180°C (350°F/Gas 4). In a large flameproof casserole dish or Dutch oven, heat oil over medium heat. Dredge chicken in the flour, shaking off excess. Add chicken to dish and fry for 4 minutes per side, or until golden brown. Transfer chicken to a plate.

2 Reduce heat to medium–low. Add capsicum and garlic to dish and cook for 5 minutes, or until capsicum is crisp-tender. Add potatoes and cook for 2 minutes.

3 Add all the mushrooms. Cover and cook, stirring occasionally, for 5 minutes, or until mushrooms begin to release their juices. Stir in stock, artichokes, 1 teaspoon salt and the tarragon and bring to a boil. Return chicken to pan and bring back to a boil. Cover, place in oven and bake for 35 minutes, or until chicken and potatoes are tender.

4 Meanwhile, in a covered saucepan, bring 2¼ cups (560 ml) water to a boil. Add rice and remaining salt. Reduce heat to a simmer, cover and cook for 17 minutes, or until rice is tender.

5 Stir lemon juice into the casserole. Serve chicken and vegetables on a bed of rice, drizzled with the sauce.

TO REDUCE THE FAT
Remove the skin from the chicken before cooking it in the stew.

Chicken 'osso buco'

Chicken 'osso buco'

2 tablespoons olive oil

8 bone-in chicken thighs, 1 kg (2 lb) in total

½ teaspoon salt

¼ teaspoon freshly ground black pepper

¼ cup (35 g) plain (all-purpose) flour

½ cup (125 ml) dry white wine

1 cup (250 g) canned chopped tomatoes

1 cup (200 g) long-grain white rice

2 cloves garlic, crushed

½ cup (15 g) chopped fresh parsley

grated zest of 1 lemon

PREPARATION 15 minutes
COOKING 40 minutes
MAKES 4 servings

PER SERVING 3414 kJ, 815 kcal, 47 g protein, 45 g fat (13 g saturated fat), 49 g carbohydrate (3 g sugars), 560 mg sodium, 3 g fibre

1 In a large heavy-based saucepan, heat oil over medium heat. Sprinkle chicken with ½ teaspoon salt and the pepper. Dredge chicken in the flour, shaking off excess.

2 Add chicken to pan and fry for 4 minutes per side, or until golden brown.

3 Add wine to pan, increase heat to high and cook for 1 minute. Add tomatoes and bring to a boil. Reduce to a simmer, cover and cook for 30 minutes, or until chicken is very tender.

4 Meanwhile, in a covered saucepan, bring 2¼ cups (560 ml) water to a boil. Add rice and remaining salt. Reduce to a simmer, cover and cook for 17 minutes, or until rice is tender.

5 In a small bowl, stir together garlic, parsley and lemon zest. Sprinkle mixture over chicken; cover and cook for 3 minutes.

6 Serve the chicken and sauce on a bed of rice.

Cardamom chicken casserole

2 tablespoons olive oil

1 large onion, finely chopped

2 cloves garlic, crushed

4 large carrots, grated

1½ cups (300 g) jasmine rice (Thai fragrant rice)

¾ teaspoon ground cardamom

½ teaspoon ground ginger

½ teaspoon salt

2 cups (500 ml) salt-reduced chicken stock (page 49)

2½ cups (375 g) diced cooked chicken breasts or thighs—leftover or poached (see Basics)

½ cup (80 g) roughly chopped raw (unblanched) almonds

½ cup (60 g) sultanas (golden raisins)

LOW FAT
PREPARATION 15 minutes
COOKING 45 minutes
MAKES 4 servings

PER SERVING 3018 kJ, 721 kcal, 37 g protein, 28 g fat (4 g saturated fat), 80 g carbohydrate (19 g sugars), 749 mg sodium, 6 g fibre

1 Preheat the oven to 180°C (350°F/Gas 4). In a flameproof casserole dish or Dutch oven, heat oil over low heat. Add onion and garlic and cook, stirring frequently, for 7 minutes, or until onion is soft. Stir in carrots and cook for 2 minutes.

2 Stir in rice, cardamom, ginger and salt until vegetables are coated. Add stock and 1½ cups (375 ml) water and bring to a boil. Stir in chicken, almonds and sultanas. Cover, place in oven and bake for 35 minutes, or until chicken and rice are tender.

Mulligatawny originated in South India; its name means 'pepper water', which suggests a spicy but thin soup. However, our interpretation is quite a hearty stew, with a touch of creaminess from coconut milk.

Chicken mulligatawny stew

1 tablespoon olive oil

2 teaspoons ground coriander

1 teaspoon ground cumin

1 teaspoon turmeric

4 bone-in chicken breast halves, about 1.25 kg (2½ lb) in total, skin removed, cut in half crosswise

3 cups (375 g) small cauliflower florets

2 cloves garlic, crushed

410 g (14 oz) can chopped tomatoes

1 teaspoon cinnamon

½ teaspoon ground ginger

1 teaspoon salt

1 cup (200 g) long-grain white rice

1½ cups (235 g) peas, fresh or frozen

⅓ cup (80 ml) light coconut milk

LOW FAT
PREPARATION 20 minutes
COOKING 50 minutes
MAKES 4 servings

PER SERVING 2249 kJ, 537 kcal, 45 g protein, 17 g fat (6 g saturated fat), 51 g carbohydrate (6 g sugars), 780 mg sodium, 4 g fibre

1 In a large heavy-based saucepan, heat oil over medium heat. Add coriander, cumin and turmeric and cook for 1 minute. Add chicken and fry for 4 minutes per side, or until golden brown. Transfer chicken to a plate.

2 Add cauliflower and garlic to pan and cook for 1 minute, or until garlic is tender. Add ⅓ cup (80 ml) water, then cover and cook for 3 minutes, or until water has evaporated.

3 Add tomatoes, cinnamon, ginger and half the salt and bring to a boil. Return chicken to pan and reduce to a simmer. Cover and cook for 30 minutes, or until chicken is cooked through and cauliflower is tender.

4 Meanwhile, in a covered saucepan, bring 2¼ cups (560 ml) water to a boil. Add rice and remaining salt. Reduce heat to a simmer, then cover and cook for 17 minutes, or until rice is tender.

5 Stir peas and coconut milk into chicken mixture. Cook, uncovered, for 5 minutes, or until peas are heated through and sauce is richly flavoured. Serve on a bed of rice.

'Tikka' means 'pieces' or 'bits'. In this Indian classic, fresh chicken breast chunks are tenderised overnight in yogurt and fragrant spices, then threaded onto skewers and cooked to perfection. Serve hot or cold, with warm naan or pita bread and a raita (try our recipe on page 45).

Chicken tikka

MARINADE

150 g (5 oz) natural (plain) yogurt

1 teaspoon cornflour (cornstarch)

1 small onion, chopped

1 clove garlic, crushed

1 tablespoon finely chopped fresh ginger

1 red chilli, finely chopped

juice of 1 lemon

2 tablespoons olive oil

2 teaspoons paprika

1 teaspoon garam masala

1 teaspoon ground cumin

½ teaspoon turmeric

2 tablespoons chopped fresh coriander
    (cilantro)

½ teaspoon salt

½ teaspoon freshly ground black pepper

500 g (1 lb) boneless, skinless chicken
    breasts, cut into large chunks

LOW FAT

PREPARATION 25 minutes, plus
    overnight marinating
COOKING 20 minutes
MAKES 4 serves

PER SERVING 1235 kJ, 295 kcal, 29 g protein, 18 g fat (4 g saturated fat), 5 g carbohydrate (3 g sugars), 401 mg sodium, 1 g fibre

1 In a food processor or blender, combine marinade ingredients. Process until smooth.

2 Place chicken in a glass or non-reactive dish. Pour marinade over and toss well until thoroughly coated. Cover and marinate in the refrigerator overnight.

3 Soak 12 wooden skewers in cold water for at least 30 minutes, to prevent scorching.

4 Heat the grill (broiler) to medium. Thread chicken onto skewers. Place on the grill rack and cook for 15 to 20 minutes, or until cooked through, turning skewers occasionally, and brushing chicken from time to time with remaining marinade to stay moist.

5 Serve hot or cold, with warm naan or pita bread and raita.

COOK'S TIPS

• These skewers can also be barbecued, or baked with the marinade in a 200°C (400°F/Gas 6) oven for 30 minutes, turning every 10 minutes or so.

• If you're baking the skewers, any leftover marinade in the baking dish can be reduced to a thick sauce by cooking it over high heat, stirring well to incorporate all the sediment and pan juices; serve drizzled over the skewers.

Most stews and casseroles benefit by being prepared ahead and then refrigerated overnight, allowing the flavours to develop and blend. If making this stew ahead of time, leave out the corn and parsley and instead add them after the stew has been gently reheated on the stovetop.

Chicken stew with lima beans

6 slices bacon, about 125 g (4 oz), cut crosswise into thick strips

4 whole chicken legs, about 1.25 kg (2½ lb) in total, cut into drumsticks and thighs (see Basics), skin removed

¼ cup (35 g) plain (all-purpose) flour

1 large onion, diced

500 g (1 lb) small red-skinned potatoes, such as desiree or pontiac, thinly sliced

¾ cup (180 ml) salt-reduced chicken stock (page 49)

410 g (14 oz) can chopped tomatoes

400 g (14 oz) can butterbeans (lima beans), rinsed and drained

1 cup (150 g) frozen corn kernels, thawed, or 1 cup (200 g) fresh corn kernels

3 tablespoons chopped fresh parsley

LOW FAT

PREPARATION 25 minutes
COOKING 1 hour 15 minutes
MAKES 4 servings

PER SERVING 2151 kJ, 514 kcal, 50 g protein, 15 g fat (5 g saturated fat), 40 g carbohydrate (8 g sugars), 958 mg sodium, 6 g fibre

1 Preheat the oven to 180°C (350°F/Gas 4). In a flameproof casserole dish or Dutch oven, cook bacon over low heat for 7 minutes, or until crisp; drain on paper towels. Remove all but 2 tablespoons bacon drippings from casserole dish.

2 Dredge chicken in the flour, shaking off excess. Add chicken to dish, increase heat to medium–high and fry in batches for 4 minutes per side, or until golden brown. Transfer chicken to a plate.

3 Add onion to dish and cook, stirring frequently, for 7 minutes, or until soft. Add potatoes and stir to coat. Add stock, tomatoes, butterbeans and bacon and bring to a boil. Cover, place in oven and bake for 35 minutes, or until chicken is tender.

4 Place dish on the stovetop and remove lid. Stir in corn and parsley and cook over medium heat for 3 minutes, or until corn is heated through. Serve hot.

French-style chicken in red wine

12 shallots (eschalots) or baby onions, unpeeled

1½ tablespoons olive oil

2 slices bacon, rind removed, cut into thin strips

12 Swiss brown or button mushrooms

1 clove garlic, crushed

4 bone-in chicken breast halves or thighs, about 625 g (1¼ lb) in total, skin removed

3 sprigs fresh parsley, stalks bruised

2 sprigs fresh thyme

1 bay leaf

150 ml (5 fl oz) salt-reduced chicken stock (page 49)

1½ cups (375 ml) full-bodied red wine, such as Burgundy

1 teaspoon freshly ground black pepper

300 g (10 oz) carrots, cut into chunks

pinch of caster (superfine) sugar

1 tablespoon cornflour (cornstarch)

2 tablespoons chopped fresh parsley

LOW FAT
PREPARATION 15 minutes
COOKING 1 hour 10 minutes
MAKES 4 servings

PER SERVING 1757 kJ, 420 kcal, 41 g protein, 18 g fat (4 g saturated fat), 9 g carbohydrate (5 g sugars), 573 mg sodium, 4 g fibre

1 Place shallots in a heatproof bowl and pour enough boiling water over to cover. Leave for 30 seconds, then drain. When cool enough to handle, peel and set aside.

2 In a large heavy-based saucepan, heat 1 tablespoon oil over medium heat. Add bacon and cook for 3 minutes, stirring frequently, or until crisp. Remove bacon and set aside. Add shallots to pan and cook, stirring frequently, over medium–high heat for 5 minutes, or until golden brown. Remove and set aside.

3 Add mushrooms and garlic to pan with remaining oil. Cook for 4 minutes, stirring often, until mushrooms are golden.

4 Add half the bacon and half the shallots. Place chicken on top and sprinkle with remaining bacon and shallots. Tie the parsley, thyme and bay leaf into a bouquet garni and add to pan with the stock, wine and pepper. Bring to a boil, then reduce to a simmer and cook for 15 minutes. Add carrots and simmer another 30 minutes, or until chicken is cooked through and carrots are tender.

5 Transfer chicken to a warmed serving platter, then the bacon, mushrooms, shallots and carrots, reserving bouquet garni. Keep platter warm.

6 Strain cooking liquid into a saucepan. Add the bouquet garni and sugar and bring to a boil. Cook until sauce has reduced to about ½ cup (375 ml). Mix the cornflour with 1 tablespoon water to make a smooth paste; add to the sauce, stirring constantly. Simmer for 2 minutes, or until thickened. Discard bouquet garni.

7 Spoon the sauce over the chicken and vegetables, sprinkle with parsley and serve.

VARIATION *Chicken with Riesling*
Instead of bone-in pieces, use 500 g (1 lb) boneless, skinless chicken breasts or thighs, cut into large chunks. In step 4, substitute Riesling for red wine; add the carrots with the chicken and simmer for 30 minutes, then add 1⅓ cups (200 g) frozen peas and simmer for another 5 minutes. Strain and reduce the cooking liquid as described in step 6, then thicken with ⅓ cup (80 ml) pouring (light) cream or sour cream. Serve with boiled pasta egg noodles, tossed with finely chopped fresh parsley or poppy seeds.

This is an interpretation of Portuguese caldo verde, a stew made with kale, potatoes and sausages. Kale, also known as 'cavolo nero' or Tuscan cabbage, is a highly nutritious member of the cabbage family with long and crinkly dark green leaves. It benefits from long, gentle cooking. Remove the tough centre stalks before using.

Portuguese chicken with greens

1 tablespoon olive oil

225 g (8 oz) spicy pork sausages, casings removed

1 leek, white part only, halved lengthwise and thinly sliced

2 carrots, thinly sliced

750 g (1½ lb) all-purpose potatoes, peeled and diced

8 cups (700 g) torn kale, spinach or silverbeet (Swiss chard) leaves, stems removed

1 cup (250 ml) salt-reduced chicken stock (page 49)

½ teaspoon dried thyme

750 g (1½ lb) boneless, skinless chicken thighs, cut into large chunks

PREPARATION 25 minutes
COOKING 40 minutes
MAKES 4 servings

PER SERVING 2829 kJ, 676 kcal, 54 g protein, 32 g fat (10 g saturated fat), 47 g carbohydrate (4 g sugars), 738 mg sodium, 9 g fibre

1 In a large heavy-based saucepan, heat oil over medium heat. Add sausages and cook for 5 minutes, or until lightly browned, turning occasionally. Transfer sausages to a plate.

2 Add leek and carrots to pan and cook, stirring frequently, for 7 minutes, or until leek is soft. Add potatoes and kale, stirring to coat in the oil. Add stock and thyme and bring to a boil.

3 Stir in chicken and sausages. Reduce to a simmer, then cover and cook for 25 minutes, or until chicken and sausages are cooked through and potatoes are tender. Serve hot.

TO REDUCE THE FAT
Substitute 225 g (8 oz) spicy fresh or cooked chicken sausages for pork sausages and 4 boneless, skinless chicken breasts for thighs. Brown sausages as directed. Add chicken breasts with stock in step 2 and cook for 10 minutes; remove chicken from pan. In step 3, cook the potatoes for 10 minutes and return chicken to pan for the last 15 minutes of cooking time.

CASSEROLES, STEWS & ONE-DISH MEALS **121**

The main ingredient in a traditional shepherd's pie is, of course, lamb, but tender chicken thighs are a worthy substitute. The mashed-potato topping can be simply spooned over the filling, or piped through a piping (icing) bag for a decorative effect. Add extra flavour by sprinkling with grated cheddar before baking.

Chicken shepherd's pie

750 g (1½ lb) all-purpose potatoes, peeled and cut into large chunks

3 cloves garlic, bruised

¼ cup (60 ml) pouring (light) cream

¾ teaspoon salt

2 tablespoons butter

1 small onion, finely chopped

3 carrots, halved lengthwise and thinly sliced

750 g (1½ lb) boneless, skinless chicken thighs, cut into small dice

2 tablespoons plain (all-purpose) flour

1 cup (250 ml) salt-reduced chicken stock (page 49)

1 cup (155 g) frozen peas

3 tablespoons chopped fresh parsley

PREPARATION 30 minutes
COOKING 1 hour
MAKES 4 servings

PER SERVING 2323 kJ, 555 kcal, 44 g protein, 28 g fat (14 g saturated fat), 31 g carbohydrate (6 g sugars), 882 mg sodium, 5 g fibre

1 In a saucepan of boiling water, cook potatoes and garlic cloves for 25 minutes, or until tender; drain. With a potato masher, mash potatoes, garlic, cream and ½ teaspoon of the salt until smooth; set aside.

2 Meanwhile, preheat the oven to 180°C (350°F/Gas 4). In a large frying pan, melt butter over low heat. Add onion and cook, stirring frequently, for 7 minutes, or until soft. Add carrots and cook, stirring frequently, for 5 minutes, or until tender. Add chicken and sauté for 4 minutes, or until no longer pink.

3 Sprinkle flour over chicken mixture and cook, stirring frequently, for 1 minute, or until no streaks of flour remain. Gradually add stock and remaining salt and bring to a boil. Reduce to a simmer and cook, stirring frequently, for 5 minutes, or until sauce is slightly thickened. Stir in peas and parsley.

4 Spoon mixture into a deep, 23 cm (9 inch) pie dish. Spoon or pipe the mashed potatoes over the top. Bake for 30 minutes, or until potato topping is golden brown and crusty. Serve hot.

VARIATION *Golden-topped shepherd's pie*
In step 1, instead of the potatoes, peel 3 parsnips, 1 turnip and 250 g (8 oz) all-purpose potatoes; cut into chunks and place in a saucepan of boiling water with 2 cups (300 g) peeled butternut pumpkin (squash) chunks and 4 bruised garlic cloves. Cook and mash as directed. In step 2, substitute 2 tablespoons olive oil for butter. Assemble and bake as directed.

Red wine tenderises chicken and infuses it with colour; the better the wine, the better the flavour. Using freshly ground (rather than pre-ground) black pepper also shines through in this simple dish. If you can't get baby onions, small quartered brown (yellow) onions work well. This braise is beautiful with mashed potato.

Chicken braised in red wine

2 tablespoons olive oil

500 g (1 lb) baby onions, fresh or frozen

12 cloves garlic, peeled

1 tablespoon sugar

500 g (1 lb) swedes (rutabaga), peeled and diced

4 carrots, chopped

1 cup (250 ml) dry red wine

750 g (1½ lb) boneless, skinless chicken thighs, cut into large chunks

2 tablespoons tomato paste (concentrated purée)

¾ teaspoon salt

¾ teaspoon freshly ground black pepper

½ teaspoon dried rosemary

LOW FAT

PREPARATION **20 minutes**

COOKING **45 minutes**

MAKES **4 servings**

PER SERVING 2153 kJ, 514 kcal, 40 g protein, 24 g fat (5 g saturated fat), 27 g carbohydrate (21 g sugars), 767 mg sodium, 9 g fibre

1 In a large heavy-based saucepan, heat oil over medium heat. Add onions and garlic, sprinkle with sugar and cook, shaking pan frequently, for 10 minutes, or until onions are lightly coloured.

2 Add swedes and carrots and cook, stirring frequently, for 5 minutes, or until swedes begin to colour.

3 Add wine, increase heat to high and cook for 2 minutes, or until liquid is slightly reduced. Stir in chicken, tomato paste, salt, pepper and rosemary and bring to a boil.

4 Reduce to a simmer, then cover and cook for 25 minutes, or until chicken is cooked through and vegetables are tender.

COOK'S TIP

Similar in appearance to a turnip, the swede (rutabaga) is a member of the turnip family and about the size of a small grapefruit. Swedes have a thin, pale yellow skin and sweet yellow flesh, while turnips have a purple tinge around their top.

VARIATION *Vermouth-braised chicken with vegetables*
Instead of swedes, use 500 g (1 lb) peeled potatoes, cut into small dice. Substitute dry white vermouth for red wine; along with the vermouth add ½ cup (125 ml) salt-reduced chicken stock (page 49). Omit tomato paste. At the end, add 1 cup (155 g) frozen peas and cook for 1 minute, or until heated through.

With two kinds of chillies, as well as beans, rice and corn, this hearty casserole is a complete meal in a bowl. It's the perfect dish to warm you up on a cold winter's night.

Chicken, chilli & bean casserole

2 tablespoons olive oil

1 large onion, finely chopped

6 cloves garlic, crushed

1 pickled jalapeño chilli, finely chopped

750 g (1½ lb) boneless chicken thighs, cut into large chunks

1 cup (200 g) long-grain white rice

1½ cups (375 ml) salt-reduced chicken stock (page 49)

¼ teaspoon salt

2 x 300 g (10 oz) cans pinto or red kidney beans, rinsed and drained

2 cups (300 g) frozen corn kernels, or 1½ cups (300 g) fresh corn kernels

3 mild green chillies, chopped

½ cup (25 g) chopped coriander (cilantro)

PREPARATION 20 minutes
COOKING 35 minutes
MAKES 4 servings

PER SERVING 3451 kJ, 824 kcal, 46 g protein, 39 g fat (10 g saturated fat), 72 g carbohydrate (9 g sugars), 926 mg sodium, 11 g fibre

1 Preheat the oven to 180°C (350°F/Gas 4). In a large heavy-based saucepan, heat oil over medium–low heat. Add onion, garlic and jalapeño and cook, stirring frequently, for 7 minutes, or until onion is soft. Increase heat to medium and add chicken, stirring to coat.

2 Stir in rice, stock, salt and 1 cup (250 ml) water and bring to a boil. Stir in beans, corn and chillies. Cover, place in oven and bake for 25 minutes, or until rice is tender and chicken is cooked through. Stir in coriander and serve.

TO REDUCE THE FAT

Use a non-stick heavy-based saucepan and reduce oil in step 1 to 1 tablespoon. Use skinless, boneless chicken breasts instead of thighs with the skin on.

Cassoulet

3 shallots (eschalots), finely chopped

3 cloves garlic, crushed

¾ teaspoon dried thyme

¼ teaspoon salt

½ teaspoon freshly ground black pepper

4 whole chicken legs, about 1.25 kg
(2½ lb) in total, cut into drumsticks
and thighs (see Basics)

¼ cup (60 ml) olive oil

2 carrots, thinly sliced

3 x 300 g (10 oz) cans cannellini beans,
rinsed and drained

1 cup (250 ml) salt-reduced chicken stock
(page 49)

175 g (6 oz) dry-cured garlic-flavoured
sausages (such as Spanish chorizo),
thinly sliced

2 slices (60 g/2 oz) firm-textured white
bread, such as ciabatta or sourdough,
crumbled

1 In a large bowl, stir together shallots, garlic, thyme, salt and pepper. Add chicken and rub herb mixture into skin. Cover and refrigerate.

2 In a large flameproof casserole dish, heat oil over low heat. Add chicken and cook very slowly, turning chicken as it colours, for 35 minutes, or until cooked through. Transfer chicken to a plate.

3 Preheat the oven to 190°C (375°F/Gas 5). Add carrots to dish and cook over low heat for 7 minutes, or until tender. Stir in beans, stock and sausages. Return chicken pieces to dish, partly covering them with the bean mixture; bring to a boil.

4 Remove dish from heat and sprinkle breadcrumbs on top then bake for 20 minutes. With the back of a spoon, break through crumb topping and spoon ¼ cup (60 ml) of the cooking liquid over crumbs. Bake for another 15 minutes, or until topping is crusty.

PREPARATION 15 minutes,
plus at least 4 hours marinating
COOKING 1 hour 20 minutes
MAKES 4 servings

PER SERVING 3865 kJ, 923 kcal, 67 g protein,
64 g fat (19 g saturated fat), 22 g carbohydrate
(5 g sugars), 1418 mg sodium, 8 g fibre

Slow-cooker honey ginger chicken

Slow-cooker honey ginger chicken

1 tablespoon vegetable oil

8 boneless, skinless chicken thighs

½ cup (175 g) honey

⅓ cup (80 ml) light soy sauce

¼ cup (60 ml) no-added-salt tomato sauce (ketchup)

440 g (15 oz) can pineapple pieces, drained, reserving juice

2 cloves garlic, crushed

1 tablespoon grated fresh ginger

2 tablespoons cornflour (cornstarch)

coriander (cilantro) leaves, to garnish

PREPARATION 20 minutes

COOKING 4 hours 15 minutes

MAKES 4 servings

1 Heat oil in a large frying pan over medium heat. Add chicken and fry for 4 minutes per side, or until golden brown. Set aside.

2 Pour honey, soy sauce, tomato sauce and reserved pineapple juice into a slow cooker. Add garlic and ginger and mix well. Add chicken and turn to coat all over.

3 Cover and cook on high for 4 hours, stirring in the pineapple pieces during the final 20 minutes of cooking.

4 Remove chicken and divide among plates or bowls. In a small bowl, mix the cornflour to a smooth paste with ⅓ cup (80 ml) water, then add to remaining sauce and stir until it thickens. Drizzle sauce over the chicken, garnish with coriander and serve.

PER SERVING 3855 kJ, 921 kcal, 89 g protein, 38 g fat (11 g saturated fat), 57 g carbohydrate (51 g sugars), 1166 mg sodium, 2 g fibre

Slow-cooker lemon garlic chicken

1 teaspoon dried oregano

½ teaspoon salt

¼ teaspoon freshly ground black pepper

1 kg (2 lb) boneless, skinless chicken breasts

1½ tablespoons butter

¼ cup (60 ml) lemon juice (about 2 lemons)

2 cloves garlic, crushed

¼ cup (60 ml) salt-reduced chicken stock (page 49)

1 teaspoon chopped fresh parsley

LOW FAT

PREPARATION 15 minutes

COOKING 3–6 hours

MAKES 6 servings

1 In a small bowl, mix together oregano, salt and pepper. Rub mixture into each chicken breast.

2 In a large frying pan, melt butter over medium heat. Add chicken and fry in batches for 4 minutes per side, or until golden brown. Transfer chicken to a slow cooker.

3 Add lemon juice, garlic and stock to pan and stir together. Bring to a boil, then pour over chicken.

4 Cover and cook on high for 3 hours, or low for 6 hours, adding parsley during the final 15 to 30 minutes of cooking.

PER SERVING 1116 kJ, 267 kcal, 36 g protein, 13 g fat (5 g saturated fat), <1 g carbohydrate (<1 g sugars), 361 mg sodium, <1 g fibre

Cajun chicken in the slow cooker

4 boneless, skinless chicken breasts

½ teaspoon salt

¼ teaspoon freshly ground black pepper

1–2 teaspoons cajun seasoning, or to taste

410 g (14 oz) can chopped tomatoes

1 stalk celery, diced

1 green capsicum (bell pepper), diced

3 cloves garlic, crushed

1 onion, diced

1⅓ cups (125 g) sliced button mushrooms

1 fresh green chilli, seeded and chopped

steamed white rice, to serve

LOW FAT
PREPARATION 15 minutes
COOKING 4–8 hours
MAKES 4 servings

1 Place chicken in slow cooker. Add salt, pepper and cajun seasoning to taste. Stir in remaining ingredients.

2 Cover and cook on low for 8 hours, or on high for 4 to 5 hours. Serve with steamed white rice.

PER SERVING 2134 kJ, 510 kcal, 76 g protein, 19 g fat (6 g saturated fat), 7 g carbohydrate (5 g sugars), 771 mg sodium, 3 g fibre

Chicken 'risotto' in the slow cooker

4 boneless, skinless chicken breasts

2 slices bacon, rind removed, cut in half

1 cup (200 g) long-grain white rice

¼ teaspoon freshly ground black pepper

pinch of ground allspice

2 cloves garlic, crushed

1 tablespoon wholegrain mustard

2 tablespoons lemon juice

2 cups (500 ml) salt-reduced chicken stock (page 49)

steamed vegetables, to serve

LOW FAT
PREPARATION 10 minutes
COOKING 8 hours
MAKES 4 servings

1 Place chicken in slow cooker; lay a bacon strip over each breast.

2 Sprinkle rice over the chicken, then sprinkle with the salt, pepper and allspice.

3 In a bowl, mix together garlic, mustard, lemon juice and stock. Pour mixture over the rice.

4 Cover and cook on low for 8 hours. Serve with steamed vegetables.

PER SERVING 2924 kJ, 699 kcal, 83 g protein, 21 g fat (7 g saturated fat), 42 g carbohydrate (2 g sugars), 844 mg sodium, <1 g fibre

Cajun chicken in the slow cooker

Chicken risotto with vegetables

3 tablespoons butter

1 small onion, finely chopped

1 red capsicum (bell pepper), diced

2 cups (300 g) butternut pumpkin
(squash), peeled and cut into
large chunks

2 cups (500 ml) salt-reduced chicken
stock (page 49)

¼ teaspoon salt

1⅓ cups (300 g) arborio rice

⅔ cup (160 ml) dry white wine

350 g (12 oz) boneless, skinless chicken
thighs, cut into small dice

1 cup (155 g) peas, fresh or frozen

½ cup (50 g) grated parmesan

6 large or 12 small amaretti biscuits
(cookies), finely crumbled (optional)

½ teaspoon freshly ground black pepper

PREPARATION 25 minutes
COOKING 45 minutes
MAKES 4 servings

PER SERVING 2847 kJ, 680 kcal, 32 g protein,
24 g fat (13 g saturated fat), 78 g carbohydrate
(10 g sugars), 719 mg sodium, 2 g fibre

1 In a large saucepan, melt 2 tablespoons butter over low heat. Add onion and cook, stirring frequently, for 7 minutes, or until soft. Add capsicum and pumpkin and cook, stirring frequently, for 10 minutes, or until pumpkin is firm-tender.

2 Meanwhile, in a separate saucepan, combine stock, salt and 1 cup (250 ml) water and bring to a simmer over low heat.

3 Add rice to sautéed vegetables and stir until well coated. Add wine and cook, stirring constantly, for 2 minutes, or until wine is reduced by half. Stir in chicken.

4 Add ½ cup (125 ml) simmering stock and stir until absorbed. Continue adding stock mixture ½ cup (125 ml) at a time, adding more liquid only when the previous amount has been absorbed. Cook, stirring constantly, until the sauce surrounding the rice is creamy. The rice will take about 25 minutes to cook.

5 Stir in peas and cook just until heated through. Stir in parmesan, amaretti crumbs if using, pepper and remaining butter. Serve hot.

COOK'S TIPS
• Risotto is traditionally made with Italian arborio rice. Arborio's plump, pearly grains have a starchy outer coat that turns creamy when cooked, while the inner kernel stays firm. This gives risotto its luxurious texture—nothing like the fluffy, separate grains that are desirable in some other rice dishes. If you use regular long- or short-grain rice in risotto, the rice will not be quite so velvety.
• Amaretti biscuits are ultra-crisp Italian macaroons. They add texture, a touch of sweetness and a subtle almond flavour to savoury dishes such as risotto. The Italians are responsible for this pairing and it is surprisingly good.

VARIATION *Chicken risotto with mushrooms*
In step 1, omit butternut pumpkin; add 225 g (8 oz) thinly sliced mushrooms with the capsicum and cook for only 7 minutes, or until capsicum is tender. Proceed as directed, but omit amaretti.

The Spanish are proud of their saffron-hued paella, and rightly so. Our low-fat version stars chicken and prawns, but you could also add other seafood or some sautéed sliced chorizo sausages to the mix. Paella takes its name from the wide, shallow two-handled pan in which it is traditionally cooked and served.

Chicken paella

¼ cup (60 ml) olive oil

8 whole chicken legs, about 2.5 kg (5 lb), cut into drumsticks and thighs (see Basics), skin and any visible fat removed

1 large onion, finely chopped

5 cloves garlic, finely chopped

1 green capsicum (bell pepper), diced

1 red capsicum (bell pepper), diced

2 cups (440 g) medium-grain white rice

3 cups (750 ml) salt-reduced chicken stock (page 49)

410 g (14 oz) can chopped tomatoes

1½ teaspoons salt

¼ teaspoon saffron threads

750 g (1½ lb) raw tiger prawns (uncooked large shrimp), peeled and deveined

LOW FAT
PREPARATION 25 minutes
COOKING 1 hour 20 minutes
MAKES 8 servings

PER SERVING 2573 kJ, 615 kcal, 57 g protein, 20 g fat (5 g saturated fat), 49 g carbohydrate (5 g sugars), 892 mg sodium, 2 g fibre

1 In a large flameproof casserole dish or Dutch oven, heat oil over medium heat. Add chicken to pan in batches and fry for 4 minutes per side, or until golden brown. Transfer chicken to a plate.

2 Add onion and garlic to dish and cook, stirring frequently, for 10 minutes, or until onion is soft and golden brown. Add capsicums and cook, stirring frequently, for 4 minutes, or until capsicums are crisp-tender.

3 Add rice and cook, stirring frequently, for 5 minutes, or until rice is pale gold. Add stock, tomatoes, salt, saffron and 1 cup (250 ml) water and bring to a boil over medium heat. Reduce to a simmer, return chicken to dish, then cover and cook for 30 minutes, or until chicken is tender.

4 Place prawns on top, then cover and cook another 10 minutes, or until prawns are cooked through and rice is tender.

Sautés & pan-fries

*An amazing variety of elegant yet simple
main dishes can be created in a humble frying
pan. From chicken marengo to raspberry
chicken breasts, here you'll find a tempting
array of wonderful meals for everyday eating
and casual entertaining.*

Serve these sautéed chicken breasts with steamed potatoes or rice and crisp-tender asparagus or green beans. Spring onions are an integral part of this dish, so choose a nice plump bunch.

Mustard-tarragon chicken sauté

2 teaspoons olive oil

4 boneless, skinless chicken breast halves, about 875 g (1¾ lb) in total, pounded 1 cm (½ inch) thick (see Basics)

2 tablespoons plain (all-purpose) flour

5 spring onions (scallions), cut into long lengths

¾ cup (180 ml) salt-reduced chicken stock (page 49)

1 tablespoon red wine vinegar

1 tablespoon dijon mustard

1 tablespoon chopped fresh tarragon, or 1 teaspoon dried

1 small tomato, seeded and diced

¼ cup (45 g) diced gherkin (pickle)

LOW FAT, QUICK
PREPARATION 10 minutes
COOKING 15 minutes
MAKES 4 servings

PER SERVING 1506 kJ, 360 kcal, 49 g protein, 15 g fat (4 g saturated fat), 7 g carbohydrate (2 g sugars), 619 mg sodium, 1 g fibre

1 In a large non-stick frying pan, heat oil over medium heat. Dredge chicken in the flour, shaking off excess. Add chicken to pan and fry for 4 minutes per side, or until golden brown. Transfer chicken to a plate.

2 Add spring onions to pan and cook for 1 minute. Add stock and vinegar, then bring to a boil. Stir in mustard and tarragon and return to a boil. Stir in tomato and gherkin.

3 Return chicken to pan, reduce to a simmer, then cover and cook for 5 minutes, or until chicken is cooked through and sauce is richly flavoured. Serve chicken with sauce spooned on top.

Chicken with mushroom sauce

2 tablespoons olive oil

1 tablespoon butter

4 small boneless, skinless chicken breast halves, about 625 g (1¼ lb) in total, pounded 5 mm (¼ inch) thick (see Basics)

2 tablespoons plain (all-purpose) flour

1 small onion, finely chopped

1 clove garlic, crushed

250 g (8 oz) fresh shiitake mushrooms, stems trimmed and caps quartered

250 g (8 oz) button mushrooms, trimmed and quartered

¼ cup (60 ml) brandy

½ cup (125 ml) salt-reduced chicken stock (page 49)

⅓ cup (80 ml) pouring (light) cream

½ teaspoon salt

½ teaspoon freshly ground black pepper

1 In a large non-stick frying pan, heat oil and butter over medium heat. Dredge chicken in the flour, shaking off excess. Add chicken to pan and fry for 1½ minutes per side, or until golden brown and cooked through. Transfer chicken to a plate.

2 Add onion and garlic to pan and cook, stirring frequently, for 5 minutes. Add shiitake and button mushrooms and cook, stirring frequently, for 7 minutes, or until mushrooms are tender.

3 Add brandy and cook for 2 minutes to evaporate alcohol. Add stock, bring to a boil and boil for 2 minutes. Add cream, salt and pepper and return to a boil. Return chicken to pan and cook for 1 minute, just until heated through. Serve topped with mushrooms and sauce.

PREPARATION 20 minutes
COOKING 20 minutes
MAKES 4 servings

PER SERVING 2105 kJ, 503 kcal, 38 g protein, 31 g fat (12 g saturated fat), 10 g carbohydrate (5 g sugars), 519 mg sodium, 2 g fibre

These chicken breasts are served with a cream-enriched sauce that balances the pungency of the pepper. You can buy coarsely ground black pepper in a jar in your supermarket, but nothing beats freshly ground black pepper from your own peppermill.

Pepper chicken with brandy cream

1 tablespoon freshly ground black pepper

½ teaspoon dried thyme

½ teaspoon salt

tiny pinch of cayenne pepper

4 boneless, skinless chicken breast halves, pounded 1 cm (½ inch) thick (see Basics)

1 tablespoon olive oil

¼ cup (60 ml) brandy, such as Cognac

½ cup (125 ml) salt-reduced chicken stock (page 49)

⅓ cup (80 ml) pouring (light) cream

2 tablespoons snipped fresh chives

QUICK

PREPARATION 10 minutes

COOKING 15 minutes

MAKES 4 servings

PER SERVING 1554 kJ, 371 kcal, 35 g protein, 22 g fat (9 g saturated fat), 2 g carbohydrate (1 g sugars), 563 mg sodium, <1 g fibre

1 In a small bowl, combine pepper, thyme, ¼ teaspoon salt and the cayenne pepper. Sprinkle mixture onto a plate. Dip chicken breasts in pepper mixture, pressing it on well.

2 In a large frying pan, heat oil over medium heat. Add chicken and fry for 3 minutes per side, or until cooked through. Transfer to serving plates.

3 Add brandy to pan and cook for 30 seconds to evaporate the alcohol. Pour in stock and boil for 1 minute. Add cream and remaining salt and boil for 3 minutes, or until slightly reduced. Stir in chives and serve over chicken.

TO REDUCE THE FAT

Use a non-stick frying pan and reduce oil to 2 teaspoons. Omit heavy cream. In step 3, boil stock for 3 minutes. Remove from heat and whisk in ¼ cup (60 g) reduced-fat sour cream.

Marmalade lends a citrus intensity to tender chicken, cut through with dijon mustard. The chicken breasts are coated with a mixture of breadcrumbs, almonds and parsley, fried until golden, then baked to perfection.

Almond-crusted orange chicken

⅓ cup (80 ml) orange juice

⅓ cup (80 ml) orange marmalade

1½ tablespoons dijon mustard

4 small boneless, skinless chicken breast halves, about 625 g (1¼ lb) in total

2 slices (60 g/2 oz) firm-textured white bread, such as ciabatta or sourdough

¾ cup (115 g) raw (unblanched) almonds

3 tablespoons fresh parsley

½ teaspoon salt

⅓ cup (80 ml) olive oil

PREPARATION 20 minutes, plus at least 1 hour chilling
COOKING 10 minutes
MAKES 4 servings

PER SERVING 2751 kJ, 657 kcal, 41 g protein, 43 g fat (6 g saturated fat), 27 g carbohydrate (21 g sugars), 642 mg sodium, 3 g fibre

1 In a shallow glass or ceramic baking dish, combine 2 tablespoons orange juice, 2 tablespoons marmalade and 1 tablespoon mustard; mix together well. Place chicken in the dish and spoon mixture over to coat. Set aside while preparing coating.

2 In a food processor, combine bread, almonds, parsley and salt. Process to a fine crumb consistency. Transfer to a shallow plate or sheet of baking (parchment) paper.

3 Lift chicken from orange mixture, discarding any mixture remaining in dish. Dip chicken in the almond-crumb mixture, pressing it on well. Transfer to a baking tray large enough to hold all the chicken in a single layer. Refrigerate, uncovered, for at least 1 hour, or up to 8 hours.

4 Preheat the oven to 180°C (350°F/Gas 4). In a small bowl, stir together remaining orange juice, marmalade and mustard to make a sauce.

5 In a large non-stick frying pan, heat 2 tablespoons oil over medium heat. Add 2 chicken breasts and cook for 1½ minutes per side, or until golden brown and cooked through. Repeat with remaining chicken and oil.

6 Transfer all the chicken to a baking dish and bake for 15 minutes, or until crust is golden and chicken is cooked through.

7 Carve chicken into thick slices and serve with the mustard marmalade sauce.

When you don't have time to roast a whole stuffed chicken—or it's too hot to turn on the oven—serve these plump chicken breasts filled with a creamy, lemon-scented pistachio stuffing. To serve, cut the stuffed breasts crosswise, arrange the slices on plates and drizzle with the sauce from the pan.

Pistachio-stuffed chicken breasts

4 boneless, skinless chicken breast halves, about 750 g (1½ lb) in total

⅓ cup (90 g) cream cheese

4 tablespoons shredded fresh basil

1 teaspoon grated lemon zest

¼ teaspoon salt

⅓ cup (50 g) shelled pistachios

2 tablespoons dry packaged breadcrumbs

1 tablespoon olive oil

¼ cup (35 g) plain (all-purpose) flour

1 cup (250 ml) salt-reduced chicken stock (page 49)

¼ cup (60 ml) lemon juice (about 2 lemons)

PREPARATION 20 minutes
COOKING 25 minutes
MAKES 4 servings

PER SERVING 2057 kJ, 491 kcal, 47 g protein, 28 g fat (9 g saturated fat), 13 g carbohydrate (3 g sugars), 718 mg sodium, 2 g fibre

1 With a sharp paring knife, make a pocket in each chicken breast half. To do this, cut a horizontal slit in the fatter side of a chicken breast, stopping 1 cm (½ inch) short of either end. Insert the blade into the slit and, with a back and forth swivelling motion, cut a pocket in the breast, without cutting through the opposite side. Repeat with the remaining chicken breasts.

2 In a food processor or blender, purée the cream cheese, basil, lemon zest and ¼ teaspoon salt until smooth. Add pistachios and breadcrumbs and process until roughly chopped. Sprinkle the remaining salt inside the chicken breast pockets and on the outsides of breasts. Spoon pistachio mixture into the pockets and secure with toothpicks.

3 In a large non-stick frying pan, heat oil over medium heat. Dredge chicken in the flour, shaking off excess. Add chicken to pan and fry for 15 minutes, or until golden brown and almost cooked through, turning chicken over as it colours.

4 Add stock and lemon juice to pan and bring to a simmer. Cover and cook for 7 minutes, or until chicken is cooked through. Remove toothpicks from chicken. Serve chicken with sauce spooned on top.

TO REDUCE THE FAT
Use reduced-fat cream cheese (or neufchâtel) instead of regular cream cheese. Reduce pistachios to ¼ cup (35 g) and increase breadcrumbs to 3 tablespoons.

If you've ever eaten saltimbocca at an Italian restaurant, you'll know the source of this recipe. Instead of veal scaloppine rolled with sage leaves and prosciutto, this appealing dish is made with pounded chicken breasts, ham, provolone cheese, and fresh basil.

Chicken rolled with ham & provolone

4 boneless, skinless chicken breast halves, about 750 g (1½ lb) in total, pounded 5 mm (¼ inch) thick (see Basics)

¼ teaspoon salt

125 g (4 oz) thinly sliced good-quality ham

60 g (2 oz) thinly sliced provolone cheese

12 large fresh basil leaves

1 tablespoon olive oil

½ cup (125 ml) salt-reduced chicken stock (page 49)

2 tablespoons lemon juice

1 tablespoon unsalted butter, chopped

PREPARATION 15 minutes
COOKING 20 minutes
MAKES 4 servings

PER SERVING 1804 kJ, 431 kcal, 51 g protein, 25 g fat (10 g saturated fat),<1 g carbohydrate (<1 g sugars), 977 mg sodium, <1 g fibre

1 Sprinkle chicken with the salt. Place chicken breasts smooth side down. Place ham on top, then top with the provolone and basil leaves. Starting at the short end, roll each chicken breast up into rolls and secure with toothpicks.

2 In a large frying pan, heat oil over medium–low heat. Add chicken rolls and fry for 10 minutes, or until golden, turning during cooking.

3 Add stock to pan. Cover and cook another 5 to 7 minutes, or until chicken is cooked through, turning during cooking. Transfer chicken to a cutting board and carve crosswise into slices 1 cm (½ inch) thick, then place on serving plates.

4 Add lemon juice and butter to pan and swirl over very low heat until creamy. Spoon over chicken and serve.

Chicken schnitzel

½ cup (75 g) plain (all-purpose) flour

2 eggs

½ teaspoon salt

½ teaspoon freshly ground black pepper

1 cup (100 g) cornflake crumbs or dry
    packaged breadcrumbs

2 large boneless, skinless chicken breasts,
    about 625 g (1¼ lb) in total

2 tablespoons olive oil

1 tablespoon butter

lemon wedges, to serve

LOW FAT
PREPARATION 10 minutes, plus 30 minutes
    chilling
COOKING 10 minutes
MAKES 4 servings

PER SERVING 2186 kJ, 522 kcal, 41 g protein,
24 g fat (7 g saturated fat), 34 g carbohydrate
(2 g sugars), 633 mg sodium, 2 g fibre

1 Place flour in a wide bowl. Beat eggs in a separate bowl with the salt and pepper. Place cornflake crumbs in a third bowl.

2 Cut each chicken breast in half horizontally, into two thin cutlets. Using a meat mallet, pound each piece 5mm (¼ inch) thick (see Basics).

3 Working one at a time, dredge each chicken breast in flour, then dip in the egg, allowing excess to drain off. Coat chicken in the crumbs and place on a baking tray in a single layer. Refrigerate, uncovered, for 30 minutes.

4 In a large frying pan, heat oil and butter over medium heat until butter foams. Add schnitzels in 2 batches and fry for 2 minutes per side, or until golden brown and cooked through. Serve hot, with lemon wedges.

COOK'S TIPS
• To vary the flavour, add 2 tablespoons grated parmesan and 2 teaspoons chopped fresh parsley (or herbs of your choice) to the crumbs.
• Serve with mashed potato and steamed broccolini.

There's quite a flavour-fest going on here, with the herb-crusted chicken served on a bed of bitter rocket and rich garlic-sautéed mushrooms. There's a pleasant contrast of temperatures and textures, too, because the salad is just warm, while the chicken breasts are hot from the pan.

Herb-crusted chicken with shiitake

3 slices (85 g/3 oz) firm-textured white bread, such as ciabatta or sourdough

½ cup (30 g) fresh basil

2 tablespoons fresh oregano, or ½ teaspoon dried

¾ teaspoon grated lemon zest

¾ teaspoon salt

1 large egg, lightly beaten with 1 tablespoon water

4 small boneless, skinless chicken breast halves, about 625 g (1¼ lb) in total, pounded 5 mm (¼ inch) thick (see Basics)

⅓ cup (80 ml) olive oil

350 g (12 oz) fresh shiitake mushrooms, stems discarded and caps thinly sliced

3 cloves garlic, crushed

500 g (1 lb) roma (plum) tomatoes, diced

1 bunch (about 150 g/5 oz) rocket (arugula), tough stems trimmed

2 tablespoons lemon juice

PREPARATION 35 minutes, plus at least 1 hour chilling
COOKING 15 minutes
MAKES 4 servings

PER SERVING 2139 kJ, 511 kcal, 41 g protein, 36 g fat (6 g saturated fat), 18 g carbohydrate (9 g sugars), 693 mg sodium, 4 g fibre

1 In a food processor or blender, combine bread, basil, oregano, lemon zest and ½ teaspoon salt. Process until bread resembles fine crumbs. Transfer to a shallow plate or sheet of baking (parchment) paper.

2 Place egg mixture in a shallow bowl. Dip chicken first in egg mixture, then in breadcrumb mixture, pressing crumbs onto chicken. Place chicken on a baking tray in a single layer. Refrigerate, uncovered, for at least 1 hour, or up to 4 hours.

3 In a large non-stick frying pan, heat 1 tablespoon oil over medium heat. Add mushrooms and garlic and cook for 7 minutes, or until mushrooms are tender. Transfer mixture to a large bowl. Add tomatoes, rocket, lemon juice, 1 tablespoon oil and remaining salt and toss to combine.

4 Wipe frying pan clean, then heat 1 tablespoon oil over medium heat. Add 2 chicken breast halves and fry for 1½ minutes per side, or until golden brown and cooked through. Repeat with remaining oil and chicken.

5 Divide mushroom mixture evenly among serving plates, top with chicken and serve.

COOK'S TIP
Wash shiitake mushrooms thoroughly but quickly, so they don't become waterlogged. Trim off the stems, which are too tough to eat; you can use these for flavouring stocks and soups.

IN A HURRY?
Omit the chilling time in step 2 and go straight to step 3, but do be sure to use a non-stick frying pan; also, be careful when turning chicken so the coating does not fall off.

Parmesan-crusted chicken cutlets

4 slices (125 g/4 oz) firm-textured white bread, such as ciabatta or sourdough

½ cup (50 g) grated parmesan

2 eggs, lightly beaten with 1 tablespoon water

4 boneless, skinless chicken breast halves, about 750 g (1½ lb) in total, pounded 1 cm (½ inch) thick (see Basics)

2 tablespoons olive oil

4 lemon wedges

LOW FAT

PREPARATION 15 minutes, plus at least 30 minutes chilling

COOKING 20 minutes

MAKES 4 servings

PER SERVING 2092 kJ, 500 kcal, 51 g protein, 27 g fat (8 g saturated fat), 14 g carbohydrate (<1 g sugars), 483 mg sodium, <1 g fibre

1 In a food processor or blender, process bread to fine crumbs. Transfer to a shallow bowl.

2 Place parmesan in a second bowl and egg mixture in a third.

3 Dip chicken first in parmesan, pressing cheese onto chicken. Dip chicken in the egg and finally in breadcrumbs, pressing crumbs onto chicken. Place on a baking tray in a single layer. Refrigerate, uncovered, for at least 30 minutes, or up to 4 hours.

4 In a large non-stick frying pan, heat oil over medium heat. Add chicken in 2 batches and fry for 5 minutes per side, or until golden brown and cooked through. Serve hot, with lemon wedges.

IN A HURRY?
Omit the chilling time in step 3 and go straight to step 4, but use a non-stick frying pan; be careful when turning chicken so the coating does not fall off.

Fragrant fresh basil is simmered with the chicken, and a handful added at the last minute. Serve the chicken with a summery vegetable accompaniment, such as steamed green or golden zucchini (courgette), yellow summer squash, or corn on the cob.

Chicken with tomato-basil sauce

2 tablespoons olive oil

4 skinless, bone-in chicken breast halves, about 1 kg (2 lb) in total

2 tablespoons plain (all-purpose) flour

1 small onion, diced

4 cloves garlic, crushed

½ cup (125 ml) dry red wine or salt-reduced chicken stock (page 49)

410 g (14 oz) can chopped tomatoes

½ cup (30 g) chopped fresh basil

½ teaspoon salt

½ teaspoon dried red chilli flakes

LOW FAT

PREPARATION 15 minutes

COOKING 35 minutes

MAKES 4 servings

PER SERVING 1370 kJ, 327 kcal, 31 g protein, 17 g fat (4 g saturated fat), 8 g carbohydrate (3 g sugars), 446 mg sodium, 2 g fibre

1 In a large frying pan, heat oil over medium heat. Dredge chicken in the flour, shaking off excess. Add chicken to pan and fry for 5 minutes per side, or until golden brown. Transfer chicken to a plate.

2 Add onion and garlic to pan and cook, stirring frequently, for 7 minutes, or until onion is soft. Add wine, increase heat to high and boil for 2 minutes.

3 Stir in tomatoes, 3 tablespoons basil, the salt and chilli flakes. Bring to a boil and return chicken to pan. Reduce to a simmer, then cover and cook for 10 minutes, or until chicken is cooked through, turning during cooking. Transfer chicken to serving plates.

4 Add remaining basil to pan and cook for 1 minute. Spoon sauce over chicken and serve.

VARIATION *Chicken breasts with spinach & mozzarella*
Fry chicken as directed in step 1. In step 2, when onion and garlic are tender, stir in 300 g (10 oz) frozen chopped spinach, thawed and squeezed dry. Omit wine, tomatoes and chilli flakes. Stir in 3 tablespoons chopped basil, ½ teaspoon salt and ⅔ cup (160 ml) chicken stock and bring to a boil. Return chicken to pan, cover and cook for 7 minutes, or until almost cooked through. Top each piece of chicken with 3 tablespoons diced fresh tomatoes, 2 basil leaves and ⅓ cup (35 g) shredded mozzarella. Cover and cook another 2 minutes, or until cheese has melted, then serve.

Lemon and dill are frequently teamed with fish, but this spring-fresh combination is equally delicious with chicken. Do use fresh lemon juice—not the juice that comes in a bottle.

Chicken breasts with lemon & dill

1 tablespoon olive oil

2 tablespoons butter

4 boneless, skinless chicken breast halves, about 750 g (1½ lb) in total

2 tablespoons plain (all-purpose) flour

2 spring onions (scallions), thinly sliced

⅔ cup (160 ml) salt-reduced chicken stock (page 49)

¼ cup (60 ml) lemon juice (about 2 lemons)

4 tablespoons snipped fresh dill

½ teaspoon salt

QUICK
PREPARATION 10 minutes
COOKING 15 minutes
MAKES 4 servings

PER SERVING 1655 kJ, 395 kcal, 42 g protein, 23 g fat (9 g saturated fat), 5 g carbohydrate (1 g sugars), 693 mg sodium, <1 g fibre

1 In a large frying pan, heat oil and 1 tablespoon butter over medium heat. Dredge chicken in the flour, shaking off excess. Add chicken to pan and fry for 12 minutes, or until golden brown and cooked through, turning it over as it colours. Transfer chicken to a plate.

2 Add spring onions to pan and cook for 1 minute. Add stock, lemon juice, dill and salt and bring to a boil. Remove from heat and swirl in remaining butter.

3 Return chicken to frying pan and spoon sauce over chicken, turning to coat. Transfer chicken to serving plates, drizzle with any remaining sauce and serve.

Manchego—a Spanish dry, salty cheese made from sheep's milk—adds a snappy tang to this family-pleasing dinner. If you can't get manchego, use freshly grated parmesan or romano. Warmed flour tortillas or squares of corn bread go very well with this dish.

Chicken, corn & broccoli sauté

1 tablespoon cornflour (cornstarch)

2 tablespoons lime juice

½ teaspoon salt

500 g (1 lb) boneless, skinless chicken breasts, cut for stir-fry (see Basics)

2 tablespoons olive oil

3 cups (180 g) small broccoli florets

2 cups (300 g) frozen corn kernels, or 1½ cups (300 g) fresh corn kernels

4 spring onions (scallions), thinly sliced

2 cloves garlic, crushed

1½ cups (375 g) mild to medium-hot bottled tomato salsa

4 tablespoons chopped fresh coriander (cilantro)

½ cup (50 g) grated aged manchego cheese, parmesan or romano

LOW FAT

PREPARATION 20 minutes

COOKING 15 minutes

MAKES 4 servings

PER SERVING 1799 kJ, 451 kcal, 39 g protein, 20 g fat (5 g saturated fat), 24 g carbohydrate (9 g sugars), 1021 mg sodium, 7 g fibre

1 In a large bowl, whisk together cornflour, lime juice and salt. Add chicken and toss to coat.

2 In a large non-stick frying pan, heat oil over medium heat. Add chicken and cook, stirring constantly, for 4 minutes, or until just cooked through. Transfer chicken to a plate.

3 Add broccoli, corn, spring onions and garlic to pan and cook for 3 minutes, or until corn is heated through. Add salsa, then cover and cook for 4 minutes, or until broccoli is crisp-tender.

4 Return chicken to pan and cook for 1 minute, or until just heated through. Stir in coriander. Spoon onto serving plates, sprinkle with the cheese and serve.

This dish was reputedly created by Napoleon Bonaparte's chef following the Battle of Marengo, waged in Italy in 1800. In this flamboyantly named dish, chicken is simply simmered in a lush tomato-wine sauce with tender mushrooms. It is wonderful served over rice, pasta noodles or polenta (cornmeal).

Chicken marengo

¼ cup (60 ml) olive oil

4 bone-in chicken breast halves, about
    1 kg (2 lb) in total, halved crosswise

¼ cup (35 g) plain (all-purpose) flour

1 red onion, finely chopped

2 cloves garlic, crushed

250 g (8 oz) mushrooms, quartered

½ cup (125 ml) dry white wine

¾ cup (185 g) canned chopped tomatoes

2 tablespoons tomato paste (concentrated
    purée)

½ teaspoon salt

LOW FAT

PREPARATION 15 minutes

COOKING 45 minutes

MAKES 4 servings

PER SERVING 1943 kJ, 464 kcal, 45 g protein,
24 g fat (5 g saturated fat), 12 g carbohydrate
(4 g sugars), 527 mg sodium, 3 g fibre

1 In a large non-stick frying pan, heat 2 tablespoons oil over medium–high heat. Dredge chicken in the flour, shaking off excess. Add chicken to pan and fry for 5 minutes per side, or until golden brown. Transfer chicken to a plate.

2 Add remaining oil to pan and heat over medium heat. Add onion and garlic and cook, stirring frequently, for 3–4 minutes, or until onion is soft. Add mushrooms and cook for 5 minutes, or until mushrooms are firm-tender.

3 Stir in wine and bring to a boil. Add tomatoes, tomato paste and salt and return to a boil. Return chicken to pan, reduce to a simmer, then cover and cook for 20 minutes, or until chicken is cooked through, turning during cooking. Serve hot.

Though festive enough for a dinner party, this dish can be on the table in about an hour. To save time, poach the apricots in advance, then refrigerate in a non-metal container until required.

Chicken thighs with sherry & apricots

1 cup (180 g) dried apricots

½ cup (125 ml) dry sherry

½ cup (125 ml) dry red wine

3 long strips orange zest

⅓ cup (75 g) sugar

2 tablespoons butter

8 bone-in chicken thighs, about 1 kg
   (2 lb) in total, skin removed

2 tablespoons plain (all-purpose) flour

300 g (10 oz) baby onions, fresh or frozen
   (thawed if frozen)

½ cup (125 ml) salt-reduced chicken stock
   (page 49)

½ teaspoon salt

½ teaspoon freshly ground black pepper

2 tablespoons snipped fresh chives

LOW FAT
PREPARATION 10 minutes
COOKING 55 minutes
MAKES 4 servings

PER SERVING 2138 kJ, 511 kcal, 30 g protein,
18 g fat (8 g saturated fat), 46 g carbohydrate
(39 g sugars), 691 mg sodium, 6 g fibre

1 In a saucepan, combine apricots, sherry, red wine, orange zest and 3 tablespoons sugar and bring to a boil over medium heat. Reduce to a simmer, then cover and cook for 20 minutes, or until apricots are tender. Remove from heat.

2 In a large non-stick frying pan, heat butter over medium heat. Dredge chicken in the flour, shaking off excess. Add chicken to pan and fry for 4 minutes per side, or until golden brown. Transfer chicken to a plate.

3 Add onions to pan, sprinkle with remaining sugar and cook, stirring frequently, for 7 minutes, or until lightly golden. Add stock, salt, pepper and apricot mixture and bring to a boil.

4 Return chicken to pan, reduce to a simmer, then cover and cook for 15 minutes, or until chicken is tender. Remove orange zest strips, stir in chives and serve.

VARIATION *Chicken thighs with prunes*
In step 1, substitute 1 cup (220 g) pitted prunes for apricots; omit sherry, increase red wine to 1 cup (250 ml) and use only 1 tablespoon sugar. Cook for only 15 minutes. Proceed with recipe as directed, adding prune mixture to chicken in step 3.

Cardamom, cloves, cumin and ground coriander are a signature blend of spices used by Indian cooks. Warming and aromatic, the spice mixture infuses the chicken, carrots and potatoes, gently rounded out with garlic towards the end.

Indian-spiced chicken & vegetables

2 tablespoons cornflour (cornstarch)

½ teaspoon ground cumin

¼ teaspoon ground cardamom

tiny pinch of ground cloves

½ teaspoon freshly ground black pepper

¾ teaspoon salt

1½ teaspoons ground coriander

¾ cup (180 ml) salt-reduced chicken stock
   (page 49)

500 g (1 lb) boneless, skinless chicken
   breasts, cut for stir-fry (see Basics)

2 tablespoons vegetable oil

3 carrots, cut into matchsticks

1 large onion, halved and thinly sliced

500 g (1 lb) all-purpose potatoes, peeled
   and finely diced

3 cloves garlic, finely sliced

1 tablespoon chopped fresh coriander
   (cilantro)

LOW FAT
PREPARATION 20 minutes
COOKING 15 minutes
MAKES 4 servings

PER SERVING 1610 kJ, 385 kcal, 32 g protein,
16 g fat (3 g saturated fat), 27 g carbohydrate
(5 g sugars), 794 mg sodium, 5 g fibre

1 In a large bowl, stir together the cornflour, cumin, cardamom, cloves, pepper, ½ teaspoon salt and 1 teaspoon coriander. Whisk in ¼ cup (60 ml) stock until smooth. Add chicken and toss to coat.

2 In a large non-stick frying pan, heat 1 tablespoon oil over medium–high heat. Remove chicken from its marinade, reserving marinade. Add chicken to pan and cook, stirring constantly, for 4 minutes, or until golden brown and cooked through. Transfer chicken to a plate.

3 Add remaining oil to pan, along with carrots, onion, potatoes, garlic and remaining coriander and salt. Cook, stirring frequently, for 5 minutes, or until carrots are crisp-tender.

4 Stir in reserved marinade and remaining stock and bring to a boil. Boil for 2 minutes, or until potatoes are tender. Return chicken to pan and cook for 1 minute, or until heated through. Serve chicken and vegetables sprinkled with coriander.

Chicken with apple & calvados

8 boneless, skinless chicken breast halves,
 about 1.5 kg (3 lb) in total, pounded
 1 cm (½ inch) thick (see Basics)

⅓ cup (35 g) plain (all-purpose) flour

2 tablespoons butter

2 tablespoons vegetable oil

1 small onion, finely chopped

4 red apples, each cut into 8 wedges

1½ teaspoons sugar

¼ cup (60 ml) calvados (apple brandy)

½ cup (125 ml) salt-reduced chicken stock
 (page 49)

½ cup (125 ml) thick (heavy/double) cream

¾ teaspoon salt

½ teaspoon freshly ground black pepper

3 tablespoons chopped fresh parsley

1 Dredge chicken in the flour, shaking off excess. In a large frying pan, heat butter and oil over medium heat. Add chicken to pan in batches and fry for 3 minutes per side, or until golden and just cooked through. Transfer chicken to a platter; cover and keep warm.

2 Add onion to pan and sauté for 5 minutes. Add apples and sugar and sauté for 5 minutes, or until apples are crisp-tender. Add calvados and cook for 1 minute to evaporate alcohol. Add stock and bring to a boil; add cream, salt and pepper and boil for 6 minutes, or until slightly thickened. Stir in parsley, spoon over chicken and serve.

PREPARATION 20 minutes
COOKING 30 minutes
MAKES 8 servings

PER SERVING 1933 kJ, 462 kcal, 41 g protein,
25 g fat (11 g saturated fat), 14 g carbohydrate
(10 g sugars), 461 mg sodium, 2 g fibre

This is a variation of the French dish 'chicken Véronique', in which green grapes are paired with chicken. (Not surprisingly, 'fish Véronique' also features green grapes.) Here, we've used red grapes to complement the heady red wine and rosemary sauce.

Chicken with red grapes & rosemary

2 tablespoons olive oil

4 bone-in chicken breast halves,
    about 1 kg (2 lb) in total, skin removed

2 tablespoons plain (all-purpose) flour

2 shallots (eschalots), finely chopped

2 cloves garlic, crushed

¼ cup (60 ml) brandy

1 cup (250 ml) dry red wine

1 tablespoon tomato paste (concentrated
    purée)

1½ teaspoons chopped fresh rosemary,
    or ½ teaspoon dried

½ teaspoon salt

2 cups (360 g) seedless red grapes, halved

2 tablespoons chopped fresh parsley

LOW FAT
PREPARATION 20 minutes
COOKING 30 minutes
MAKES 4 servings

PER SERVING 1761 kJ, 421 kcal, 31 g protein,
17 g fat (4 g saturated fat), 19 g carbohydrate
(14 g sugars), 434 mg sodium, 2 g fibre

1 In a large frying pan, heat oil over medium heat. Dredge chicken in the flour, shaking off excess. Add chicken to pan and fry for 4 minutes per side, or until golden brown. Transfer chicken to plate.

2 Reduce heat to medium–low. Add shallots and garlic and stir-fry for 3 minutes, or until shallots are tender. Add brandy and cook for 30 seconds to evaporate alcohol. Add wine, bring to a boil and cook for 2 minutes, or until liquid is slightly reduced.

3 Stir in tomato paste, rosemary and salt. Add chicken and grapes and reduce to a simmer. Cover and cook for 12 minutes, or until chicken is cooked through, turning chicken halfway during cooking.

4 Transfer chicken to serving plates, leaving sauce in pan. Stir parsley into sauce, spoon over chicken and serve.

Raspberry sauce is a sophisticated step up from apple sauce, and it's wonderful with chicken. Here, raspberry vinegar forms the tart basis of the lightly thickened sauce, with sweet fresh berries added as a final flourish.

Raspberry chicken breasts

2 tablespoons olive oil

4 boneless, skinless chicken breast halves, about 750 g (1½ lb) in total

2 tablespoons plain (all-purpose) flour

4 spring onions (scallions), thinly sliced

1 tablespoon sugar

⅓ cup (80 ml) raspberry vinegar or red wine vinegar

¾ cup (180 ml) salt-reduced chicken stock (page 49)

½ teaspoon dried tarragon

½ teaspoon salt

1½ teaspoons cornflour (cornstarch)

350 g (12 oz) raspberries

LOW FAT, QUICK
PREPARATION 10 minutes
COOKING 20 minutes
MAKES 4 servings

PER SERVING 1750 kJ, 418 kcal, 43 g protein, 20 g fat (5 g saturated fat), 16 g carbohydrate (10 g sugars), 653 mg sodium, 5 g fibre

1 In a large frying pan, heat oil over medium heat. Dredge chicken in the flour, shaking off excess. Add chicken to pan and fry for 4 minutes per side, or until golden brown. Transfer chicken to a plate.

2 Add spring onions to pan and cook for 1 minute, or until soft. Add sugar and cook for 4 minutes, or until sugar has melted and is amber in colour. Add vinegar and bring to a boil.

3 Add stock, tarragon and salt and bring to a boil. Return chicken to pan, reduce to a simmer, then cover and cook for 5 minutes, or until chicken is cooked through.

4 Transfer chicken to serving plates. Return sauce to a boil. Whisk the cornflour with 1 tablespoon water until smooth, then add to the sauce and cook, stirring constantly, for 1 minute, or until sauce is slightly thickened.

5 Stir in the raspberries, spoon sauce over chicken and serve.

Pasta & noodles

Pasta and noodles are very versatile and for many people are the ultimate comfort food. Pasta and noodle dishes are generally quick and simple to prepare, and there's no end to the variations you can create. Here's a great selection to inspire you.

Round out this simple yet elegant dish with a green salad tossed with a lemon vinaigrette. If you're using fresh tarragon for this dish, chop some to toss into the salad. A light fruit dessert, such as pears poached in white wine, would be a beautiful ending to this meal.

Chicken braised in herb cream sauce

2 tablespoons olive oil

1 whole chicken (about 1.75 kg/3½ lb), cut into 8 serving pieces (see Basics), skin removed

¼ cup (35 g) plain (all-purpose) flour

1 large onion, finely chopped

3 cloves garlic, crushed

½ cup (125 ml) dry vermouth or white wine

½ cup (125 ml) salt-reduced chicken stock (page 49)

2 tablespoons snipped fresh chives

½ teaspoon salt

225 g (8 oz) ribbon pasta or tagliatelle

1 cup (155 g) frozen peas

¼ cup (60 ml) pouring (light) cream

2 tablespoons chopped fresh tarragon, or 1 teaspoon dried

PREPARATION 20 minutes
COOKING 1 hour 5 minutes
MAKES 4 servings

PER SERVING 3172 kJ, 758 kcal, 53 g protein, 34 g fat (11 g saturated fat), 52 g carbohydrate (4 g sugars), 566 mg sodium, 3 g fibre

1 Preheat the oven to 180°C (350°F/Gas 4). In a large flameproof casserole dish or Dutch oven, heat oil over medium heat. Dredge chicken in the flour, shaking off excess. Add chicken to dish in batches and fry for 4 minutes per side, or until golden brown. Transfer chicken to a plate.

2 Reduce heat to low. Add onion and garlic to dish and cook, stirring frequently, for 5 minutes, or until softened. Add vermouth, increase heat to high and cook for 2 minutes. Add stock, chives and salt and bring to a boil. Return chicken to dish and bring to a boil. Cover, place in the oven and bake for 35 minutes, or until chicken is cooked through.

3 Meanwhile, in a large pot of boiling water, cook pasta until al dente, following packet instructions. Drain and place in a large serving bowl. When chicken is cooked, add it to the pasta.

4 Add peas, cream and tarragon to the casserole dish and cook over high heat for 5 minutes, or until sauce is slightly reduced and peas are heated through. Spoon sauce over chicken and pasta and serve hot.

VARIATION *Chicken paprikash*
In step 1, sauté chicken in 3 tablespoons oil. In step 2, when onion is soft, stir in 2 tablespoons paprika and cook for 2 minutes. Add vermouth and cook as directed. Add stock, substitute ½ teaspoon caraway seeds for chives, and increase salt to 1 teaspoon. Bake chicken and cook noodles as directed. In a small bowl, blend together ½ cup (125 g) reduced-fat sour cream and 1 tablespoon flour. In step 4, omit cream and tarragon. Stir sour-cream mixture into dish and simmer for 2 minutes, or until no floury taste remains. Stir in peas and heat through, then spoon over chicken and noodles.

Lasagne is universally popular and lasagne fans will welcome this hearty variation. There are tomatoes in the chicken-and-eggplant filling, but instead of being tomato-based, the sauce is a creamy 'balsamella', or Italian white sauce.

Chicken & eggplant lasagne

⅓ cup (80 ml) olive oil

1 onion, finely chopped

3 cloves garlic, crushed

2 eggplant (aubergine), about 375 g
    (12 oz) each, cut into chunks

2 x 410 g (14 oz) cans chopped tomatoes

½ cup (125 g) salt-free tomato paste
    (concentrated purée)

500 g (1 lb) minced (ground) chicken

¾ teaspoon salt

2 tablespoons butter

¼ cup (35 g) plain (all-purpose) flour

2½ cups (625 ml) milk

9 instant lasagne sheets (no-cook lasagne
    noodles)

1½ cups (225 g) grated reduced-fat
    mozzarella

¼ cup (25 g) grated parmesan

PREPARATION 25 minutes
COOKING 1 hour 10 minutes
MAKES 6 servings

PER SERVING 2740 kJ, 655 kcal, 40 g protein,
37 g fat (15 g saturated fat), 40 g carbohydrate
(15 g sugars), 839 mg sodium, 7 g fibre

1 Preheat the oven to 180°C (350°F/Gas 4). In a large frying pan, heat 1 tablespoon oil over medium–low heat. Add onion and garlic and cook, stirring frequently, for 4 minutes, or until onion is soft.

2 Add remaining oil to pan and increase heat to medium. Add eggplant and cook for 5 minutes, or until eggplant are firm-tender. Add tomatoes, tomato paste and ½ cup (125 ml) water. Bring to a boil, then reduce to a simmer and cook for 5 minutes. Stir in chicken and ½ teaspoon salt and cook for 7 minutes, or until chicken is cooked through. Set aside.

3 In a saucepan, melt butter over low heat. Whisk in flour and stir until well combined. Gradually whisk in milk. Add remaining salt and cook, stirring frequently, for 5 minutes, or until sauce is slightly thickened and coats the back of a spoon.

4 Spoon ½ cup (125 g) of eggplant mixture into the bottom of a 23 x 33 cm (9 x 13 inch) glass baking dish. Lay 3 lasagne sheets on top, overlapping slightly. Spoon half the remaining eggplant mixture over the lasagne. Spoon one-third of the white sauce and one-third of the mozzarella on top. Top with 3 lasagne sheets, the remaining eggplant mixture, half the remaining white sauce and half the remaining mozzarella. Top with remaining lasagne sheets, white sauce, parmesan and mozzarella.

5 Cover loosely with foil and bake for 30 minutes. Remove foil and bake for 5 minutes, or until sauce is bubbly and cheese has melted.

VARIATION *Chicken & mushroom lasagne*
In step 1, increase garlic to 4 cloves and sauté with the onion. In step 2, substitute 750 g (1½ lb) thinly sliced Swiss brown (porcini) mushrooms for eggplant and decrease oil used to cook mushrooms to 2 tablespoons. After cooking mushrooms, drain off excess liquid from frying pan. Add tomatoes, tomato paste, ½ teaspoon dried rosemary and ½ cup (125 ml) water to frying pan and cook as directed. Make the white sauce, layer and bake as directed.

This simple but hearty Greek casserole, known as 'pastitsio', calls for tubular pasta, such as ditalini ('little thimbles'). The chicken is cooked in a spicy tomato sauce, then layered with the pasta and a white sauce, creating a homely, comforting meal.

Chicken pasta bake

2 tablespoons olive oil

1 large onion, finely chopped

2 cloves garlic, crushed

500 g (1 lb) minced (ground) chicken

2 cups (500 g) canned chopped tomatoes

1 teaspoon ground cinnamon

½ teaspoon salt

½ teaspoon freshly ground black pepper

¼ teaspoon ground allspice

tiny pinch of ground cloves

200 g (7 oz) ditalini, penne or ziti

2 tablespoons butter

¼ cup (35 g) plain (all-purpose) flour

2 cups (500 ml) low-fat milk

½ cup (50 g) grated parmesan

PREPARATION 20 minutes
COOKING 1 hour 5 minutes
MAKES 4 servings

PER SERVING 2880 kJ, 688 kcal, 43 g protein, 32 g fat (12 g saturated fat), 56 g carbohydrate (14 g sugars), 810 mg sodium, 5 g fibre

1 In a large frying pan, heat oil over medium heat. Add onion and garlic and cook, stirring frequently, for 4 minutes, or until onion is soft. Stir in chicken, tomatoes, cinnamon, salt, pepper, allspice and cloves. Reduce heat and simmer for 20 minutes, or until mixture is thick and almost dry.

2 Meanwhile, in a large pot of boiling water, cook pasta until al dente, following packet instructions; drain.

3 Preheat the oven to 180°C (350°F/Gas 4). In a saucepan, melt butter over low heat. Whisk in flour until well combined. Gradually whisk in milk, stirring until well combined and smooth. Cook, stirring constantly, for 5 minutes, or until sauce is slightly thickened.

4 Spoon ¼ cup (60 ml) of the sauce into a 23 cm (9 inch) square baking dish. Spoon half the pasta over the top, spreading to form an even layer. Spoon half the chicken mixture on top, then sprinkle with half the parmesan. Top with remaining pasta, chicken mixture and white sauce. Sprinkle with remaining parmesan.

5 Transfer to the oven and bake, uncovered, for 35 minutes, or until topping is crusty and golden brown.

Fettuccine with chicken & asparagus

500 g (1 lb) asparagus, cut on the diagonal into long lengths

300 g (10 oz) fettuccine

1 tablespoon butter

¼ cup (40 g) finely chopped onion

350 g (¾ lb) boneless, skinless chicken breasts, cut into chunks

½ cup (125 ml) salt-reduced chicken stock (page 49)

½ cup (125 ml) pouring (light) cream

½ teaspoon salt

½ teaspoon dried tarragon

½ teaspoon freshly ground black pepper

⅓ cup (35 g) grated parmesan

QUICK
PREPARATION 15 minutes
COOKING 15 minutes
MAKES 4 servings

1 In a large pot of boiling water, cook asparagus for 3 minutes. With a slotted spoon, remove asparagus and rinse under cold water to stop it cooking. In the same pot of boiling water, cook pasta until al dente, following packet instructions; drain, reserving ¼ cup (60 ml) of pasta cooking water.

2 Meanwhile, in a large frying pan, melt butter over low heat. Add onion and cook, stirring frequently, for 5 minutes, or until onion is softened. Add chicken and cook for 1 minute.

3 Increase heat to medium. Add stock, cream, salt, tarragon and pepper and bring to a boil. Cook for 3 minutes, or until the sauce is slightly thickened and chicken is cooked through. Add asparagus and cook for 30 seconds, just until heated through.

4 Transfer mixture to a large bowl. Add hot pasta, parmesan and reserved pasta cooking water and toss well to combine.

PER SERVING 2219 kJ, 530 kcal, 35 g protein, 18 g fat (10 g saturated fat), 55 g carbohydrate (4 g sugars), 612 mg sodium, 5 g fibre

Sicilian chicken & broccoli linguine

300 g (10 oz) linguine

¼ cup (60 ml) olive oil

3 cloves garlic, finely sliced

500 g (1 lb) broccoli (or broccoli rabe), trimmed and chopped

175 g (6 oz) fully cooked spicy chicken sausages, roughly chopped

350 g (¾ lb) boneless, skinless chicken breast halves, cut for stir-fry (see Basics)

¼ teaspoon salt

⅔ cup (65 g) grated parmesan

½ cup (60 g) sultanas (golden raisins)

½ cup (70 g) oil-packed sun-dried tomatoes, drained and roughly chopped

¼ cup (40 g) pine nuts

1 In a large pot of boiling water, cook pasta until al dente, following packet instructions. Drain, reserving 1 cup (250 ml) of pasta cooking water.

2 Meanwhile, in a large frying pan, heat oil over low heat. Add garlic and cook for 2 minutes. Add broccoli and sausages and cook, stirring, for 12 minutes, or until broccoli is very tender.

3 Add chicken and salt and cook for 5 minutes, or until chicken is cooked through. Stir in reserved pasta cooking water and bring to a boil. Transfer to a large bowl, add hot cooked pasta and remaining ingredients and toss well.

PREPARATION 25 minutes
COOKING 20 minutes
MAKES 4 servings

PER SERVING 3590 kJ, 858 kcal, 51 g protein, 41 g fat (10 g saturated fat), 72 g carbohydrate (18 g sugars), 892 mg sodium, 13 g fibre

Fettuccine with chicken & asparagus

Radiatore, a ruffle-edged ridged pasta, is perfect for bakes, but fusilli or a similar sturdy, spiral-shaped pasta will work just as well.

Baked radiatore with smoked chicken

300 g (10 oz) radiatore or fusilli pasta

2 tablespoons butter

1 small red capsicum (bell pepper), diced

2 tablespoons plain (all-purpose) flour

2½ cups (625 ml) low-fat milk

½ teaspoon freshly ground black pepper

½ teaspoon salt

tiny pinch of ground nutmeg

250 g (8 oz) skinless smoked chicken, diced

175 g (6 oz) fontina or gruyère cheese, cut into small chunks

2 tablespoons pine nuts

¼ cup (25 g) grated parmesan

PREPARATION 15 minutes
COOKING 35 minutes
MAKES 4 servings

PER SERVING 3256 kJ, 778 kcal, 49 g protein, 35 g fat (17 g saturated fat), 67 g carbohydrate (12 g sugars), 755 mg sodium, 3 g fibre

1 Preheat the oven to 180°C (350°F/Gas 4). In a large pot of boiling water, cook pasta until al dente, following packet instructions; drain.

2 Meanwhile, in a saucepan, melt butter over medium heat. Add capsicum and cook for 4 minutes, or until crisp-tender. Whisk in flour until well combined. Gradually whisk in milk, pepper, salt and nutmeg. Cook, whisking constantly, for 5 minutes, or until sauce is lightly thickened. Remove from heat and stir in smoked chicken, cheese and pine nuts.

3 In a large bowl, stir together drained pasta and chicken mixture. Transfer to an 18 x 28 cm (7 x 11 inch) baking dish. Sprinkle with parmesan and bake for 25 minutes, or until top is golden brown and pasta is piping hot.

VARIATION *Baked rigatoni with sausage & manchego*
Substitute rigatoni for radiatore pasta, fully cooked sliced chicken sausages for the smoked chicken and aged manchego cheese (or parmesan) for fontina. Omit pine nuts. Add 2 teaspoons chilli powder and 2 cups (300 g) thawed frozen corn kernels to chicken mixture in step 2. Assemble and bake as directed.

Wine is often used as a cooking ingredient, but spirits have their place, too. This dish gets a subtly smoky flavour from a shot of tequila. If you prefer not to cook with spirits, simply substitute chicken stock for the tequila in step 2.

Tequila chicken over pepper linguine

300 g (10 oz) pepper-flavoured or regular
  linguine

¼ cup (60 ml) olive oil

500 g (1 lb) boneless, skinless chicken
  breasts, cut for stir-fry (see Basics)

¼ cup (60 ml) tequila

1 red onion, finely chopped

2 red capsicums (bell peppers), finely diced

2 cups (300 g) frozen corn kernels, or
  1½ cups (300 g) fresh corn kernels

2 roma (plum) tomatoes, finely diced

½ cup (125 ml) orange juice

1 teaspoon salt

4 tablespoons chopped fresh coriander
  (cilantro)

LOW FAT

PREPARATION 10 minutes, plus at least
  1 hour marinating
COOKING 15 minutes
MAKES 4 servings

PER SERVING 3011 kJ, 719 kcal, 40 g protein,
23 g fat (4 g saturated fat), 77 g carbohydrate
(10 g sugars), 776 mg sodium, 7 g fibre

1 In a large pot of boiling water, cook linguine until al dente, following packet instructions; drain.

2 Meanwhile, in a large deep frying pan, heat 1 tablespoon oil over medium heat. Stir-fry the chicken in 2 batches for 4 minutes per batch, or until golden brown and cooked through. Return all the chicken to the pan. Add tequila and cook for 2 minutes to evaporate the alcohol.

3 Add onion, capsicums, corn, tomatoes, orange juice, salt, coriander and remaining oil. Add the hot pasta, toss well and serve.

COOK'S TIPS

• A visit to a pasta shop or specialty food store will reveal an array of flavoured and coloured pastas. Some are tinted with vegetables such as tomato, spinach or beetroot (beet), while others are flavoured with herbs and spices, such as saffron, basil or pepper.

• Tequila is a fiery Mexican liquor made from the sweet sap of the agave plant, also known as the century plant as it was once thought to bloom only once every hundred years.

In its native Italy, 'cacciatore' means 'hunter style'. Dishes bearing this name are simmered in a lush tomato sauce enriched with onions, mushrooms and sometimes wine. Chicken is especially good cooked in this manner, and not surprisingly is widely popular.

Chicken cacciatore with spaghetti

½ cup (10 g) dried porcini mushrooms

2 tablespoons olive oil

1 whole chicken (about 1.75 kg/3½ lb), cut into 8 serving pieces (see Basics), skin removed

¼ cup (35 g) plain (all-purpose) flour

1 onion, finely chopped

3 cloves garlic, crushed

250 g (8 oz) button mushrooms, trimmed

410 g (14 oz) can chopped tomatoes

¾ teaspoon salt

¼ teaspoon freshly ground black pepper

3 long strips orange zest

300 g (10 oz) spaghetti

LOW FAT

PREPARATION 25 minutes, plus 20 minutes soaking

COOKING 1 hour 10 minutes

MAKES 4 servings

PER SERVING 3091 kJ, 739 kcal, 55 g protein, 28 g fat (7 g saturated fat), 65 g carbohydrate (5 g sugars), 700 mg sodium, 7 g fibre

1 In a small bowl, soak porcini in ½ cup (125 ml) boiling water for 20 minutes, or until softened. Remove porcini from soaking liquid; reserve liquid. Roughly chop porcini, then set aside.

2 Preheat the oven to 180°C (350°F/Gas 4). In a large flameproof casserole dish or Dutch oven, heat oil over medium–high heat. Dredge chicken in the flour, shaking off excess. Add chicken to the dish in batches and fry for 4 minutes per side, or until golden brown. Transfer chicken to a plate.

3 Reduce heat to medium–low, add onion and garlic to dish and cook, stirring frequently, for 4 minutes, or until onion is soft. Add button mushrooms and cook for 5 minutes, or until mushrooms begin to give off liquid. Add porcini and reserved soaking liquid, increase heat to high and cook for 2 minutes. Add tomatoes, salt, pepper and orange zest strips.

4 Return chicken to the dish and bring to a boil. Cover, place in the oven and bake for 35 minutes, or until chicken is cooked through.

5 Meanwhile, in a large pot of boiling water, cook spaghetti until al dente, following packet instructions; drain.

6 Divide spaghetti among serving bowls, top with cacciatore mixture and serve.

To preserve every drop of the delicious lemony garlic butter, the sautéed chicken breasts are served on wide ribbon pasta to soak up the sauce. You could also serve the chicken and sauce with other types of pasta, potatoes or bread.

Chicken breasts in lemon garlic butter

1 head garlic

⅔ cup (160 ml) chicken stock (page 49)

1 teaspoon grated lemon zest

1 tablespoon lemon juice

¼ teaspoon salt

¼ teaspoon freshly ground black pepper

2 teaspoons olive oil

4 boneless, skinless chicken breast halves, about 750 g (1½ lb) in total

2 tablespoons plain (all-purpose) flour

250 g (8 oz) broad ribbon pasta, such as pappardelle

1 tablespoon cold butter, finely diced

3 tablespoons snipped fresh chives

LOW FAT
PREPARATION 10 minutes
COOKING 45 minutes
MAKES 4 servings

PER SERVING 2292 kJ, 548 kcal, 49 g protein, 18 g fat (6 g saturated fat), 48 g carbohydrate (<1 g sugars), 509 mg sodium, 3 g fibre

1 Preheat the oven to 200°C (400°F/Gas 6). Wrap garlic in foil and bake for 30 minutes, or until packet feels soft when squeezed. When cool enough to handle, remove foil, snip off top of garlic bulb and squeeze garlic pulp into a small bowl. Whisk in stock, lemon zest, lemon juice, salt and pepper; set aside.

2 In a large frying pan, heat oil over medium heat. Dredge chicken in the flour, shaking off excess. Add chicken to pan and fry for 4 minutes per side, or until golden brown. Transfer chicken to a plate.

3 Whisk the lemon and garlic mixture again, then pour into the frying pan. Bring to a boil, return the chicken to the pan, then reduce to a simmer. Cover and cook for 5 minutes, or until chicken is cooked through. Cover until ready to serve.

4 Meanwhile, in a large pot of boiling water, cook pasta until al dente, following packet instructions. Drain and divide among serving plates.

5 With a slotted spoon, arrange chicken pieces over plates of pasta. Return sauce to a simmer, then remove from heat and swirl in butter until creamy. Stir in chives, spoon sauce over chicken and pasta and serve.

Orzo, chicken & vegetable salad

1 cup (220 g) orzo or risoni

⅓ cup (80 ml) balsamic vinegar

⅓ cup (80 ml) olive oil

¾ teaspoon salt

⅓ cup (60 g) kalamata olives, pitted and roughly chopped

4 boneless, skinless chicken breast halves, about 750 g (1½ lb) in total

1 zucchini (courgette), quartered lengthwise

1 golden zucchini (courgette), quartered

4 red capsicums (bell peppers), cut lengthwise into flat pieces

PREPARATION 10 minutes
COOKING 30 minutes
MAKES 4 servings

PER SERVING 2881 kJ, 688 kcal, 46 g protein, 32 g fat (6 g saturated fat), 53 g carbohydrate (7 g sugars), 764 mg sodium, 2 g fibre

1 In a large pot of boiling water, cook orzo until al dente, following packet instructions. Drain and set aside.

2 Meanwhile, preheat grill (broiler) to medium–high. In a large bowl, whisk together vinegar, 2 tablespoons oil and ½ teaspoon salt. Stir in olives and set aside.

3 On a plate, stir together 1 tablespoon oil and remaining salt. Add chicken, turning to coat. Brush zucchini with remaining oil.

4 Arrange chicken and zucchini on the grill rack and place under grill, 15 cm (6 inches) from the heat. Cook for 3 minutes each side, or until chicken is just done and zucchini are tender. When cool enough to handle, cut chicken crosswise into small chunks and cut zucchini into short lengths.

5 Grill (broil) the capsicum pieces, skin side down, for 10 minutes, or until skins are blackened. When cool enough to handle, peel capsicums and cut into strips 1 cm (½ inch) wide.

6 Add chicken, zucchini, capsicums and orzo to the bowl with the olives and vinaigrette, then toss well. Serve immediately or chilled.

When summer arrives, pick up a big bunch of fresh basil and some cherry tomatoes and treat yourself to this superb chicken-and-pasta dish. Use the pesto for any kind of pasta; add other vegetables and thin slices of smoked chicken for a variation on this meal.

Penne pesto with chicken & tomatoes

1 cup (50 g) firmly packed fresh basil leaves

⅓ cup (80 ml) olive oil

2 tablespoons pine nuts

1 large clove garlic

¾ teaspoon salt

½ cup (50 g) grated parmesan

300 g (10 oz) penne

350 g (¾ lb) boneless, skinless chicken breasts, cut for stir-fry (see Basics)

2 cups (340 g) cherry tomatoes, halved

QUICK
PREPARATION 15 minutes
COOKING 15 minutes
MAKES 4 servings

PER SERVING 2710 kJ, 647 kcal, 34 g protein, 33 g fat (7 g saturated fat), 54 g carbohydrate (2 g sugars), 700 mg sodium, 5 g fibre

1 In a food processor or blender, purée basil, ¼ cup (60 ml) oil, the pine nuts, garlic and salt until smooth. Add half the parmesan and process until combined.

2 In a large pot of boiling water, cook pasta until al dente, following packet instructions. Drain, reserving ¼ cup (60 ml) of pasta cooking water.

3 Meanwhile, in a large frying pan, heat remaining oil over medium heat. Add chicken and stir-fry for 2 minutes, or until no longer pink. Add cherry tomatoes and cook for 3 minutes, or until chicken is cooked through and cherry tomatoes have started to collapse. Add pesto and reserved pasta cooking water and toss to coat well.

4 Transfer chicken mixture to a large bowl. Add hot pasta and remaining parmesan. Toss well and serve.

VARIATION *Coriander pesto with chicken*
Cook the pasta as directed. In step 2, substitute 1 cup (30 g) coriander (cilantro) leaves and tender stems for basil and ¼ cup (40 g) almonds for pine nuts; increase salt to 1 teaspoon and garlic to 2 cloves. Process as directed, but omit the ¼ cup parmesan. In step 3, sauté chicken as directed, but omit cherry tomatoes. Add coriander pesto and reserved pasta cooking water and cook for 1 minute. In step 4, substitute ¾ cup grated cheddar cheese for the parmesan and add 1 cup (145 g) thinly sliced roasted red capsicums (bell peppers), from a jar; toss well.

You can easily double this recipe to serve eight. If you'd like to make it ahead of time and freeze, line the baking dish with heavy-duty foil before filling. Bake as directed, allow to cool, then wrap tightly with the foil and freeze. Reheat the frozen, foil-covered dish in the oven at 150°C (300°F/Gas 2) for 25 minutes, or until hot.

Chicken and provolone manicotti

8 manicotti or cannelloni tubes
   (about 175 g/6 oz)

2 tablespoons olive oil

2 large onions, finely chopped

350 g (¾ lb) minced (ground) chicken

¼ cup (25 g) grated parmesan

3 cups (350 g) grated provolone cheese

⅔ cup (40 g) chopped fresh basil leaves

¼ teaspoon salt

½ teaspoon freshly ground black pepper

1 large egg yolk

2 x 410 g (14 oz) cans chopped tomatoes

1 teaspoon sugar

¼ teaspoon dried red chilli flakes

PREPARATION 25 minutes
COOKING 40 minutes
MAKES 4 servings

PER SERVING 3294 kJ, 787 kcal, 52 g protein, 45 g fat (21 g saturated fat), 43 g carbohydrate (11 g sugars), 1328 mg sodium, 6 g fibre

1 In a large pot of boiling water, cook the pasta tubes until al dente, following packet instructions. Drain and rinse under cold running water.

2 Meanwhile, in a large frying pan, heat oil over medium heat. Add onions and cook, stirring frequently, for 10 minutes, or until golden brown. Transfer half the onions to a large bowl. Remove frying pan with remaining onions from the heat and set aside.

3 Preheat the oven to 190°C (375°F/Gas 5). Allow onions in the bowl cool to room temperature, then stir in chicken, parmesan, half the provolone, half the basil, ¼ teaspoon salt, the pepper and egg yolk. Fill a piping (icing) bag or large sturdy zip-seal bag with the chicken mixture. (If using a zip-seal bag, snip a 1 cm/½ inch piece off one corner.) Pipe mixture into one end of the manicotti until half full, then pipe filling into the other end.

4 Add tomatoes, remaining basil, remaining salt, the sugar and chilli flakes to the onions in the frying pan. Bring to a boil, reduce to a simmer and cook for 5 minutes, or until sauce is slightly thickened.

5 Spoon ½ cup (125 ml) of the tomato sauce into the bottom of an 18 x 28 cm (7 x 11 inch) glass baking dish. Arrange manicotti on top, then spoon remaining sauce over. Place in the oven and bake for 20 minutes. Sprinkle remaining provolone on top and bake another 5 minutes, or until cheese is bubbly.

COOK'S TIP
Rinsing the manicotti after cooking removes the surface starch and stops them sticking together after they're cooked.

IN A HURRY?
Replace minced (ground) chicken with 2 cups (300 g) finely chopped cooked chicken thigh; add as directed in step 3. Use 3 cups (750 ml) of ready-made pasta sauce (preferably basil-flavoured) and add to the sautéed onions in step 4. Omit remainder of sauce-making step.

Pesto is the fragrant Genoese pasta sauce made from fresh basil, pine nuts and parmesan. As tasty as it is on fettuccine or penne (see our recipe on page 187), pesto is also a delicious seasoning for these meatballs, which are simmered in a tomato and oregano sauce.

Pesto chicken meatballs with ziti

2 cloves garlic, peeled

1 cup (50 g) firmly packed fresh basil leaves

⅓ cup (35 g) grated parmesan

¼ cup (60 ml) pouring (light) cream

¼ cup (40 g) pine nuts

¼ teaspoon salt

500 g (1 lb) minced (ground) chicken

1 large egg

¼ cup (25 g) dry packaged breadcrumbs

¼ cup (35 g) plain (all-purpose) flour

¼ cup (60 ml) olive oil

2 x 410 g (14 oz) cans chopped tomatoes

3 tablespoons chopped fresh oregano, or 1 teaspoon dried

300 g (10 oz) ziti (or rigatoni or penne)

PREPARATION 20 minutes
COOKING 15 minutes
MAKES 4 servings

PER SERVING 3433 kJ, 820 kcal, 43 g protein, 41 g fat (10 g saturated fat), 70 g carbohydrate (8 g sugars), 726 mg sodium, 7 g fibre

1 In a small pan of boiling water, blanch garlic cloves for 2 minutes. Transfer garlic to a food processor or blender. Add basil, parmesan, cream, pine nuts and ½ teaspoon salt and process until combined.

2 Transfer pesto mixture to a large bowl; add chicken, egg and breadcrumbs and mix well to combine. With moistened hands, shape into 24 meatballs. Dredge meatballs in the flour, shaking off excess.

3 In a large frying pan, heat oil over medium heat. Add meatballs and cook for 4 minutes, or until golden brown, turning often. Stir in tomatoes, oregano and remaining salt and bring to a boil. Reduce to a simmer, then cover and cook for 5 to 7 minutes, or until meatballs are cooked through and sauce is flavoursome.

4 Meanwhile, in a large pot of boiling water, cook pasta until al dente, following packet instructions. Drain pasta and serve topped with the meatballs and sauce.

Marsala is a Sicilian wine that has been fortified with unfermented grape juice and grape syrup, then aged. It marries wonderfully with chicken and adds a rich, deep, dark, smoky, almost nutty flavour to this beautiful sauce. This is a great dinner-party dish.

Chicken marsala over noodles

2 tablespoons olive oil

3 tablespoons butter

8 boneless, skinless chicken breast halves, about 1.5 kg/3 lb in total, pounded 1 cm (½ inch) thick (see Basics), then cut crosswise into 6 pieces each

⅓ cup (50 g) plain (all-purpose) flour

1 cup (250 ml) dry Marsala

⅔ cup (160 ml) salt-reduced chicken stock (page 49)

½ teaspoon salt

¼ teaspoon freshly ground black pepper

1½ teaspoons cornflour (cornstarch)

500 g (1 lb) fresh pasta egg noodles

2 tablespoons snipped fresh chives

LOW FAT, QUICK
PREPARATION 10 minutes
COOKING 20 minutes
MAKES 8 servings

PER SERVING 2421 kJ, 578 kcal, 47 g protein, 22 g fat (8 g saturated fat), 41 g carbohydrate (4 g sugars), 377 mg sodium, 1 g fibre

1 In a large frying pan, heat oil and 1 tablespoon butter until foam subsides. Dredge chicken in the flour, shaking off excess. Add half the chicken to pan and sauté for 6 minutes, or until golden brown and cooked through. Transfer chicken to a large plate. Repeat with remaining chicken.

2 Pour off any fat remaining in frying pan. Add Marsala to pan, scraping up any browned bits. Bring to a boil over high heat and cook for 2 minutes. Add stock, salt and pepper; return to a boil and boil for 1 minute. Mix the cornflour with 1 tablespoon water to make a smooth paste; add to pan and cook, stirring constantly, for 1 minute, or until sauce is slightly thickened. Remove from heat and swirl in 1 tablespoon butter.

3 Meanwhile, in a large pot of boiling water, cook pasta until al dente, following packet instructions. Drain, reserving ½ cup (125 ml) of pasta cooking water.

4 Return hot pasta to the pot and toss with reserved cooking water and remaining butter.

5 Divide pasta among serving plates, arrange chicken on top and spoon sauce over. Sprinkle with chives and serve.

Chicken & soba noodle salad

¾ cup (180 ml) salt-reduced chicken stock (page 49)

2 cloves garlic, crushed

½ teaspoon ground ginger

¼ teaspoon dried red chilli flakes

375 g (¾ lb) boneless, skinless chicken breasts

300 g (10 oz) soba (buckwheat) noodles

250 g (8 oz) green beans, halved

2 carrots, cut into thin matchsticks

1½ tablespoons dark brown sugar

1 tablespoon salt-reduced soy sauce

3 teaspoons peanut or other vegetable oil

2 cups (150 g) finely shredded cabbage

LOW FAT
PREPARATION 20 minutes
COOKING 15 minutes
MAKES 4 servings

1 In a large frying pan, bring stock, garlic, ginger and chilli flakes to a boil over medium heat. Reduce to a simmer, add chicken, then cover and cook for 10 minutes, or until chicken is cooked through, turning chicken over halfway during cooking. Transfer chicken to a plate, reserving cooking liquid. When the chicken is cool enough to handle, shred it.

2 Meanwhile, in a large pot of boiling water, cook noodles until firm-tender, according to packet directions, adding beans and carrots for the last minute of cooking. Drain.

3 In a large bowl, whisk together sugar, soy sauce, oil and reserved cooking liquid. Add shredded chicken, noodles, beans, carrots and cabbage, tossing to combine. Serve at room temperature or chilled.

PER SERVING 2001 kJ, 478 kcal, 32 g protein, 10 g fat (2 g saturated fat), 62 g carbohydrate (9 g sugars), 1068 mg sodium, 7 g fibre

One of Thailand's most famous dishes, pad Thai is a festival of tastes and textures. Look for rice noodles (slender white noodles that come coiled in 'nests') in Asian grocery stores and supermarkets.

Chicken pad Thai

125 g (4 oz) thin rice stick noodles

2 tablespoons vegetable oil

3 spring onions (scallions), thinly sliced

2 cloves garlic, crushed

350 g (¾ lb) boneless, skinless chicken breasts, cut into small dice

8 tiger prawns (large shrimp), peeled and deveined

¼ cup (55 g) firmly packed soft brown sugar

2 tablespoons tomato sauce (ketchup)

2 tablespoons rice vinegar

1 tablespoon fish sauce

2 large eggs, lightly beaten

2 cups (180 g) fresh bean sprouts, tails trimmed

3 tablespoons chopped fresh coriander (cilantro)

¼ cup (40 g) peanuts, roughly chopped

lime or lemon wedges, to serve

LOW FAT, QUICK
PREPARATION 20 minutes
COOKING 10 minutes
MAKES 4 servings

PER SERVING 2258 kJ, 539 kcal, 36 g protein, 23 g fat (4 g saturated fat), 45 g carbohydrate (18 g sugars), 714 mg sodium, 4 g fibre

1 In a heatproof bowl, soak noodles in boiling water for 5 to 10 minutes, or until softened. (Don't let them get too soft or they will fall apart when added to the pan.) Drain well.

2 Meanwhile, in a large wok or non-stick frying pan, heat oil over medium heat. Add spring onions and garlic and cook for 1 minute. Add chicken and cook for 2 minutes, or until chicken is almost cooked through.

3 Add prawns, sugar, tomato sauce, vinegar and fish sauce and toss to coat. Add drained noodles and cook, tossing frequently, for 3 minutes, or until prawns and chicken are cooked through and noodles are hot. Pour eggs into the frying pan and toss to scramble.

4 Place bean sprouts on a large platter and top with noodles. Sprinkle with coriander and peanuts and serve with lime or lemon wedges.

A perennial favourite at Singaporean food stalls and a popular dish all over the world, this tasty, home-cooked version will feed the family for much less than noodles from a restaurant—and they'll taste far fresher and less oily, too.

Singapore noodles

175 g (6 oz) rice vermicelli noodles

2 tablespoons peanut oil

200 g (7 oz) peeled small raw prawns (uncooked shrimp)

200 g (7 oz) boneless, skinless chicken breasts, thinly sliced

6 spring onions (scallions), thinly sliced diagonally

3 teaspoons grated fresh ginger

1 small red capsicum (bell pepper), thinly sliced

2 teaspoons curry powder

1 teaspoon ground turmeric

3 teaspoons Chinese rice wine

2 tablespoons light soy sauce

2 tablespoons chicken stock (page 49)

¾ cup (115 g) frozen peas, thawed

3 eggs, beaten

fresh coriander (cilantro) sprigs, to garnish

lime wedges, to serve

LOW FAT
PREPARATION 20 minutes
COOKING 15 minutes
MAKES 4 serving

PER SERVING 1668 kJ, 399 kcal, 26 g protein, 13 g fat (3 g saturated fat), 42 g carbohydrate (3 g sugars), 606 mg sodium, 2 g fibre

1 In a heatproof bowl, soak noodles for 5 to 10 minutes, or according to packet instructions. Drain and set aside.

2 Meanwhile, in a wok or large non-stick frying pan, heat 1 tablespoon oil. Add prawns and stir-fry for 2 minutes, or until just cooked; remove to a plate. Add chicken to pan and stir-fry for 3 minutes, or until just cooked; remove and add to the prawns.

3 Heat remaining oil in wok and stir-fry spring onions, ginger and capsicum for 3 minutes, or until capsicum is just beginning to soften. Stir in curry powder and turmeric and cook for 1 minute.

4 Pour in rice wine, soy sauce and stock; toss until combined. Add peas and drained noodles and cook, tossing frequently, for 3 minutes, or until peas are tender.

5 Push noodles to one side of the wok and pour in beaten eggs. Cook stirring, for 1 minute, then mix the egg through the noodles.

6 Return prawns and chicken to the wok and toss until warmed through and well combined. Divide among serving bowls, garnish with coriander and serve with lime wedges.

Stir-fries

Stir-fries are so easy to dish up: the trick is to have all your ingredients measured out and chopped to the same size for quick, even cooking. Toss them together in a sizzling hot wok and before you know it, dinner's on the table in the most spectacular fashion.

An array of crisp vegetables and lean, tender chicken breast strips turn a quick stir-fry into a colourful and health-giving meal. Orange zest and orange juice add a clean, sweet refreshing tang to the mix.

Orange chicken and vegetable stir-fry

1½ teaspoons cornflour (cornstarch)

1 teaspoon grated orange zest

½ cup (125 ml) orange juice

¼ cup (60 ml) salt-reduced soy sauce

¼ teaspoon salt

2 tablespoons vegetable oil

2 tablespoons grated fresh ginger

3 cloves garlic, crushed

2 cups (125 g) broccoli florets

1 red capsicum (bell pepper), cut into large chunks

1 green capsicum (bell pepper), cut into large chunks

125 g (4 oz) snow peas (mangetout), halved crosswise

375 g (¾ lb) skinless, boneless chicken breasts, cut for stir-fry (see Basics)

LOW FAT, QUICK

PREPARATION 20 minutes

COOKING 10 minutes

MAKES 4 servings

PER SERVING 1102 kJ, 263 kcal, 25 g protein, 15 g fat (3 g saturated fat), 8 g carbohydrate (5 g sugars), 768 mg sodium, 3 g fibre

1 In small bowl, whisk together cornflour, orange zest, orange juice, soy sauce and salt; set aside.

2 In a wok or large non-stick frying pan, heat oil over medium heat. Add ginger and garlic and cook for 30 seconds. Add broccoli, capsicums, snow peas and ¼ cup (60 ml) water, then stir-fry for 4 minutes, or until broccoli is crisp-tender.

3 Stir in chicken and increase heat to medium–high; stir-fry for 2 minutes, or until chicken is just cooked through.

4 Whisk orange juice mixture again and pour into wok. Bring to a boil and cook, stirring, for 1 minute, or until sauce is slightly thickened. Serve hot.

Try this quick and easy dish when you're after something a little different. Lime juice, soy sauce, ground ginger and peanut butter blend together into a slightly tangy sauce that's spooned over the chicken.

Chicken with peanut sauce

4 small boneless, skinless chicken breast halves, 625 g (1¼ lb) in total, pounded 5 mm (¼ inch) thick (see Basics)

2 tablespoons plain (all-purpose) flour

2 tablespoons olive oil

1 yellow capsicum (bell pepper), chopped

2 spring onions (scallions), thinly sliced

½ cup (125 g) canned chopped tomatoes

½ cup (125 ml) salt-reduced chicken stock (page 49)

¼ cup (60 g) peanut butter

1 tablespoon salt-reduced soy sauce

1 tablespoon lime juice

¾ teaspoon ground ginger

½ teaspoon salt

½ teaspoon sugar

3 tablespoons chopped fresh coriander (cilantro)

LOW FAT, QUICK
PREPARATION 15 minutes
COOKING 15 minutes
MAKES 4 servings

PER SERVING 1798 kJ, 430 kcal, 39 g protein, 26 g fat (5 g saturated fat), 10 g carbohydrate (4 g sugars), 776 mg sodium, <1 g fibre

1 Dredge chicken in the flour, shaking off excess. In a wok or large non-stick frying pan, heat oil over medium–high heat. Add chicken and cook for 1½ minutes per side, or until golden brown and cooked through. Transfer chicken to a plate.

2 Add capsicum and spring onions to wok and stir-fry for 3 minutes, or until crisp-tender. Add remaining ingredients except coriander and bring to a boil. Reduce to a simmer and cook for 5 minutes. Return chicken to wok and cook for 1 minute, or until just heated through.

3 Transfer chicken to serving plates. Stir coriander into the sauce, spoon over chicken and serve.

Thai chicken stir-fry

4 cloves garlic, roughly chopped

4 spring onions (scallions), cut into short lengths

4 tablespoons fresh coriander (cilantro) leaves

¼ teaspoon salt

½ teaspoon dried red chilli flakes

¼ cup (60 ml) vegetable oil

500 g (1 lb) boneless, skinless chicken breast halves, cut for stir-fry (see Basics)

1⅓ cups (250 g) baby corn

2 roma (plum) tomatoes, diced

1½ tablespoons salt-reduced soy sauce

¾ tablespoon fish sauce

1½ teaspoons sugar

½ cup (25 g) firmly packed fresh basil leaves, roughly chopped

1 In a food processor or blender, combine garlic, spring onions, coriander, salt, chilli flakes, 1 tablespoon oil and 2 teaspoons water. Process to a smooth paste.

2 In a wok or large non-stick frying pan, heat remaining oil over medium–high heat. Add herb paste and cook for 1 minute. Add chicken and stir-fry for 4 minutes, or until chicken is no longer pink.

3 Add remaining ingredients and cook, stirring constantly, for 2 minutes, or until chicken is just cooked through. Serve hot.

LOW FAT, QUICK
PREPARATION 15 minutes
COOKING 10 minutes
MAKES 4 servings

PER SERVING 1417 kJ, 339 kcal, 30 g protein, 21 g fat (4 g saturated fat), 7 g carbohydrate (4 g sugars), 855 mg sodium, 4 g fibre

The wonderful flavour of Chinese fermented black beans is a shortcut to tasty stir-fries. Made by fermenting beans with salt and spices, this versatile ingredient is sold in many supermarkets. Once you open the container, transfer the contents to an airtight jar. The beans will keep indefinitely.

Chicken with black bean sauce

500 g (1 lb) boneless, skinless chicken breasts, cut for stir-fry (see Basics)

¼ cup (60 ml) salt-reduced soy sauce

1 tablespoon dry sherry

1 tablespoon cornflour (cornstarch)

2 teaspoons sesame oil

¼ cup (60 ml) peanut (groundnut) oil or other vegetable oil

2 tablespoons fermented black beans

1 red capsicum (bell pepper), cut into thin strips

1 mild green chilli, chopped (optional)

2 tablespoons grated fresh ginger

2 cloves garlic, crushed

3 baby bok choy, trimmed, leaves separated

LOW FAT, QUICK
PREPARATION 20 minutes
COOKING 10 minutes
MAKES 4 servings

PER SERVING 1532 kJ, 366 kcal, 30 g protein, 23 g fat (5 g saturated fat), 8 g carbohydrate (4 g sugars), 1063 mg sodium, 2 g fibre

1 In a large bowl, combine chicken, 2 tablespoons soy sauce, the sherry and cornflour and toss together until chicken is well coated. Add 1 teaspoon sesame oil and toss again.

2 In a wok or large non-stick frying pan, heat 2 tablespoons peanut oil over medium–high heat. Add chicken mixture and stir-fry for 4 minutes, or until chicken is lightly browned and cooked through. Transfer chicken to a plate.

3 Meanwhile, rinse black beans in several changes of cold water. Drain well; mash half the black beans with the flat side of a knife.

4 Add remaining peanut oil to wok, along with capsicum, chilli if using, ginger, garlic and black beans; stir to combine. Add remaining soy sauce, sesame oil and ½ cup (125 ml) water and stir-fry for 2 minutes. Add bok choy and stir-fry for 1 minute, or until leaves are just starting to wilt.

5 Return chicken to the wok and stir-fry for 1 minute, or until heated through. Serve hot.

Asparagus and chicken are a timeless pairing, brightened with a hint of lemon zest. This simple stir-fry is especially enjoyable in spring, when asparagus and peas are at their sweetest and freshest.

Asparagus & chicken stir-fry

1 tablespoon vegetable oil

3 spring onions (scallions), thinly sliced

375 g (¾ lb) boneless, skinless chicken breasts, cut for stir-fry (see Basics)

350 g (12 oz) asparagus, trimmed and cut into long lengths on the diagonal

250 g (8 oz) sugarsnap peas or snow peas (mangetout)

½ cup (125 ml) chicken stock (page 49)

½ teaspoon grated lemon zest, plus extra, to garnish

1 tablespoon light soy sauce

1 teaspoon cornflour (cornstarch)

LOW FAT, QUICK
PREPARATION 15 minutes
COOKING 10 minutes
MAKES 4 servings

PER SERVING 896 kJ, 214 kcal, 25 g protein, 10 g fat (2 g saturated fat), 6 g carbohydrate (4 g sugars), 406 mg sodium, 3 g fibre

1 In a wok or large non-stick frying pan, heat half the oil over medium heat. Add spring onions and stir-fry for 1 minute, or until just wilted. Add chicken and stir-fry for 3 minutes, or until chicken is no longer pink.

2 Add remaining oil and the asparagus and toss for 2 minutes to coat the asparagus.

3 Add peas, stock, lemon zest, soy sauce and ½ cup (125 ml) water and bring to a boil. Reduce to a simmer and stir-fry for 2 minutes, or until chicken and asparagus are just cooked through.

4 Mix the cornflour with 1 tablespoon water to make a smooth paste; add to wok and stir until blended. Bring to a boil and cook, stirring constantly, for 1 minute, or until sauce is slightly thickened. Divide among bowls, garnish with extra lemon zest and serve.

Sweet, crunchy glazed almonds are the surprising and delicious garnish for this stir-fry. The almonds are pretty irresistible: it's a good idea to move them out of reach while you cook the chicken or you may find that you have none left when your stir-fry is ready to serve!

Chicken with almonds

¼ cup (55 g) sugar, plus ½ teaspoon

½ teaspoon salt

1 cup (155 g) blanched almonds

1½ teaspoons cornflour (cornstarch)

½ cup (125 ml) chicken stock (page 49)

2 tablespoons salt-reduced soy sauce

1 tablespoon dry sherry

2 tablespoons vegetable oil

2 tablespoons grated fresh ginger

2 cloves garlic, crushed

750 g (1½ lb) boneless, skinless chicken thighs, cut into large chunks

2 red capsicums (bell peppers), cut into large chunks

2 spring onions (scallions), thinly sliced on the diagonal

steamed white rice, to serve

PREPARATION 20 minutes
COOKING 15 minutes
MAKES 4 servings

PER SERVING 2734 kJ, 653 kcal, 44 g protein, 44 g fat (7 g saturated fat), 20 g carbohydrate (18 g sugars), 638 mg sodium, 5 g fibre

1 In a non-stick frying pan, heat ¼ cup (55 g) sugar, ¼ teaspoon salt and the almonds over medium heat. Stir-fry for 3 minutes, or until almonds are crisp and glazed. Transfer almonds to a plate.

2 In a small bowl, whisk together cornflour, stock, soy sauce, sherry and remaining sugar and salt; set aside.

3 In a large wok or non-stick frying pan, heat oil over medium–high heat. Add ginger and garlic and cook for 30 seconds. Add chicken and stir-fry for 5 minutes, or until just cooked through. Add capsicums and stir-fry for 3 minutes, or until crisp-tender.

4 Whisk stock mixture again and add to wok. Bring to a boil, then boil for 1 minute, or until sauce is of coating consistency.

5 Serve on a bed of steamed white rice, sprinkled with the glazed almonds and spring onions.

Whoever first thought of teaming chicken with creamy, nutty cashews was clearly onto a winner. In this delightfully healthy stir-fry, crisp vegetables contribute colour, texture and crunch, with ginger, garlic and chilli sauce rounding out a perfect match.

Chicken & cashew stir-fry

1 tablespoon salt-reduced soy sauce

1 tablespoon dry sherry

375 g (¾ lb) boneless, skinless chicken thighs, cut into large chunks

3 cups (180 g) small broccoli florets

2 teaspoons vegetable oil

3 teaspoons grated fresh ginger

3 cloves garlic, crushed

1 red capsicum (bell pepper), cut into large chunks

½ cup (125 ml) chicken stock (page 49)

2 tablespoons chilli (pepper) sauce

2 teaspoons cornflour (cornstarch)

2 spring onions (scallions), sliced into long lengths on the diagonal

¼ cup (40 g) cashew nuts, chopped

LOW FAT, QUICK
PREPARATION 20 minutes
COOKING 10 minutes
MAKES 4 servings

PER SERVING 1077 kJ, 258 kcal, 23 g protein, 15 g fat (3 g saturated fat), 8 g carbohydrate (4 g sugars), 583 mg sodium, 4 g fibre

1 In a bowl, mix together soy sauce and sherry. Add chicken and toss until well coated.

2 In a steamer or microwave, cook broccoli for 3 minutes, or until crisp-tender. Set aside.

3 Meanwhile, in a wok or large non-stick frying pan, heat oil over medium heat. Add chicken and stir-fry for 3 minutes, or until just cooked through. Transfer chicken to a plate.

4 Add ginger and garlic to the wok and stir-fry for 30 seconds. Add broccoli and capsicum and stir-fry for 2 minutes.

5 Add stock and chilli sauce and bring to a boil. Mix the cornflour with 1 tablespoon water to make a smooth paste; add to wok and stir for 1 minute, or until sauce is slightly thickened.

6 Return chicken to wok, add spring onions and toss for 1 minute. Stir in cashews just before serving.

Traditionally, this dish would be made with a deep red, salty, dry-cured Chinese ham, which is most commonly diced or thinly sliced and used as a flavouring. You can use a good-quality slow-cured, wood-smoked, country-style ham instead.

Chinese chicken with walnuts

1 cup (100 g) walnut halves

⅓ cup (80 ml) salt-reduced soy sauce

1 tablespoon dry sherry

1 tablespoon cornflour (cornstarch)

1 teaspoon sugar

½ teaspoon salt

1.25 kg (2½ lb) boneless, skinless chicken breasts, cut into large chunks

⅓ cup (80 ml) vegetable oil

3 leeks, white part only, cut into thick strips

500 g (1 lb) asparagus, cut on the diagonal into long lengths

1 red capsicum (bell pepper), thinly sliced

125 g (4 oz) Chinese or country-style ham, cut into long strips

3 cloves garlic, finely chopped

½ cup (125 ml) chicken stock (page 49)

steamed white rice, to serve

LOW FAT

PREPARATION 20 minutes
COOKING 20 minutes
MAKES 8 servings

PER SERVING 1743 kJ, 416 kcal, 39 g protein, 27 g fat (4 g saturated fat), 5 g carbohydrate (4 g sugars), 700 mg sodium, 3 g fibre

1 Preheat the oven to 180°C (350°F/Gas 4). Spread walnuts out on a baking tray and bake for 7 minutes, or until slightly crisp and fragrant.

2 Meanwhile, in a large bowl, whisk together soy sauce, sherry, cornflour, sugar and salt. Add chicken and toss to coat well.

3 In a wok or large non-stick frying pan, heat 2 tablespoons oil over medium heat. Add chicken and stir-fry for 5 minutes, or until golden brown and almost cooked through. Transfer chicken to a plate.

4 Add remaining oil to wok and heat over medium heat. Add leeks, asparagus, capsicum, ham and garlic and stir-fry for 4 minutes, or until asparagus is crisp-tender. Add stock and cook for 2 minutes.

5 Return chicken to wok and cook for 2 minutes, or until cooked through. Serve on a bed of steamed white rice, sprinkled with toasted walnuts.

COOK'S TIP
Instead of Chinese ham, you could also use prosciutto. Add whole prosciutto slices to the baking tray in step 1 and bake for 4 minutes, or until crisp. When cool enough to handle, tear into shreds. Sprinkle over the stir-fry with the toasted walnuts just before serving.

Don't wait for your next trip to a Chinese restaurant—cook up a batch of fried rice at home and enjoy it fresh and sizzling hot. Serve the rice in deep bowls, which hold the heat. Have fun experimenting: replace the asparagus with snow peas (mangetout), use brown rice instead of white, or add some prawns (shrimp).

Fried rice with chicken

2 large eggs

½ small red capsicum (bell pepper), finely diced

¼ cup (60 ml) salt-reduced soy sauce

1½ teaspoons sugar

2 teaspoons sesame oil

2 tablespoons vegetable oil

2 tablespoons grated fresh ginger

2 cloves garlic, crushed

500 g (1 lb) asparagus, thinly sliced on the diagonal

6 spring onions (scallions), sliced

3 cups (450 g) shredded cooked chicken breasts or thighs—leftover or poached (see Basics)

3 cups (550 g) cooked long-grain white rice

¼ cup (60 ml) rice vinegar

1½ cups (235 g) frozen peas, thawed

LOW FAT
PREPARATION 25 minutes
COOKING 15 minutes
MAKES 4 servings

PER SERVING 3881 kJ, 927 kcal, 53 g protein, 25 g fat (5 g saturated fat), 119 g carbohydrate (7 g sugars), 702 mg sodium, 4 g fibre

1 In a small bowl, whisk together eggs, capsicum, 1 tablespoon soy sauce and ½ teaspoon sugar. In a small frying pan, heat sesame oil over medium–high heat. Add egg mixture and cook, without stirring, for 2 minutes, or until set. Transfer omelette to a cutting board and cut into strips 1 cm (½ inch) wide.

2 In a wok or large non-stick frying pan, heat vegetable oil over medium–high heat. Add ginger and garlic and cook for 30 seconds. Add asparagus and spring onions and stir-fry for 3 minutes, or until asparagus is crisp-tender.

3 Add chicken and rice, stirring to coat. In a small bowl, whisk together vinegar and remaining soy sauce and sugar. Pour over rice mixture and stir-fry for 7 minutes, or until rice is piping hot and slightly crusty.

4 Stir in peas and egg strips and cook for 1 minute, or until peas are heated through. Serve hot.

VARIATION *Creole fried rice*
Omit step 1 and omelette ingredients. In step 2, fry 125 g (4 oz) diced chorizo sausages in the oil over medium heat for 5 minutes, or until slightly crisp. Omit ginger and increase garlic to 3 cloves; add as directed. Instead of asparagus, use 1 large diced green capsicum (bell pepper); add with spring onions and stir-fry for 5 minutes, or until crisp-tender. In step 3, add chicken and rice as directed; omit vinegar, soy sauce and sugar, but stir in ¼ teaspoon salt, 2 teaspoons ground turmeric and 2 teaspoons hot chilli (pepper) sauce. Stir-fry for 7 minutes, or until rice is piping hot and slightly crusty. In step 4, omit peas, but stir in 3 tablespoons chopped fresh parsley and serve.

Roasts &
oven-baked dishes

*There's no mistaking the tantalising aroma
of chicken roasting in the oven. If you don't
have time to roast a whole bird, never fear: try
our succulent shortcuts using oven-baked
breasts or crusted chicken legs.*

Fragrant with rosemary, thyme and lemon, our plump, golden roast chicken will be welcome at any dinner table. You can experiment with other fresh herbs in the herb butter. Some great combinations to try are fresh sage and parsley; ground cumin and finely chopped coriander (cilantro); and oregano and hot paprika.

Perfect roast herb & lemon chicken

60 g (2 oz) butter, at room temperature

1 tablespoon finely chopped fresh
    rosemary

1 tablespoon finely chopped fresh thyme

1 shallot (eschalot), finely chopped

1 teaspoon salt

½ teaspoon freshly ground black pepper

1 whole chicken, about 1.75 kg (3½ lb),
    giblets removed (reserve for
    another use)

1 large lemon

2 cloves garlic, unpeeled

PREPARATION 10 minutes
COOKING 50 minutes
MAKES 4 servings

PER SERVING 2320 kJ, 554 kcal, 39 g protein,
44 g fat (18 g saturated fat), 2 g carbohydrate
(<1 g sugars), 879 mg sodium, 2 g fibre

1 Preheat the oven to 200°C (400°F/Gas 6). In a small bowl, mash together butter, rosemary, thyme, shallot, ½ teaspoon of the salt and the pepper. With your fingers, gently loosen skin from chicken breast and legs without removing it, then rub the herb butter under skin around legs and breast of chicken.

2 With a fork, prick lemon in several places. Rub cavity of chicken with another ½ teaspoon of salt and place lemon and garlic cloves in cavity. With kitchen string, tie chicken legs together. Lift wings up towards the neck, then fold the wing tips under back of chicken so wings stay in place. Sprinkle remaining salt over chicken.

3 Place chicken, breast side up, on a rack in a 23 x 33 cm (9 x 13 inch) roasting pan. Roast for 50 minutes, basting frequently with pan drippings, until chicken is cooked through and richly browned. Transfer chicken to a platter or carving board.

4 Pour pan drippings from the roasting pan into a cup or gravy separator; spoon (or pour) off and discard fat. Pour 1 cup (250 ml) water (or salt-reduced chicken stock; see page 49) into roasting pan and stir with a whisk to scrape up any browned bits (caramelised meat juices) from the bottom and sides of pan. Whisk in the de-fatted pan drippings and serve with the chicken.

TO REDUCE THE FAT
Remove the skin from the chicken before eating.

VARIATION *Orange-chilli roast chicken*
In step 1, add 1 tablespoon chilli powder and 2 teaspoons grated orange zest to the butter mixture. In step 2, substitute 1 navel orange, quartered, for the lemon. Complete the dish as directed.

Duck à l'orange may not be your idea of a simple family dinner, but with this lovely chicken dish you can enjoy similar flavours with far less effort. The sweetness of the honey is cleverly balanced with soy sauce and paprika. Serve the chicken with steamed brussels sprouts or cabbage and brown or white rice.

Orange-honey glazed chicken

1 tablespoon olive oil

¼ cup (40 g) finely chopped onion

2 cloves garlic, crushed

½ cup (125 ml) orange juice

¼ cup (90 g) honey

2 tablespoons salt-reduced soy sauce

2 teaspoons paprika

½ teaspoon salt

¾ teaspoon freshly ground black pepper

½ teaspoon ground ginger

1 whole chicken, about 1.75 kg (3½ lb), split in half lengthwise (see Cook's Tips)

PREPARATION 10 minutes
COOKING 50 minutes
MAKES 4 servings

PER SERVING 2357 kJ, 563 kcal, 40 g protein, 36 g fat (10 g saturated fat), 23 g carbohydrate (22 g sugars), 839 mg sodium, 1 g fibre

1 Preheat the oven to 190°C (375°F/Gas 5). In a frying pan, heat oil over low heat. Add onion and garlic and cook, stirring frequently, for 5 minutes, or until onion has softened. Increase heat to medium, stir in orange juice, honey, soy sauce, paprika, salt, pepper and ginger. Bring to a boil and cook for 3 minutes, or until mixture has thickened slightly.

2 Place chicken, skin side up, in a roasting pan large enough to hold it in a single layer. Spoon half the orange mixture over the chicken. Roast for 20 minutes.

3 Spoon remaining orange mixture over the chicken and roast for another 20 minutes, basting twice, until cooked through. Transfer chicken to a platter or carving board.

4 Pour pan juices into a cup or gravy separator. Spoon (or pour) off and discard fat. Serve the pan juices with the chicken.

TO REDUCE THE FAT
Remove the skin from the chicken before eating.

COOK'S TIPS
• A split chicken cooks a little faster than a whole one.
• To split a chicken in half lengthwise, place it on a chopping board breast side up. Starting at the tail end, use poultry shears to cut through the rib bones along one side of the breast bone. Next, still using the poultry shears, cut along both sides of the backbone to separate the two halves of the chicken. Discard the backbone, or reserve for making stock.
• For this recipe, it's a good idea to line the roasting pan with foil because the sugary glaze is likely to burn onto the pan. For a more intense flavour, try using a wildflower honey in this recipe.

Make the most of a hot oven by roasting some vegetables to serve with a roast bird. You can vary the vegetables according to what's in season; simply adjust the cooking time to suit. For juicy results, allow the chicken to rest for 10 minutes before carving it.

Roast thyme chicken with pan gravy

1 whole chicken, about 1.6 kg (3 lb)

½ teaspoon salt

a few sprigs fresh thyme

1 small onion, halved

2 tablespoons olive oil

1 teaspoon freshly ground black pepper

1 tablespoon melted butter

½ cup (125 ml) salt-reduced chicken stock (page 49), plus ½ cup (125 ml) extra, for basting

4 baking (floury) potatoes, peeled and cut in half

300 g (10 oz) pumpkin (winter squash), cut into chunks (leave the skin on if you like)

2 carrots, cut in half horizontally

PAN GRAVY

2 tablespoons plain (all-purpose) flour

1–1½ cups (250–375 ml) salt-reduced chicken stock (page 49)

PREPARATION 15 minutes
COOKING 1 hour 30 minutes
MAKES 4 servings

PER SERVING 2769 kJ, 662 kcal, 43 g protein, 42 g fat (13 g saturated fat), 29 g carbohydrate (7 g sugars), 856 mg sodium, 4 g fibre

1 Preheat the oven to 180°C (350°F/Gas 4). Rub cavity of chicken with ½ teaspoon of the salt and place thyme sprigs and onion in cavity. With kitchen string, tie chicken legs together. Lift wings up towards the neck, then fold the wing tips under back of chicken so wings stay in place. Rub half the oil over chicken, then sprinkle with half the pepper and another ½ teaspoon salt.

2 Place chicken, breast side up, in a roasting pan. Drizzle with the melted butter and pour stock into the pan. Cover with foil and roast for 45 minutes.

3 Remove pan from the oven. Discard foil and baste chicken with extra stock. Move chicken around a bit so it doesn't stick to the pan. Place vegetables in another large roasting pan, drizzle with remaining oil and sprinkle with remaining salt and pepper.

4 Roast chicken and vegetables for 30 minutes, leaving chicken uncovered and basting occasionally. Turn vegetables and roast another 15 minutes, or until chicken is cooked through and vegetables are golden and tender. Transfer chicken to a platter or carving board and cover loosely with foil to keep warm.

5 To make pan gravy, place roasting pan on stovetop over medium heat. Stir in flour with a whisk to scrape up any browned bits (caramelised meat juices) from the bottom and sides of pan. Slowly whisk in stock and bring to a boil; reduce heat and simmer for a few minutes to thicken.

6 Carve chicken into serving pieces. Serve with the pan gravy and roasted vegetables.

TO REDUCE THE FAT
Remove the skin from the chicken before eating.

This one-dish meal roasts for a little over an hour. There's very little to prepare, so you can get it into the oven in practically no time and put your feet up while the oven does all the work.

Country roast chicken & vegetables

1 whole chicken, about 1.75 kg (3½ lb), cut into 8 serving pieces (see Basics)

16 small red-skinned potatoes, such as desiree (about 750 g/1½ lb), cut into large chunks

1 zucchini (courgette), cut into large chunks

1 golden zucchini or yellow summer squash, cut into large chunks

225 g (8 oz) baby carrots, peeled

1 garlic bulb, loose outer skin removed, and the top quarter sliced off

2 dried bay leaves

½ teaspoon dried sage

½ teaspoon dried thyme

¾ teaspoon salt

¼ teaspoon freshly ground black pepper

2 tablespoons vegetable oil

PREPARATION 15 minutes
COOKING 1 hour 15 minutes
MAKES 4 servings

PER SERVING 3116 kJ, 744 kcal, 48 g protein, 41 g fat (11 g saturated fat), 47 g carbohydrate (6 g sugars), 653 mg sodium, 9 g fibre

1 Preheat the oven to 200°C (400°F/Gas 6). Place chicken pieces in a large roasting pan. Add vegetables, garlic bulb and bay leaves, then sprinkle with the dried herbs, salt and pepper. Drizzle with oil and gently toss to coat.

2 Place in oven and roast, turning chicken and tossing vegetables every 15 minutes, for 1 hour 15 minutes, or until chicken is cooked through and vegetables are golden and tender.

3 Transfer chicken to a platter and vegetables to a bowl. Discard bay leaves. Squeeze roasted garlic pulp from garlic cloves and toss with vegetables. Arrange vegetables around chicken and serve.

TO REDUCE THE FAT
Remove the skin from the chicken before eating.

VARIATION *Southwestern roast chicken & vegetables*
Omit bay leaves. Substitute ½ teaspoon ground cumin for the sage, and ½ teaspoon dried oregano for the thyme. If you like, sprinkle with chopped coriander (cilantro) after roasting.

ROASTS & OVEN-BAKED DISHES

The chicken and vegetables are lavished with butter that has been infused with toasted fennel seeds; as a delicious change, try dill seeds instead of fennel seeds and add some finely chopped fresh dill. Spoon the beautiful buttery pan juices over the chicken and vegetables and mop them up with crusty bread.

Roast chicken with fennel butter

1 tablespoon fennel seeds

125 g (4 oz) butter, at room temperature

1 teaspoon grated lemon zest

10 carrots, quartered crosswise

8 small onions, about 500 g (1 lb), peeled

8 cloves garlic, unpeeled

¾ teaspoon salt

1 whole chicken, about 1.75 kg (3½ lb),
    giblets removed (reserve for
    another use)

PREPARATION 25 minutes
COOKING 55 minutes
MAKES 4 servings

PER SERVING 2992 kJ, 715 kcal, 41 g protein,
57 g fat (27 g saturated fat), 11 g carbohydrate
(8 g sugars), 912 mg sodium, 5 g fibre

1 Preheat the oven to 200°C (400°F/Gas 6). In a small dry frying pan, toast fennel seeds over low heat for 3 minutes, or until fragrant and lightly crisped. When cool, transfer to a zip-seal plastic bag and lightly crush with a rolling pin. Transfer to a large bowl, add butter and lemon zest and mix to thoroughly combine. Measure out 4 tablespoons of fennel butter and set aside.

2 Add carrots, onions, garlic cloves and ¾ teaspoon of the salt to the bowl and toss to combine. Transfer mixture to a baking dish or roasting pan large enough to hold vegetables in a single layer.

3 With your fingers, gently loosen skin from chicken breast and legs without removing it. Rub the reserved 4 tablespoons of fennel butter under skin around legs and breast of chicken. Season cavity and skin of chicken with remaining salt. With kitchen string, tie chicken legs together. Lift wings up towards the neck, then fold the wing tips under back of chicken so wings stay in place.

4 Place chicken, breast side down, on top of vegetables. Roast for 25 minutes. Turn vegetables over, and turn chicken breast side up. Roast for another 25 minutes, or until chicken is cooked through and vegetables are golden and tender.

TO REDUCE THE FAT
In step 1, decrease butter to 60 g (2 oz) and blend with half the toasted fennel seeds. Use this fennel butter to rub under skin of chicken in step 3. In step 2, toss vegetables with 2 tablespoons olive oil and remaining toasted fennel seeds instead of fennel butter. Roast chicken and vegetables in two separate roasting pans.

This Indian-inspired dish dates back to the nineteenth century. Perhaps, as the name implies, a ship's captain or a military officer procured the recipe and spirited it home across the seas, but it's possible that residents of a port city simply made creative use of the new spices brought in on passing sailing ships.

Country captain

½ cup currants (75 g) or raisins (60 g)

½ cup (60 g) slivered almonds

⅓ cup (80 ml) olive oil

2 whole chickens, each about 1.75 kg (3½ lb), cut into 10 pieces each (see Basics)

½ cup (75 g) plain (all-purpose) flour

1 large onion, finely chopped

3 cloves garlic, finely chopped

1 red capsicum (bell pepper), finely diced

4 teaspoons curry powder

1 teaspoon dried thyme

1 teaspoon salt

4 cups (1 kg) canned chopped tomatoes

steamed white rice, to serve

PREPARATION 20 minutes, plus 10 minutes soaking
COOKING 1 hour 10 minutes
MAKES 8 servings

PER SERVING 2290 kJ, 547 kcal, 43 g protein, 35 g fat (10 g saturated fat), 16 g carbohydrate (6 g sugars), 546 mg sodium, 4 g fibre

1 Preheat the oven to 180°C (350°F/Gas 4). In a small bowl, soak currants in ½ cup (125 ml) hot water for 10 minutes, or until softened.

2 Meanwhile, place almonds on a baking tray and roast in the oven for 5 minutes, or until golden brown. Remove from oven. When cool enough to handle, roughly chop and set aside.

3 In a large frying pan, heat oil over medium heat. Dredge chicken in the flour, shaking off excess. Fry one-third of the chicken for 4 minutes per side, or until golden brown. Transfer to a roasting pan large enough to hold all the chicken in a single layer. Fry two more batches in the same way, transferring each batch to the roasting pan.

4 Add onion and garlic to frying pan and sauté for 5 minutes, or until onion has softened. Add capsicum and cook for 4 minutes, or until crisp-tender. Stir in curry powder, thyme and salt and cook for 1 minute, then add tomatoes and currants and their soaking liquid and bring to a boil.

5 Pour sauce over chicken in roasting pan. Cover with foil and bake for 30 minutes, or until chicken is cooked through. Serve chicken sprinkled with the roasted almonds, with steamed white rice.

TO REDUCE THE FAT
Remove the skin from the chicken before eating.

Like garlic, shallots become sweeter the longer they cook. These whole roasted ones are irresistible—there are enough for three per person, but you can toss in a few more if you like. You can eat them as a vegetable, or mash them with your fork to spread on bites of chicken or on bread.

Roast chicken with shallots

¼ cup (60 ml) olive oil

12 shallots (eschalots), about 225 g (8 oz) in total, peeled

3 sprigs fresh rosemary

1 teaspoon salt

¾ teaspoon freshly ground black pepper

1 whole chicken, about 1.75 kg (3½ lb), giblets removed (reserve for another use)

2 tablespoons plain (all-purpose) flour

PREPARATION 15 minutes
COOKING 55 minutes
MAKES 4 servings

PER SERVING 2460 kJ, 588 kcal, 40 g protein, 45 g fat (12 g saturated fat), 7 g carbohydrate (2 g sugars), 825 mg sodium, 2 g fibre

1 Preheat the oven to 200°C (400°F/Gas 6). Pour oil into a 23 x 33 cm (9 x 13 inch) roasting pan. Add whole shallots and rosemary sprigs and toss to coat.

2 In a small bowl, combine 1¼ teaspoons of the salt with ½ teaspoon of the pepper. With your fingers, gently loosen skin from chicken breast and legs without removing it, then rub the salt mixture under skin, inside cavity and over skin of chicken. With kitchen string, tie chicken legs together. Lift wings up towards the neck, then fold the wing tips under back of chicken so wings stay in place.

3 Place chicken, breast side up, on a rack in the roasting pan. Roast for 50 minutes, basting frequently with pan drippings, until skin is crisp and chicken is cooked through. Transfer chicken and shallots to a serving platter. Discard rosemary sprigs.

4 Pour fat from roasting pan into a small bowl and set aside. Pour 1 cup (250 ml) water into the roasting pan and stir with a whisk to scrape up any browned bits (caramelised meat juices) from the bottom and sides of pan. Set roasting pan aside.

5 Spoon 2 tablespoons of the reserved fat into a small saucepan. Heat over medium heat. Whisk in flour until well combined and cook for 2 to 3 minutes, or until lightly browned. Whisk in pan juices from roasting pan along with remaining salt and pepper and cook over low heat until slightly thickened.

6 Serve chicken and shallots with the gravy.

TO REDUCE THE FAT
Remove the skin from the chicken before eating.

COOK'S TIP
Shallots, also known as eschalots or French shallots, are mild-flavoured members of the onion family. Like garlic, shallots grow in 'heads' comprising several cloves, each wrapped in a papery skin.

Treat your garlic-loving friends to this modern classic.
Even those who normally shy away from garlic may
enjoy it with this meal, as the garlic's bite is tamed by
slow cooking, becoming richly mellow and sweet.
You don't even have to eat the garlic cloves as they'll
already have done a nice job of flavouring the chicken.

Chicken baked with 40 garlic cloves

½ cup (125 ml) olive oil

2 whole chickens, each about 1.75 kg
    (3½ lb), cut into 8 serving pieces each
    (see Basics)

⅓ cup (50 g) plain (all-purpose) flour

40 cloves garlic, unpeeled

3 stalks celery, halved lengthwise and
    cut crosswise into large chunks

4 sprigs fresh rosemary, or ¾ teaspoon
    dried

3 sprigs fresh thyme, or ½ teaspoon dried

¾ cup (180 ml) dry vermouth or white
    wine

¾ cup (180 ml) salt-reduced chicken stock
    (page 49)

1½ teaspoons salt

8 slices wholegrain bread, about 1 cm
    (½ inch) thick

PREPARATION 25 minutes
COOKING 1 hour 15 minutes
MAKES 8 servings

PER SERVING 2844 kJ, 679 kcal, 44 g protein,
47 g fat (12 g saturated fat), 14 g carbohydrate
(2 g sugars), 754 mg sodium, 7 g fibre

1 Preheat the oven to 180°C (350°F/Gas 4). In a large frying pan, heat half the oil over medium heat. Dredge chicken in the flour, shaking off excess. Fry one-third of the chicken for 4 minutes per side, or until golden brown. Transfer to a large roasting pan. Fry two more batches in the same way, transferring each batch to the roasting pan.

2 Add garlic cloves, celery, rosemary and thyme to frying pan and cook for 1 minute. Add vermouth, increase heat to high, bring to a boil and cook for 2 minutes to evaporate alcohol. Add stock and salt and bring to a boil. Pour mixture over chicken in roasting pan.

3 Cover pan with foil and bake for 45 minutes, or until chicken is cooked through and garlic is meltingly tender.

4 Meanwhile, in a large frying pan, heat remaining oil over medium heat. Add bread slices and fry for 1 minute per side, or until golden brown. Cut each piece in half.

5 Spoon chicken and garlic cloves onto serving plates. Serve with the bread slices, for spreading the roasted garlic over.

TO REDUCE THE FAT
Remove the skin from the chicken before eating. Serve with baguettes rather than the fried bread.

It takes very little effort to stuff a plump chicken. The sausage and mushroom stuffing used here adds an extra element of comfort and deliciousness during the coldest months of the year. If you can't find shiitake mushrooms, just use more button mushrooms.

Roast chicken with sausage stuffing

225 g (8 oz) coarse-textured wholegrain bread, cut into 2.5 cm (1 inch) cubes (about 6 cups)

2 tablespoons olive oil

150 g (5 oz) sweet, mildly spiced Italian sausages, casings removed

1 large onion, finely chopped

3⅓ cups (300 g) thinly sliced button mushrooms

225 g (8 oz) fresh shiitake mushrooms, stems trimmed and caps thinly sliced

¼ teaspoon freshly ground black pepper

½ teaspoon salt

¾ cup (180 ml) salt-reduced chicken stock (page 49)

2 tablespoons butter, at room temperature

1 whole chicken, about 1.75 kg (3½ lb), giblets removed (reserve for another use)

PREPARATION 25 minutes
COOKING 1 hour 20 minutes
MAKES 4 servings

PER SERVING 3624 kJ, 866 kcal, 55 g protein, 60 g fat (20 g saturated fat), 23 g carbohydrate (7 g sugars), 1068 mg sodium, 11 g fibre

1 Preheat the oven to 190°C (375°F/Gas 5). Spread bread cubes on a baking tray and toast in the oven, shaking the tray once, for 7 minutes, or until golden brown. Transfer to a large bowl.

2 In a large frying pan, heat oil over medium heat. Crumble sausages into the pan and sauté for 5 minutes, or until just cooked through. Add to the bread cubes.

3 Add onion to pan and cook, stirring frequently, for 7 minutes, or until soft. Add button and shiitake mushrooms, sprinkle with pepper and ¼ teaspoon of the salt and sauté for 7 minutes, or until mushrooms are tender. Add to the bread cubes with the stock and butter and stir until butter has melted. Set aside to cool slightly before stuffing chicken.

4 Loosely spoon stuffing into neck and body cavities of chicken. (If there is any stuffing left over, spoon it into a small baking dish; cover with foil and cook alongside chicken during final 25 minutes of roasting.) Tie chicken legs together with kitchen string. Lift wings up towards the neck, then fold wing tips under back of chicken so wings stay in place. Sprinkle remaining salt over chicken.

5 Place chicken, breast side up, on a rack in a 23 x 33 cm (9 x 13 inch) baking dish. Roast chicken for 20 minutes. Baste with pan drippings and roast for another 30 minutes, basting twice more, until chicken is cooked through.

TO REDUCE THE FAT
In step 2, omit olive oil and sausages. In step 3, omit butter and increase stock to 1 cup (250 ml); stir in 225 g (8 oz) fully cooked chicken sausages, roughly chopped. Stuff and roast as directed. Also, remove the skin from the chicken before eating.

Carving a whole bird in the kitchen is the easy way to go, but carving at the table definitely adds a note of drama to a dinner party. No matter how you serve this stuffed chicken, it will look and taste sensational.

Apricot-glazed roast chicken

1 whole chicken, about 2.7 kg (6 lb), giblets removed (reserve for another use)

1 teaspoon salt

½ cup (160 g) apricot jam

1 tablespoon lemon juice

APRICOT PECAN COUSCOUS STUFFING
1⅔ cups (7 oz) instant couscous

2 cups (500 ml) salt-reduced chicken stock (page 49), heated

2 tablespoons butter

1 large onion, finely chopped

2 stalks celery, quartered lengthwise and thinly sliced

½ cup (50 g) pecans, chopped

½ cup (30 g) chopped fresh parsley

½ cup (90 g) dried apricots, finely chopped

PREPARATION 15 minutes
COOKING 1 hour 45 minutes
MAKES 8 servings

PER SERVING 2467 kJ, 589 kcal, 35 g protein, 32 g fat (10 g saturated fat), 40 g carbohydrate (20 g sugars), 645 mg sodium, 3 g fibre

1 Preheat the oven to 200°C (400°F/Gas 6). To make the stuffing, soak couscous in the hot stock in a heatproof bowl for 5 to 10 minutes, until stock is absorbed. Meanwhile, melt butter in a large frying pan over medium heat and sauté onion for 7 minutes, or until soft. Stir in celery and cook for 5 minutes, or until celery is crisp-tender. Add onion mixture to couscous with remaining stuffing ingredients and mix together well.

2 Rub chicken inside and out with the salt. Loosely spoon stuffing into neck and body cavities of chicken. Spoon remaining stuffing into a small baking dish; cover with foil and set aside. Tie chicken legs together with kitchen string. Lift wings up towards the neck, then fold wing tips under back of chicken so wings stay in place.

3 Place chicken, breast side up, on a rack in a 28 x 38 cm (11 x 15 inch) roasting pan. Roast chicken for 1 hour.

4 Place dish of stuffing alongside chicken in oven. In a small bowl, stir together jam and lemon juice, then brush half the mixture over chicken and roast for 10 minutes.

5 Brush remaining apricot mixture over chicken and roast for another 20 minutes, or until skin is glazed and chicken is cooked through. Serve with the stuffing.

VARIATION
Currant-glazed chicken with cranberry & almond stuffing
In step 1, prepare stuffing mixture as directed, but substitute ⅔ cup (85 g) toasted almonds for the pecans, and ⅔ cup (80 g) dried cranberries for the apricots. Prepare and stuff chicken as directed in steps 2 and 3, but in steps 4 and 5, substitute ½ cup (160 g) redcurrant jelly for the apricot jam-lemon juice mixture. Roast and baste as directed.

A soy sauce marinade, its taste and colour further enhanced with brown sugar and cinnamon, yields a Chinese-style roast chicken with mahogany-brown skin. As an attractive glaze, and for an extra flavour dimension, fragrant dark sesame oil is brushed on the chicken when it comes out of the oven.

Mahogany chicken with rice stuffing

¼ cup (60 ml) salt-reduced soy sauce

¼ cup (60 ml) dry sherry

¼ cup (45 g) brown sugar

1 teaspoon ground cinnamon

1 whole chicken, about 1.75 kg (3½ lb), giblets removed (reserve for another use)

1 tablespoon vegetable oil

2 spring onions (scallions), thinly sliced

1 clove garlic, finely chopped

1 carrot, quartered lengthwise, then thinly sliced crosswise

1 cup (200 g) long-grain white rice

½ cup (125 ml) salt-reduced chicken stock (page 49)

2 teaspoons sesame oil

PREPARATION 10 minutes, plus
    at least 1 hour marinating
COOKING 1 hour 30 minutes
MAKES 4 servings

PER SERVING 3113 kJ, 744 kcal, 43 g protein, 38 g fat (11 g saturated fat), 54 g carbohydrate (13 g sugars), 832 mg sodium, 1 g fibre

1 In a small bowl, whisk together soy sauce, sherry, sugar and cinnamon. Place chicken in a large bowl, pour in soy-sauce mixture, then turn to coat. Cover and refrigerate for at least 1 hour or overnight, turning chicken several times to coat with marinade.

2 In a large saucepan, heat vegetable oil over low heat. Add spring onions and garlic and sauté for 2 minutes, or until garlic is soft. Stir in carrots and cook, stirring frequently, for 4 minutes or until crisp-tender. Stir in rice, stock and 1½ cups (375 ml) water and bring to a boil. Reduce to a simmer, then cover and cook for 17 minutes, or until rice is tender. Cool to room temperature.

3 Preheat the oven to 200°C (400°F/Gas 6). Lift chicken from marinade, reserving marinade. Loosely stuff neck and body cavities of chicken with rice mixture. (If there is any rice remaining, spoon it into a baking dish, cover with foil and cook alongside chicken during last 15 minutes of roasting.) Tie chicken legs together with kitchen string. Lift wings up towards the neck, then fold wing tips under back of chicken so wings stay in place.

4 Place chicken, breast side up, on a rack in a 28 x 38 cm (11 x 15 inch) roasting pan. Roast for 15 minutes. Brush with half the reserved marinade and roast for another 30 minutes.

5 Brush chicken with remaining marinade and roast for a final 15 to 20 minutes, until chicken is cooked through. Check frequently that chicken isn't becoming too brown; if it is, cover with a sheet of foil, leaving the two ends unsealed to keep the skin crisp.

6 Transfer chicken to a platter or carving board. Brush with sesame oil and let stand for 10 minutes before carving.

The generous use of herbs is a keynote of the cuisines of the Mediterranean. Here, fresh basil combines with tapenade, the pungent Provençal condiment made of ripe olives, capers, anchovies, olive oil and lemon juice.

Baked basil and tapenade chicken

¼ cup (60 ml) olive oil

6 cloves garlic, crushed

500 g (1 lb) artichoke hearts, frozen,
    or canned and drained

500 g (1 lb) asparagus, trimmed

½ teaspoon dried rosemary

1 dried bay leaf

½ teaspoon salt

¼ cup (60 g) tapenade (olive spread)

3 tablespoons chopped fresh basil

4 bone-in chicken breast halves, about
    1.25 kg (2½ lb) in total

lemon wedges, to serve

PREPARATION 15 minutes

COOKING 40 minutes

MAKES 4 servings

PER SERVING 2007 kJ, 479 kcal, 38 g protein,
34 g fat (8 g saturated fat), 4 g carbohydrate
(3 g sugars), 787 mg sodium, 4 g fibre

1 Preheat the oven to 200°C (400°F/Gas 6). Combine oil and garlic in a 23 x 33 cm (9 x 13 inch) baking dish. Heat dish in oven for 5 minutes, or until oil begins to sizzle. Stir in artichokes, asparagus, rosemary, bay leaf and half the salt. Bake for 10 minutes.

2 Meanwhile, in a small bowl, mix together tapenade and basil. With your fingers, gently loosen skin from chicken breasts without removing it, then spoon tapenade mixture under skin.

3 Place chicken breasts, skin side up, on top of the roasted vegetables. Sprinkle chicken with remaining salt. Bake, uncovered, for 25 minutes, or until chicken is cooked through and vegetables are tender. Discard bay leaf and serve with lemon wedges.

COOK'S TIP
You can buy jars of ready-made tapenade from delicatessens, specialist grocers and larger supermarkets.

This sophisticated dish takes its inspiration from saltimbocca—veal with prosciutto and fresh sage. The pounded chicken breasts are rolled around a sage-scented gorgonzola-pecan spread and a slice of good ham. Halved cherry tomatoes, sautéed in olive oil and tossed with snipped chives, is an ideal side dish.

Ham & asparagus chicken rolls

12 thin spears asparagus

175 g (6 oz) gorgonzola cheese or other blue cheese

2 tablespoons cream cheese

⅓ cup (35 g) pecans, finely chopped

½ teaspoon freshly ground black pepper

tiny pinch of dried sage

4 small boneless, skinless chicken breast halves, about 625 g (1¼ lb) in total, pounded 5 mm (¼ inch) thick (see Basics)

125 g (4 oz) thinly sliced black forest ham or prosciutto

1 large egg

1 cup (100 g) dry packaged breadcrumbs

2 tablespoons olive oil

PREPARATION 25 minutes
COOKING 30 minutes
MAKES 4 servings

PER SERVING 2845 kJ, 680 kcal, 56 g protein, 42 g fat (15 g saturated fat), 19 g carbohydrate (2 g sugars), 1280 mg sodium, 2 g fibre

1 Preheat the oven to 200°C (400°F/Gas 6). In a pot of boiling water, blanch asparagus for 2 minutes. Drain and rinse under cold water, then set aside.

2 In a bowl, using an electric mixer, beat gorgonzola and cream cheese until well combined. Stir in pecans, pepper and sage.

3 Place chicken halves on a work surface, smooth (skinned side) down, with one short end facing you. Cover the entire surface with ham slices. Spread cheese mixture over ham, leaving a 1 cm (½ inch) border all around. Place 3 asparagus spears crosswise over each breast, so the ends protrude, then roll up chicken from one short end. Secure with toothpicks to keep filling in place.

4 In a shallow bowl, beat the egg with 1 tablespoon water. In another shallow bowl, toss together breadcrumbs and oil. Dip each chicken roll first in egg mixture, then in breadcrumb mixture, patting crumbs onto chicken.

5 Place chicken rolls, seam side down, on a lightly greased baking tray. Bake for 25 minutes, or until topping is golden and chicken is firm to the touch. Remove toothpicks before serving.

TO REDUCE THE FAT
In step 2, reduce gorgonzola to 85 g (3 oz), use 4 tablespoons reduced-fat cream cheese (neufchâtel) instead of the regular cream cheese and reduce pecans to ¼ cup (25 g). In step 4, omit oil; instead, in step 5, spray chicken rolls lightly with olive oil cooking spray before baking.

Rosemary chicken breasts with garlic

Chicken breasts with parsley-butter

3 slices firm-textured white bread
    (about 85 g/3 oz)

60 g (2 oz) butter

2 shallots (eschalots), finely chopped

2 cloves garlic, crushed

½ cup (30 g) chopped fresh parsley

⅓ cup (80 ml) salt-reduced chicken stock
    (page 49)

4 bone-in chicken breast halves, with skin,
    about 1.25 kg (2½ lb) in total

½ teaspoon salt

¼ teaspoon freshly ground black pepper

PREPARATION 15 minutes
COOKING 45 minutes
MAKES 4 servings

PER SERVING 1769 kJ, 423 kcal, 33 g protein,
28 g fat (13 g saturated fat), 10 g carbohydrate
(1 g sugars), 662 mg sodium, 1 g fibre

1 Preheat the oven to 190°C (375°F/Gas 5). Cut bread into 1 cm (½ inch) cubes and spread on a baking tray. Bake for 7 minutes, or until golden brown.

2 Meanwhile, in a small frying pan, melt butter over medium heat. Add shallots and garlic and cook, stirring frequently, for 5 minutes, or until shallots are soft. Transfer to a large bowl. Add parsley, stock and toasted bread cubes and mix together.

3 With your fingers, gently loosen skin from chicken breasts without removing it, then rub salt and pepper under skin. Spoon bread mixture under skin, gently pulling skin back over to cover bread. Place chicken, skin side up, in a deep-sided baking tray. Bake for 35 minutes, or until cooked through.

TO REDUCE THE FAT
Reduce butter to 1 tablespoon and increase stock to ½ cup (125 ml).

Rosemary chicken breasts with garlic

2 tablespoons chopped fresh rosemary,
    or 2 teaspoons dried

1 teaspoon salt

½ teaspoon freshly ground black pepper

4 bone-in chicken breast halves, with skin,
    about 1.25 kg (2½ lb) in total

¼ cup (60 ml) olive oil

16 cloves garlic, unpeeled

LOW FAT
PREPARATION 10 minutes
COOKING 45 minutes
MAKES 4 servings

PER SERVING 1724 kJ, 412 kcal, 32 g protein,
30 g fat (7 g saturated fat), 4 g carbohydrate
(<1 g sugars), 701 mg sodium, 4 g fibre

1 Preheat the oven to 190°C (375°F/Gas 5). Place oil and garlic in a 23 x 33 cm (9 x 13 inch) baking dish. Toss to coat garlic with oil. Heat in oven for 5 minutes, or until oil begins to sizzle.

2 Meanwhile, in a small bowl, mix together rosemary, salt and pepper. With your fingers, gently loosen skin from chicken breasts without removing it. Rub rosemary mixture under the skin.

3 Add chicken to baking dish, skin side down. Bake for 20 minutes. Turn chicken skin side up and bake for another 20 minutes, or until chicken is cooked through. Serve chicken with roasted garlic, drizzled with pan juices.

Italian cooks typically use veal scaloppine for this type of dish, but pounded chicken breast halves are an ideal substitute—and far less expensive. While the chicken is in the oven, cook a pot of spaghetti or linguine to serve with it, and throw together a crisp green salad.

Stuffed chicken breasts parmesan

¾ cup (110 g) grated mozzarella

2 tablespoons finely chopped fresh parsley

4 small boneless, skinless chicken breast halves, about 625 g (1¼ lb) in total, pounded 5 mm (¼ inch) thick (see Basics)

¼ cup (35 g) plain (all-purpose) flour

½ cup (50 g) grated parmesan

2 tablespoons olive oil

2 cups (500 ml) bottled pasta sauce

PREPARATION 15 minutes
COOKING 25 minutes
MAKES 4 servings

PER SERVING 2226 kJ, 532 kcal, 49 g protein, 28 g fat (11 g saturated fat), 19 g carbohydrate (8 g sugars), 803 mg sodium, <1 g fibre

1 Preheat the oven to 200°C (400°F/Gas 6). In a small bowl, mix together mozzarella and parsley. Place chicken halves on a work surface, smooth (skinned side) down, with one short end facing you. Dividing evenly, spread mozzarella mixture over each chicken half, leaving a 2.5 cm (1 inch) border all around. Roll up chicken from one short end. Secure with toothpicks to keep filling in place.

2 In a shallow bowl, combine flour and half the parmesan. Dredge each chicken roll in the flour mixture, pressing it onto chicken. In a non-stick frying pan, heat oil over medium heat. Add chicken rolls and cook, turning, for 6 to 8 minutes, or until golden brown and crisp on all sides. Remove toothpicks.

3 Spread 1 cup (250 ml) pasta sauce in a 20 cm (8 inch) square baking dish. Add chicken rolls. Top with remaining pasta sauce and sprinkle with remaining parmesan. Bake for 15 minutes, or until sauce is bubbly. Let stand for 5 minutes before serving.

TO REDUCE THE FAT
Use low-fat mozzarella. Roll chicken up as directed in step 1, but omit dredging and frying in step 2; instead, skip straight to step 3. Increase amount of parmesan on top of chicken to ⅓ cup (35 g). Bake for 20 to 30 minutes, or until chicken is cooked through.

COOK'S TIPS
• You can stuff and roll the chicken breasts and dredge them in the flour mixture ahead of time. Place them on a platter, then cover and refrigerate for up to 4 hours before continuing.
• If you enjoy sharp cheese, try this recipe using half romano cheese, which is stronger than parmesan.

To trim some fat from this recipe, you can use fat-free (rather than fat-reduced) mayonnaise in the horseradish cream. The assertive horseradish will compensate for any reduction in flavour.

Crumbed horseradish cream chicken

3 slices firm-textured white bread
(about 85 g/3 oz)

¼ cup (60 g) reduced-fat sour cream

¼ cup (60 g) reduced-fat mayonnaise

3 tablespoons bottled grated
horseradish, drained

¼ teaspoon salt

4 boneless, skinless chicken breast halves,
about 750 g (1½ lb) in total

2 tablespoons butter, melted

CREAMY CUCUMBER SALSA

1 small cucumber, peeled, seeded and
finely diced

½ cup (125 g) reduced-fat sour cream

1 tablespoon bottled grated horseradish,
drained

2 tablespoons finely chopped red onion

1 tablespoon lemon juice

PREPARATION 15 minutes
COOKING 30 minutes
MAKES 4 servings

PER SERVING 2442 kJ, 583 kcal, 44 g protein, 37 g fat (20 g saturated fat), 18 g carbohydrate (8 g sugars), 1024 mg sodium, 1 g fibre

1 Preheat the oven to 190°C (375°F/Gas 5). Lightly grease a baking tray and heat in oven for 5 minutes.

2 Meanwhile, in a food processor or blender, process bread to fine crumbs; set aside. In a shallow bowl, mix together sour cream, mayonnaise, horseradish and salt. In a large bowl, toss breadcrumbs and melted butter. Coat chicken with sour-cream mixture, then dip into breadcrumb mixture, patting crumbs gently onto chicken.

3 Place chicken on heated baking tray and bake for 10 minutes. Turn chicken over and bake for 10 to 15 minutes, or until coating is crisp and chicken is cooked through.

4 Meanwhile, combine the creamy cucumber salsa ingredients in a small bowl and mix together. Serve with chicken.

VARIATION *Sour cream chicken with pears*
In step 2, omit the horseradish from the sour cream mixture. Coat and bake chicken as directed. Instead of the creamy cucumber salsa, mix together ½ cup (125 g) sour cream, 1 tablespoon lemon juice, 1 tablespoon honey, 1 tablespoon snipped chives and 2 ripe pears, peeled and cut into wedges 2.5 cm (1 inch) thick. Serve with the chicken.

Here's a no-shopping-trip special. For all its enticing spiciness, this recipe is made with ingredients that are probably on your kitchen shelves right now. Do make sure the use-by dates for the herbs and spices haven't expired, though. Rub a little of each between your fingers and sniff to be sure it's still potent.

Ginger-fennel chicken breasts

2 teaspoons fennel seeds

1 teaspoon dried sage

1 teaspoon ground ginger

¾ teaspoon salt

½ teaspoon freshly ground black pepper

½ teaspoon sugar

1 large egg

4 boneless, skinless chicken breast halves, about 625 g (1¼ lb) in total

2 tablespoons butter, melted

4 lemon wedges

LOW FAT, QUICK
PREPARATION 10 minutes
COOKING 20 minutes
MAKES 4 servings

PER SERVING 1335 kJ, 319 kcal, 36 g protein, 18 g fat (8 g saturated fat), 2 g carbohydrate (1 g sugars), 637 mg sodium, <1 g fibre

1 Preheat the oven to 180°C (350°F/Gas 4). Place fennel seeds in a small bag and lightly crush with a rolling pin. Transfer to a shallow bowl and stir in sage, ginger, salt, pepper and sugar. In a separate shallow bowl, beat egg with 1 tablespoon water.

2 Dip chicken in egg mixture, then sprinkle fennel mixture over, pressing it firmly onto chicken. Place on a lightly greased baking tray.

3 Drizzle butter over chicken and bake for 20 minutes, or until cooked through. Serve with lemon wedges.

Baked chicken breasts with caponata

200 g (7 oz) can or jar caponata
  (see Cook's Tip)

½ cup (125 g) canned chopped tomatoes

½ cup (60 ml) chicken stock (page 49)

½ cup (60 ml) orange juice

4 tablespoons chopped fresh basil leaves

4 small boneless, skinless chicken breast
  halves, about 625 g (1¼ lb) in total

¼ teaspoon salt

1 cup (150 g) grated mozzarella

LOW FAT
PREPARATION 10 minutes
COOKING 40 minutes
MAKES 4 servings

1691 kJ, 404 kcal, 45 g protein, 21 g fat
(8 g saturated fat), 9 g carbohydrate
(9 g sugars), 489 mg sodium, 2 g fibre

1 Preheat the oven to 180°C (350°F/Gas 4). In a bowl, stir together caponata, tomatoes, stock and orange juice. Stir in half the basil. Place chicken in an 18 x 28 cm (7 x 11 inch) glass baking dish. Sprinkle chicken with salt.

2 Spoon caponata mixture over chicken and bake for 35 minutes. Sprinkle mozzarella over chicken and bake for 5 minutes, or until chicken is cooked through. Sprinkle remaining basil over chicken just before serving.

COOK'S TIP
Look in the Italian food aisle of your supermarket for jars or cans of caponata, a tasty Sicilian appetiser made from vegetables —usually eggplant (aubergine), onions, celery and tomatoes— flavoured with capers and vinegar. Keep a jar or two on your shelf to serve as an instant first course or sandwich filling.

Chicken breasts with goat's cheese

125 g (4 oz) soft goat's cheese

2 tablespoons reduced-fat cream cheese

1 large egg

¼ cup (35 g) oil-packed sun-dried
  tomatoes, drained and finely chopped

¼ cup (25 g) pecans, roughly chopped

1 spring onion (scallion), thinly sliced

¼ teaspoon freshly ground black pepper

4 bone-in chicken breast halves, with skin,
  about 1.25 kg (2½ lb) in total

2 tablespoons lemon juice

1 tablespoon olive oil

½ teaspoon salt

PREPARATION 20 minutes
COOKING 30 minutes
MAKES 4 servings

1 Preheat the oven to 190°C (375°F/Gas 5). In a bowl, beat together goat's cheese and cream cheese until soft and well combined. Beat in egg. Stir in sun-dried tomatoes, pecans, spring onion and pepper.

2 With your fingers, gently loosen skin from chicken breasts without removing it. Spread goat's cheese mixture under skin.

3 Place chicken, stuffed side up, in a baking dish. In a small bowl, whisk together lemon juice, oil and salt. Drizzle lemon juice mixture over chicken. Bake for 30 minutes, or until stuffing is set and chicken is cooked through.

PER SERVING 2035 kJ, 486 kcal, 40 g protein, 35 g fat (12 g saturated fat), 3 g carbohydrate (3 g sugars), 566 mg sodium, 1 g fibre

Baked chicken breasts with caponata

Party-perfect in just an hour, these filled, rolled chicken breasts are handsome when sliced crosswise for a colourful pinwheel effect. Creamy scalloped potatoes make an elegant accompaniment. To avoid watering down the filling, be sure to squeeze all the liquid out of the frozen spinach.

Chicken, spinach, fontina & raisin rolls

4 small boneless, skinless chicken breast halves, about 625 g (1¼ lb) in total, pounded 5 mm (¼ inch) thick (see Basics)

½ teaspoon salt

300 g (10 oz) frozen spinach leaves, thawed and squeezed dry

125 g (4 oz) fontina cheese, sliced

⅓ cup (35 g) pecans, finely chopped

¼ cup (30 g) raisins

½ teaspoon dried sage

2 slices firm-textured white bread (about 60 g/2 oz)

2 tablespoons grated parmesan

1 large egg

2 tablespoons olive oil

PREPARATION 25 minutes
COOKING 30 minutes
MAKES 4 servings

PER SERVING 2442 kJ, 583 kcal, 48 g protein, 37 g fat (12 g saturated fat), 14 g carbohydrate (7 g sugars), 823 mg sodium, 2 g fibre

1 Preheat the oven to 190°C (375°F/Gas 5). Sprinkle chicken halves on both sides with ¼ teaspoon of the salt. Place on a work surface, smooth (skinned side) down, with one short end facing you. Dividing evenly, spread spinach over each chicken half, leaving a 1 cm (½ inch) border all around. Top with fontina, then sprinkle with the pecans, raisins and sage. Roll up chicken from one short end, then secure with toothpicks to keep filling in place.

2 In a food processor or blender, process bread to fine crumbs. Add parmesan and remaining salt and process to combine. Transfer mixture to a plate. In a shallow bowl, beat egg with 1 teaspoon water. Dip chicken into egg mixture, then into breadcrumbs, patting crumbs onto chicken.

3 Place chicken on a baking tray and drizzle with oil. Bake for 25 to 30 minutes, until crust is golden brown and chicken is cooked through. Remove toothpicks before serving.

COOK'S TIPS
• Fontina, a buttery, semi-soft cheese, originated in the Aosta Valley in northern Italy. The finest fontina, labelled Fontina Val d'Aosta, comes from this region, but fontina from other parts of Italy is nearly as good and less expensive.
• You can replace the pecans with pine nuts or almonds.

Potato-crusted baked chicken

⅓ cup (35 g) grated parmesan

½ teaspoon salt

½ teaspoon freshly ground black pepper

½ teaspoon dried sage

2 large eggs

⅔ cup (45 g) dried instant mashed
  potatoes

4 boneless, skinless chicken breast halves,
  about 625 g (1¼ lb) in total

2 tablespoons olive oil

LOW FAT
PREPARATION 15 minutes
COOKING 30 minutes
MAKES 4 servings

1 Preheat the oven to 190°C (375°F/Gas 5). Lightly grease
a baking tray and heat in oven for 5 minutes.

2 Meanwhile, in a shallow bowl, stir together parmesan, salt,
pepper and sage. In another shallow bowl, beat eggs with
1 tablespoon water. Place instant mashed potatoes in a third bowl.
Dip chicken into parmesan mixture, pressing it on well. Dip chicken
into egg mixture, then into mashed potatoes, pressing on well.

3 Place chicken on heated baking tray; drizzle olive oil over chicken.
Bake for 10 minutes, then turn chicken over and bake for another
10 to 15 minutes, or until coating is crusty and golden brown and
chicken is cooked through.

PER SERVING 1725 kJ, 412 kcal, 41 g protein, 24 g fat (7 g saturated fat),
7 g carbohydrate (<1 g sugars), 662 mg sodium, 1 g fibre

Tahini is sometimes referred to as the 'butter' of the Middle East. With its soft, rich texture and nutty flavour, it's a delicious sauce or spread. Before using tahini, give it a stir to reincorporate its natural oils.

Oven-poached chicken tahini breasts

1 cup (250 ml) chicken stock (page 49)

8 cloves garlic, crushed

1 teaspoon grated lemon zest

4 boneless, skinless chicken breast halves, about 625 g (1¼ lb) in total

¼ cup (65 g) tahini (sesame paste), stirred well

2 teaspoons lemon juice

½ teaspoon salt

¼ teaspoon cayenne pepper

¼ cup (60 g) natural (plain) yogurt

3 tablespoons chopped fresh mint, or 1 teaspoon dried

1 tablespoon sesame seeds

LOW FAT
PREPARATION 15 minutes
COOKING 25 minutes
MAKES 4 servings

PER SERVING 1494 kJ, 357 kcal, 40 g protein, 21 g fat (5 g saturated fat), 3 g carbohydrate (2 g sugars), 744 mg sodium, 4 g fibre

1 Preheat the oven to 180°C (350°F/Gas 4). In a 23 x 33 cm (9 x 13 inch) glass baking dish, stir together stock, garlic and lemon zest. Place chicken in dish in a single layer, then cover with foil.

2 Bake for 15 to 20 minutes, or until chicken is just cooked through. Reserving the poaching liquid and 6 garlic cloves, remove chicken to a warm platter and cover chicken with foil to keep warm.

3 Pour ⅓ cup (80 ml) of the reserved poaching liquid into a food processor or blender. Add reserved garlic cloves, tahini, lemon juice, salt and cayenne pepper and process until smooth. Transfer to a bowl, then stir in yogurt and mint.

4 In a small dry frying pan, toast sesame seeds over low heat for 2 minutes, or until fragrant. Place chicken on serving plates and spoon sauce on top. Sprinkle with sesame seeds and serve.

VARIATION *Chicken pita breads*
Oven-poach chicken as directed. When cool enough to handle, shred chicken. Make tahini sauce as directed in step 3. In a bowl, combine shredded chicken with 2 cups (80 g) shredded lettuce, 2 chopped tomatoes and the tahini sauce. Spoon chicken mixture into 4 large pita breads. Omit sesame seeds and step 4.

The French call this oven-poaching technique 'en papillote', where food is sealed in individual parcels and cooked in its own cloud of fragrant steam. Food baked in this way retains all its juices and flavours, ensuring tender, flavoursome results—and the table presentation always impresses.

Chicken & vegetable parcels

625 g (1¼ lb) small red-skinned potatoes, such as desiree, thinly sliced

225 g (8 oz) sugar snap peas, strings removed

2 carrots, cut into matchsticks

1 teaspoon grated lemon zest

1 teaspoon salt

50 g (1¾ oz) butter, at room temperature

2 shallots (eschalots), finely chopped, or 2 spring onions (scallions), thinly sliced

4 small boneless, skinless chicken breast halves, about 625 g (1¼ lb) in total

½ teaspoon dried tarragon

LOW FAT
PREPARATION 25 minutes
COOKING 30 minutes
MAKES 4 servings

PER SERVING 1807 kJ, 432 kcal, 39 g protein, 19 g fat (9 g saturated fat), 25 g carbohydrate (4 g sugars), 809 mg sodium, 5 g fibre

1 Preheat the oven to 200°C (400°F/Gas 6). In a large pot of boiling salted water, blanch potato slices for 3 minutes. Drain and transfer to a large bowl. Add sugar snap peas, carrots, lemon zest and ¾ teaspoon salt to potatoes and toss to combine.

2 In a small bowl, mix together butter and shallots until well combined. Set aside.

3 Tear off four pieces of foil, each 38 cm (15 inches) long. Fold each rectangle of foil crosswise in half to make a centre-line. Open up the foil and place potato mixture on one half of each sheet. Place chicken breasts on top of vegetables, then sprinkle with tarragon and remaining salt. Divide butter mixture into four portions and place on the middle of each chicken breast.

4 Starting with one long edge, fold foil over tightly several times, about 1 cm (½ inch) each time, but do not fold foil all the way up to the chicken as it needs some steaming room. Fold the two short ends over in the same manner, sealing tightly, and leaving some space around chicken.

5 Place parcels on a baking tray and bake for 25 minutes, or until chicken and vegetables are cooked through. (To test, simply unfold the end of one packet.) Transfer parcels to serving plates and serve, allowing diners to open their own parcels.

TO REDUCE THE FAT
Omit the butter. Instead, toss shallots with 2 tablespoons olive oil, then assemble and bake the parcels as directed.

The sesame oil called for here is the dark Asian-style oil sold in small bottles. Made from toasted sesame seeds, it has an intense flavour and is mostly used as a seasoning, not a cooking oil. Try a little of it in salad dressings, or as a final flourish when stir-frying.

Breaded chicken with lime

3 slices firm-textured white bread (about 85 g/3 oz)

½ cup (80 g) salted peanuts

½ cup (25 g) chopped coriander (cilantro) leaves and stems

1 tablespoon sesame seeds

1 teaspoon grated lime zest

1½ tablespoons sesame oil

2 eggwhites

8 chicken drumsticks, about 1.25 kg (2½ lb) in total, skin removed

½ cup (125 ml) lime juice

¼ cup (60 ml) salt-reduced soy sauce

2 teaspoons sugar

2 spring onions (scallions), thinly sliced

LOW FAT
PREPARATION 15 minutes
COOKING 25 minutes
MAKES 4 servings

PER SERVING 2056 kJ, 491 kcal, 41 g protein, 29 g fat (5 g saturated fat), 17 g carbohydrate (5 g sugars), 983 mg sodium, 3 g fibre

1 Preheat the oven to 190°C (375°F/Gas 5). In a food processor or blender, combine bread, peanuts, coriander, sesame seeds and lime zest and process to fine crumbs.

2 Divide crumb mixture among two shallow bowls. Add 1 tablespoon sesame oil to each bowl, then toss each to combine. (It's best to coat half the chicken in one bowl and the rest in the other bowl so the crumb mixture doesn't get too mushy.)

3 In a shallow bowl, lightly beat eggwhites with 1 tablespoon water. Dip half the chicken first in eggwhite mixture, then in one bowl of breadcrumb mixture, pressing coating on well. Dip remaining chicken in eggwhite mixture, then the other bowl of breadcrumb mixture, pressing coating on well.

4 Transfer chicken to a lightly greased baking tray. Bake for 25 minutes, or until coating is crisp and golden and chicken is cooked through.

5 Meanwhile, in a small saucepan, combine lime juice, soy sauce and sugar and stir over low heat for 30 seconds, or until sugar has dissolved. Carefully transfer dipping sauce to four small bowls and garnish each with some spring onion.

6 Serve the hot chicken with individual bowls of dipping sauce.

Instead of breadcrumbs, why not try tortilla crumbs for breading chicken? Here the crumbs are seasoned with chilli powder, coriander and cayenne pepper, for an intriguing hint of spice. Serve with a colourful salsa of corn, tomatoes and spring onions (scallions).

Baked tortilla-crusted chicken legs

2 cups (500 ml) buttermilk

½ teaspoon grated lime zest

4 whole chicken legs, about 1.25 kg
    (2½ lb) in total, cut into drumsticks
    and thighs (see Basics), skin removed

8 corn tortillas (15 cm/6 inch diameter),
    torn into pieces

1 tablespoon chilli powder

1 teaspoon ground coriander

¾ teaspoon salt

¼ teaspoon cayenne pepper

2 tablespoons olive oil

2 tablespoons lime juice

lime wedges (optional)

PREPARATION 10 minutes, plus
    at least 1 hour marinating
COOKING 30 minutes
MAKES 4 servings

PER SERVING 2338 kJ, 558 kcal, 37 g protein,
35 g fat (10 g saturated fat), 24 g carbohydrate
(9 g sugars), 755 mg sodium, 3 g fibre

1 In a large bowl, whisk together buttermilk and lime zest. Add chicken and toss to coat. Cover and refrigerate overnight, or for at least 1 hour.

2 Preheat the oven to 180°C (350°F/Gas 4). In a food processor or blender, combine tortillas, chilli powder, coriander, salt and cayenne pepper. Process to fine crumbs, then tip into a large bowl.

3 Lift chicken from buttermilk mixture. Dredge in tortilla mixture, pressing mixture onto chicken. Place on a lightly greased baking tray and drizzle with oil.

4 Bake for 30 minutes, or until coating is crisp and golden brown, turning chicken halfway during cooking. Sprinkle with the lime juice and serve with lime wedges, if desired.

TO REDUCE THE FAT

Instead of chicken legs, use bone-in chicken breast halves, with the skin removed. Omit the oil in step 3; instead spray the chicken with olive oil cooking spray before baking.

A ripe avocado isn't always easy to find. A few days ahead of time, buy yourself a firm, unbruised avocado, and leave it at room temperature in a loosely closed paper bag until it yields to thumb pressure and your patience will be rewarded. Soft, ripe avocado is a creamy treat with these chicken thighs.

Baked chicken with avocado relish

1½ teaspoons ground cumin

1 teaspoon ground coriander

1 teaspoon chilli powder

¾ teaspoon dried oregano

½ teaspoon salt

4 bone-in chicken breast halves, with
    skin on, about 1.25 kg (2½ lb) in total

AVOCADO RELISH

500 g (1 lb) roma (plum) tomatoes,
    chopped

1 avocado, diced

4 tablespoons chopped coriander (cilantro)

¼ cup (40 g) finely chopped red onion

2 tablespoons red wine vinegar

½ teaspoon salt

PREPARATION 15 minutes
COOKING 25 minutes
MAKES 4 servings

PER SERVING 1874 kJ, 448 kcal, 28 g protein,
36 g fat (10 g saturated fat), 4 g carbohydrate
(3 g sugars), 747 mg sodium, 3 g fibre

1 Preheat the oven to 180°C (350°F/Gas 4). In a small bowl, stir together spices and salt. Spread mixture over both sides of chicken, rubbing it in well.

2 Place chicken on a baking tray and bake for 25 minutes, or until coating is crisp and golden brown and chicken is cooked through.

3 Meanwhile, in a large bowl, combine the avocado relish ingredients. Gently stir together.

4 Divide chicken among serving plates. Drizzle with pan juices and serve with avocado relish.

In this simple recipe, a spinach and fetta mixture—enhanced with lemon and fresh dill—is stuffed under the skin of chicken thighs, making them moist and flavoursome. (You can also use chicken breasts, if you prefer.) Orzo, the pasta shape most associated with Greece, is a natural choice to serve on the side.

Greek baked chicken with fetta & dill

1 tablespoon olive oil

¼ cup (40 g) finely chopped onion

2 cloves garlic, crushed

300 g (10 oz) frozen chopped spinach, thawed and squeezed dry

1¼ cups (175 g) crumbled reduced-fat fetta

3 tablespoons snipped fresh dill

½ teaspoon grated lemon zest

8 bone-in chicken thighs, with skin, about 1 kg (2 lb) in total

2 tablespoons lemon juice

¼ teaspoon salt

PREPARATION 20 minutes
COOKING 50 minutes
MAKES 4 servings

PER SERVING 1792 kJ, 428 kcal, 36 g protein, 30 g fat (11 g saturated fat), 3 g carbohydrate (2 g sugars), 775 mg sodium, <1 g fibre

1 Preheat the oven to 190°C (375°F/Gas 5). In a small frying pan, heat oil over low heat. Add onion and garlic and cook, stirring frequently, for 5 minutes, or until onion has softened. Add spinach and cook, stirring frequently, for 2 minutes, or until spinach is dry. Transfer mixture to a large bowl. Stir in fetta, dill and lemon zest.

2 With your fingers, gently loosen skin from chicken thighs without removing it. Push fetta mixture under skin.

3 Place chicken in an 18 x 28 cm (7 x 11 inch) baking dish and sprinkle with the lemon juice and salt. Bake for 40 minutes, or until chicken is cooked through. Serve hot.

Baked chicken legs with basil & lemon

2 tablespoons olive oil

1 clove garlic, peeled

½ teaspoon dried tarragon

¼ teaspoon dried red chilli flakes

4 whole chicken legs, about 1.25 kg (2½ lb) in total, cut into drumsticks and thighs (see Basics)

1 teaspoon salt

⅔ cup (40 g) chopped fresh basil

1½ teaspoons grated lemon zest

2 tablespoons lemon juice

PREPARATION 15 minutes
COOKING 30 minutes
MAKES 4 servings

PER SERVING 1664 kJ, 398 kcal, 29 g protein, 31 g fat (8 g saturated fat), <1 g carbohydrate (<1 g sugars), 754 mg sodium, <1 g fibre

1 In a small frying pan, heat oil over low heat. Add garlic, tarragon and chilli flakes. Cook very slowly, turning garlic as it colours, for 5 minutes, or until oil is fragrant and garlic is golden brown. Discard garlic. Transfer herb oil to a large bowl and allow to cool to room temperature.

2 Preheat the oven to 180°C (350°F/Gas 4). With your fingers, gently loosen skin from chicken drumsticks and thighs without removing it. Add chicken legs to the herb oil and toss to coat, making sure some marinade gets under the skin.

3 Place chicken in a baking dish and sprinkle with ¾ teaspoon of the salt. Bake for 25 minutes, or until skin is golden brown and chicken is cooked through, turning chicken halfway during cooking.

4 Meanwhile, in a small bowl, stir together basil, lemon zest and remaining salt.

5 Divide chicken among serving plates. Sprinkle lemon juice over chicken. Scatter the basil mixture over and serve.

A tangy blend of maple syrup, vinegar and spices flavours these chicken thighs and the sweet potatoes baked with them. The sweet potatoes need longer cooking than the chicken, so they are given a head start in the oven. Just before serving, the baked chicken is flashed under a hot grill (broiler) to caramelise the skin.

Maple syrup baked chicken thighs

2 tablespoons olive oil

1 kg (2 lb) sweet potatoes, peeled and cut into 1 cm (½ inch) dice

⅓ cup (80 ml) maple syrup

¼ cup (60 ml) tomato sauce (ketchup)

2 tablespoons cider vinegar

1 tablespoon butter

2 cloves garlic, crushed

1 teaspoon ground ginger

¾ teaspoon salt

½ teaspoon freshly ground black pepper

¼ teaspoon cayenne pepper

8 bone-in chicken thighs, about 1 kg (2 lb) in total, skin removed

LOW FAT

PREPARATION 15 minutes

COOKING 50 minutes

MAKES 4 servings

PER SERVING 2453 kJ, 586 kcal, 30 g protein, 23 g fat (7 g saturated fat), 60 g carbohydrate (35 g sugars), 792 mg sodium, 5 g fibre

1 Preheat the oven to 190°C (375°F/Gas 5). Pour oil into a 23 x 33 cm (9 x 13 inch) baking dish. Add sweet potatoes and toss to coat. Bake for 20 minutes.

2 Meanwhile, in a small saucepan, stir together maple syrup, tomato sauce, vinegar, butter, garlic, ginger, salt, pepper and cayenne pepper. Bring to a simmer over low heat, then gently cook for 10 minutes to develop flavours, stirring now and then. Set aside.

3 Place chicken on top of sweet potatoes and spoon maple-syrup mixture over them all. Bake for 25 minutes, or until chicken is cooked through and sweet potatoes are tender.

4 Meanwhile, preheat grill (broiler) to high. Transfer baked chicken to a grill tray and place 20 cm (8 inches) from heat. Cook for 1 to 2 minutes, until chicken skin is nicely caramelised. Serve with the sweet potatoes.

IN A HURRY?

Substitute 1 cup (250 ml) bottled tomato-based barbecue sauce for the sauce made in step 2.

Barbecues & picnics

A picnic basket packed to the brim is a delightful option for eating al fresco. If barbecuing is your big thing, go beyond burgers with juicy chicken skewers, honey-mustard barbecued chicken and Mexican-style fajitas.

Many cooks claim to have a 'secret' for perfect fried chicken. But all you really need is a simple, foolproof recipe like this one. The chicken pieces are soaked in buttermilk for optimal tenderness and flavour; after flouring, they're left to 'rest' so the coating won't flake off when the chicken is fried.

Southern fried chicken

1½ cups (375 ml) buttermilk

½ teaspoon freshly ground black pepper

¾ teaspoon salt

4 whole chicken legs, about 1.25 kg (2½ lb) in total, cut into drumsticks and thighs (see Basics)

1 cup (150 g) plain (all-purpose) flour

½ cup (125 ml) vegetable oil

PREPARATION 5 minutes, plus
at least 30 minutes marinating
and at least 30 minutes chilling
COOKING 30 minutes
MAKES 4 servings

PER SERVING 3149 kJ, 752 kcal, 37 g protein, 53 g fat (12 g saturated fat), 32 g carbohydrate (5 g sugars), 657 mg sodium, 1 g fibre

1 In a large bowl, stir together buttermilk, pepper and ¼ teaspoon salt. Add chicken pieces and mix them around to coat. Cover and refrigerate for up to 8 hours, or at least 30 minutes.

2 In a large shallow bowl, mix together flour and another ¼ teaspoon of the salt. Lift chicken from marinade and dip into the flour, patting it onto the chicken. Place chicken on a plate and refrigerate, uncovered, for 30 minutes, or up to 4 hours, for the coating to set.

3 Divide oil among two large, deep frying pans and heat over medium–low heat. The oil is ready for frying when a piece of bread sizzles as it hits the surface.

4 Add chicken and cook, carefully turning pieces as they colour, for 30 minutes, or until richly browned and cooked through.

5 Transfer chicken to paper towels to drain. Sprinkle remaining salt over chicken and serve.

Honey-mustard barbecued chicken

Honey-mustard barbecued chicken

⅓ cup (115 g) honey

1½ tablespoons dijon mustard

⅓ cup (80 ml) cider vinegar

¾ teaspoon freshly ground black pepper

1 whole chicken, about 1.75 kg (3½ lb),
    cut into 8 serving pieces (see Basics)

¾ teaspoon salt

⅓ cup (105 g) apple jelly

4 granny smith or golden delicious apples,
    cut horizontally into 4 thick slices each

PREPARATION 15 minutes
COOKING 20 minutes
MAKES 4 servings

PER SERVING 2859 kJ, 683 kcal, 39 g protein,
32 g fat (10 g saturated fat), 63 g carbohydrate
(61 g sugars), 798 mg sodium, 4 g fibre

1 In a large bowl, whisk together honey, mustard, 2 tablespoons of the vinegar and the pepper. With your fingers, gently loosen skin from chicken pieces without removing it, then rub the salt over and under skin. Rub mustard mixture under chicken skin.

2 In a small saucepan, melt apple jelly over low heat with remaining vinegar. Place apple slices in a bowl, pour jelly mixture over, then toss to coat well.

3 Preheat a barbecue to medium–high. Barbecue chicken and apples 15 cm (6 inches) from the heat for the following amounts of time: barbecue chicken, turning often, for 20 minutes, or until cooked through; barbecue apples for 10 minutes, turning several times, until tender.

Grilled rosemary chicken

⅓ cup (80 ml) olive oil

3 tablespoons roughly chopped fresh
    rosemary, or 4 teaspoons dried
    rosemary, crumbled

3 long thin orange zest strips

¾ teaspoon freshly ground black pepper

1 whole chicken, about 1.75 kg (3½ lb),
    halved lengthwise (see Cook's Tips
    for Orange-honey glazed chicken,
    page 223)

1 teaspoon salt

PREPARATION 10 minutes
COOKING 30 minutes
MAKES 4 servings

PER SERVING 2489 kJ, 595 kcal, 38 g protein,
49 g fat (12 g saturated fat), 1 g carbohydrate
(<1 g sugars), 768 mg sodium, <1 g fibre

1 In a small frying pan, heat oil over low heat. Add rosemary, orange zest strips and pepper and cook for 5 minutes, or until oil is fragrant and flavourful. Cool to room temperature, then strain through a fine-meshed sieve set over a small bowl. Measure out 2 tablespoons rosemary oil and set aside for serving.

2 With your fingers, gently loosen chicken skin from chicken breast and legs without removing it. Rub salt under and over skin, then rub remaining rosemary oil under skin.

3 Preheat a barbecue to medium. Barbecue chicken, skin side up, 15 cm (6 inches) from the heat for 12 minutes, or until nicely browned. Turn chicken over and barbecue for another 12 minutes, or until cooked through.

4 Cut each chicken piece in half crosswise. Brush with reserved rosemary oil and serve.

Crunchy and slightly sweet, shredded coconut gives these spiced chicken legs a very special texture. Hidden underneath the coconut is a curry-like coating —a mixture of coriander, turmeric, ginger and cumin. Serve with blanched green beans and a potato salad.

Indonesian coconut chicken legs

2 teaspoons ground coriander

2 teaspoons dried turmeric

1 teaspoon ground ginger

1 teaspoon ground cumin

1 teaspoon salt

½ teaspoon freshly ground black pepper

2 eggwhites

1⅓ cups (120 g) shredded coconut

4 whole chicken legs, about 1.25 kg (2½ lb) in total, cut into drumsticks and thighs (see Basics), skin removed

¼ cup (60 ml) vegetable oil

PREPARATION 15 minutes, plus
    at least 1 hour chilling
COOKING 30 minutes
MAKES 4 servings

PER SERVING 2320 kJ, 554 kcal, 35 g protein, 45 g fat (23 g saturated fat), 4 g carbohydrate (2 g sugars), 799 mg sodium, 5 g fibre

1 In a shallow bowl, stir together coriander, turmeric, ginger, cumin, salt and pepper. In another shallow bowl, beat eggwhites with 1 tablespoon water. Spread coconut on a plate.

2 Dip chicken first in egg mixture, then spice mixture, then coconut. Place on a plate and refrigerate, uncovered, for at least 1 hour, or up to 8 hours, for coating to set.

3 Preheat the oven to 200°C (400°F/Gas 6). Place chicken on a lightly greased deep-sided baking tray. Drizzle oil over chicken.

4 Bake for 30 minutes, turning chicken halfway during cooking, until coating is crisp and chicken is cooked through. Cool to room temperature before packing.

Marinated chicken legs with plums

HOISIN-SOY MARINADE

¼ cup (60 ml) hoisin sauce

2 tablespoons salt-reduced soy sauce

1 tablespoon lemon juice

2 teaspoons vegetable oil

½ teaspoon freshly ground black pepper

½ teaspoon ground cinnamon

4 whole chicken legs, about 1.25 kg (2½ lb) in total, cut into drumsticks and thighs (see Basics), skin removed

2 teaspoons butter

500 g (1 lb) plums, pitted and diced

1 tablespoon sugar

¼ teaspoon freshly ground black pepper

1 spring onion (scallion), thinly sliced

1 In a large non-reactive bowl, whisk together the marinade ingredients. Add chicken and toss to coat. Cover and refrigerate for at least 1 hour, turning chicken occasionally if possible.

2 Preheat the oven to 200°C (400°F/ Gas 6). Place chicken on a deep-sided baking tray and drizzle marinade over. Bake for 25 minutes, or until chicken is cooked through.

3 Meanwhile, in a large frying pan, heat butter over medium heat. Add plums, sugar and pepper and cook, stirring frequently, for 10 minutes, or until plums are tender. Add spring onion and gently mix through. Cool chicken and plums in the refrigerator before packing for a picnic. Pack chicken and plums separately.

LOW FAT
PREPARATION 15 minutes, plus marinating
COOKING 25 minutes
MAKES 4 servings

PER SERVING 1531 kJ, 366 kcal, 33 g protein, 17 g fat (5 g saturated fat), 20 g carbohydrate (18 g sugars), 799 mg sodium, 5 g fibre

This oven-baked chicken, crumbed with a mixture of flour and polenta, is delicious cold and the coating is sturdy enough to stand up to a little off-road travel. For a real camp-style meal, make some on-the-spot accompaniments over an open fire, such as corn on the cob, barbecued vegetables or roast potatoes.

Perfect picnic chicken

1½ cups (375 g) natural (plain) yogurt

2 tablespoons cider vinegar

2 teaspoons salt

2 whole chickens, each about 1.75 kg (3½ lb), cut into 10 pieces each (see Basics)

1½ cups (225 g) plain (all-purpose) flour

⅔ cup (100 g) polenta

1 teaspoon freshly ground black pepper

PREPARATION 15 minutes, plus at least 1 hour marinating
COOKING 45 minutes
MAKES 8 servings

PER SERVING 2524 kJ, 603 kcal, 45 g protein, 33 g fat (11 g saturated fat), 31 g carbohydrate (2 g sugars), 794 mg sodium, 2 g fibre

1 In a large bowl, stir together yogurt, vinegar and ¾ teaspoon of the salt until well combined. Add chicken and toss to coat. Cover and refrigerate for at least 1 hour, or up to 4 hours.

2 Preheat the oven to 220°C (425°F/Gas 7). On a plate, combine flour, polenta, pepper and another 1 teaspoon of the salt. Dredge chicken in the flour mixture, shaking off excess.

3 Place the chicken on two generously greased, deep-sided baking trays, leaving space in between. Bake for 20 minutes, or until the bottom crust is set. Turn pieces over and bake for another 20 to 25 minutes, until cooked through.

4 Sprinkle remaining salt over chicken. Cool in the refrigerator, before individually wrapping.

VARIATIONS

Chilli-spiced picnic chicken
Marinate chicken as directed in step 1. In step 2, add 1½ teaspoons chilli powder, 1 teaspoon ground cumin and 1 teaspoon ground coriander to the flour mixture. Dredge and bake chicken as directed.

Honey-citrus picnic chicken
In step 1, substitute 2 tablespoons lemon juice for the vinegar; add 3 tablespoons honey, 1 teaspoon grated lime zest and 1 teaspoon grated lemon zest to the yogurt mixture. Marinate, dredge and bake chicken as directed.

Moroccan-style picnic chicken
In step 1, substitute 2 tablespoons lemon juice for the vinegar. Marinate chicken as directed. In step 2, add 2 teaspoons paprika, 1½ teaspoons dried turmeric, 1 teaspoon ground coriander and 1 teaspoon ground ginger to the flour mixture. Dredge and bake chicken as directed.

Barbecued chicken with corn salsa

4 corn cobs, husks and silks removed

¼ cup (60 ml) olive oil

1 tablespoon chilli powder

1 teaspoon salt

2 tablespoons red wine vinegar

1 large tomato, halved, seeded and diced

4 tablespoons chopped coriander (cilantro)

⅓ cup (50 g) finely chopped red onion

4 boneless, skinless chicken breast halves,
    about 750 g (1½ lb) in total

LOW FAT

PREPARATION 15 minutes

COOKING 25 minutes

MAKES 4 servings

1 Preheat a barbecue to medium. Barbecue corn cobs 15 cm (6 inches) from the heat, turning frequently, for 15 minutes, or until golden brown. When cool enough to handle, use a sharp paring knife to scrape corn kernels into a large bowl.

2 Add 1 tablespoon of the oil, half the chilli powder and half the salt to the corn. Add vinegar, tomato, coriander and onion, then toss and refrigerate until serving time.

3 Toss chicken with remaining oil, chilli powder and salt. Barbecue chicken 15 cm (6 inches) from the heat for 3 minutes per side, or until cooked through. Serve chicken with corn salsa.

PER SERVING 2264 kJ, 541 kcal, 48 g protein,
26 g fat (5 g saturated fat), 28 g carbohydrate
(4 g sugars), 747 mg sodium, 9 g fibre

Both the chicken and vegetables here are seasoned with a lively blend of chilli powder, cumin, coriander and oregano. For a clear, true flavour, use pure chilli powder, which doesn't contain other spices. While the chicken cooks, pop some thickly sliced bread on the barbecue—that's 'Texas toast'.

Tex-Mex chicken & vegetables

TEX-MEX SPICE RUB

1 tablespoon ground cumin

2 teaspoons ground coriander

1½ teaspoons dried oregano

1½ teaspoons chilli powder

1 teaspoon salt

¾ teaspoon freshly ground black pepper

4 bone-in chicken breast halves, skin-on, about 1.25 kg (2½ lb) in total

2 corn cobs, husks and silks removed, halved crosswise

1 zucchini (courgette), halved lengthwise, then crosswise

1 golden zucchini (courgette) or yellow summer squash, halved lengthwise, then crosswise

1 very large onion, cut into 4 thick rounds

2 tablespoons olive oil

lime wedges, to serve

LOW FAT

PREPARATION 15 minutes

COOKING 30 minutes

MAKES 4 servings

PER SERVING 1977 kJ, 472 kcal, 39 g protein, 28 g fat (7 g saturated fat), 18 g carbohydrate (4 g sugars), 721 mg sodium, 6 g fibre

1 In a large bowl, mix together the Tex-Mex spice rub ingredients. Measure out 4½ teaspoons of spice mixture and set aside to rub over chicken, leaving remaining mixture in the bowl.

2 With your fingers, gently loosen skin from chicken breasts without removing it. Rub reserved spice mixture under and over skin of chicken.

3 Add corn, zucchini and onion to the bowl with remaining spice mixture. Toss gently to coat. Add oil and toss again.

4 Preheat a barbecue to medium–high. Barbecue vegetables 15 cm (6 inches) from the heat for 10 minutes, turning them as they colour, until zucchini and red onion are crisp-tender and corn is lightly charred and hot. Transfer to a platter and cover with foil to keep warm.

5 Barbecue chicken, skin side up, for 10 minutes. Turn chicken and barbecue for another 5 to 7 minutes, until chicken is cooked through. Serve chicken and vegetables with lime wedges.

Outdoor entertaining just doesn't get any easier. You can make the barbecue glaze a day in advance and the same goes for the traditional side dishes—coleslaw, potato salad and cornbread. Even iced tea can brew in the refrigerator overnight. The barbecue chef can then perform, unharried by last-minute details.

Barbecued chicken for a crowd

SWEET TOMATO BARBECUE GLAZE

¼ cup (60 ml) vegetable oil

2 onions, finely chopped

6 cloves garlic, finely chopped

3¼ cups (800 g) canned chopped tomatoes

½ cup (115 g) dark brown sugar

½ cup (125 ml) white vinegar or cider vinegar

1 tablespoon worcestershire sauce

1¼ teaspoons salt

1 teaspoon ground ginger

½ teaspoon cayenne pepper

2 whole chickens, each about 1.75 kg (3½ lb), cut into 10 pieces each (see Basics)

½ teaspoon salt

PREPARATION 10 minutes
COOKING 50 minutes
MAKES 8 servings

PER SERVING 2410 kJ, 576 kcal, 40 g protein, 38 g fat (11 g saturated fat), 19 g carbohydrate (19 g sugars), 792 mg sodium, 2 g fibre

1 To make the glaze, heat oil in a large frying pan over medium heat and sauté onions and garlic for 10 minutes, or until onion is soft. Add remaining glaze ingredients and bring to a boil. Reduce to a simmer, then cover and cook for 15 minutes, or until richly flavoured and reduced to 4 cups (1 litre). Transfer to a food processor or blender and process until smooth. Measure out 2 cups (500 ml) to use as a glaze; set aside remainder to serve with the chicken.

2 Preheat a barbecue to medium. Sprinkle the salt over chicken. Barbecue chicken 15 cm (6 inches) from the heat for 15 minutes, turning often, until browned all over.

3 Brush chicken pieces with 1 cup (250 ml) glaze, turn over, then brush with remaining glaze. Barbecue, without turning, for 5 to 7 minutes, until chicken is cooked through.

4 Serve chicken with the reserved barbecue sauce.

COOK'S TIPS

• Discard any unused glaze that remains after the chicken is cooked. Don't add it to the sauce you're serving at the table, because the glaze has been in contact with raw chicken via the basting brush and will contain bacteria.

• Cut-up whole chickens are a good choice for a crowd because there's something to please everyone. As you're barbecuing, be sure to check the white-meat (breast) portions first for doneness, as they cook more quickly than dark (leg) meat.

Caribbean chicken

2½ teaspoons freshly ground black pepper

2½ teaspoons curry powder

1 tablespoon brown sugar

2½ teaspoons ground ginger

¾ teaspoon salt

banana chutney (page 287)

8 boneless, skinless chicken thighs, about 750 g (1½ lb) in total

LOW FAT

PREPARATION 20 minutes, plus at least 1 hour marinating

COOKING 1 hour

MAKES 4 servings

PER SERVING 2466 kJ, 589 kcal, 40 g protein, 19 g fat (5 g saturated fat), 67 g carbohydrate (60 g sugars), 792 mg sodium, 7 g fibre

1 In a large bowl, mix together pepper, curry powder, sugar, ginger and salt. Add chicken and toss well to coat. Cover and refrigerate overnight, or for at least 1 hour.

2 Meanwhile, make the banana chutney.

3 Preheat the oven to 200°C (400°F/Gas 6). Place chicken on a baking tray and bake for 30 minutes, or until skin is crisp and chicken is cooked through.

4 Cool chicken in the refrigerator before packing for a picnic. Pack chutney and chicken separately.

Chicken sausages & green chilli sauce

1 green capsicum (bell pepper), cut lengthwise into flat pieces

1 cup (50 g) chopped fresh coriander (cilantro) leaves and stems

3 mild green chillies, chopped

2 pickled jalapeño chillies

2 tablespoons lime juice

¼ cup (40 g) chopped onion

¼ teaspoon cayenne pepper

750 g (1½ lb) chicken sausages

4 crusty bread rolls, split

PREPARATION 10 minutes
COOKING 25 minutes
MAKES 4 servings

PER SERVING 3508 kJ, 838 kcal, 34 g protein, 46 g fat (16 g saturated fat), 72 g carbohydrate (4 g sugars), 2182 mg sodium, 10 g fibre

1 Preheat a barbecue to medium–high. Place capsicum pieces, skin side down, on the barbecue and cook 15 cm (6 inches) from the heat for 10 minutes, or until skins are blackened. When cool enough to handle, peel capsicums and transfer to a food processor or blender. Add coriander, green chillies, jalapeños, lime juice, onion, salt and cayenne pepper. Process until smooth; set aside.

2 Barbecue the sausages 15 cm (6 inches) from the heat for 10 minutes, or until cooked through, turning them as they cook.

3 Barbecue the bread rolls, cut side down, until lightly toasted. Place sausages in rolls and drizzle with the sauce.

Banana chutney

1 tablespoon olive oil

1 large onion, finely chopped

2 cloves garlic, finely chopped

1 red capsicum (bell pepper), finely diced

⅓ cup (60 g) brown sugar

⅓ cup (80 ml) red wine vinegar

1 teaspoon freshly ground black pepper

1 teaspoon curry powder

½ teaspoon ground ginger

¼ teaspoon salt

⅓ cup (40 g) raisins

750 g (1½ lb) ripe bananas, peeled and sliced 1 cm (½ inch) thick

1 Heat oil in a large frying pan over medium heat and sauté onion and garlic for 7 minutes, or until onion is soft. Stir in capsicum and cook for 5 minutes, or until crisp-tender.

2 Stir in sugar, vinegar, pepper, curry powder, ginger and salt; bring to a boil. Add raisins and bananas and cook, stirring occasionally, for 15 minutes, or until chutney is thick and fully flavoured.

3 Cool chutney to room temperature, then cover and refrigerate until required. Serve with Caribbean chicken (page 286).

Calzones could be described as pizza turnovers: they're circles of dough, stuffed with pizza-like fillings and folded to make half-rounds. These hefty calzones contain shredded chicken, spinach, fresh basil and lots of cheese. If there's a barbecue at your picnic, reheat the calzones for 2 minutes to re-melt the cheese.

Chicken calzones with two cheeses

1 tablespoon olive oil

1 small onion, finely chopped

2 cloves garlic, finely chopped

1 red capsicum (bell pepper), finely chopped

300 g (10 oz) frozen chopped spinach, thawed and squeezed dry

¼ teaspoon salt

2 cups (300 g) shredded cooked chicken thighs or breasts—leftover or poached (see Basics)

1 cup (125 g) grated fontina cheese

1 cup (150 g) shredded mozzarella

4 tablespoons fresh basil

500 g (1 lb) ready-made pizza or bread dough, cut into 4 pieces

1 large egg

PREPARATION 30 minutes

COOKING 30 minutes

MAKES 4 servings

PER SERVING 3424 kJ, 818 kcal, 54 g protein, 36 g fat (15 g saturated fat), 70 g carbohydrate (8 g sugars), 1373 mg sodium, 5 g fibre

1 In a large frying pan, heat oil over medium heat. Add onion and garlic and sauté for 7 minutes, or until onion is tender. Add capsicum and cook for 5 minutes, or until crisp-tender. Stir in spinach and salt and cook for 2 minutes, or until spinach is heated through. Transfer to a large bowl and cool to room temperature. Stir in chicken, fontina, mozzarella and basil.

2 Preheat the oven to 220°C (425°F/Gas 7). On a lightly floured surface, roll each piece of dough out to a 20 cm (8 inch) round. Mound chicken mixture on the bottom half of each round, leaving a 1 cm (½ inch) border. Brush bottom half with water along the edge. Fold top half over the filling, then press edge with your thumb or a fork to seal the dough and give a decorative edge.

3 With a sharp paring knife, make two short slashes in the top of each calzone for steam to escape; do not cut through to the bottom dough. Place on a lightly greased baking tray.

4 In a small bowl, whisk the egg and 1 tablespoon water, then brush over calzones. Bake for 15 minutes, or until top is crisp and golden.

VARIATION *Chicken & broccoli calzones with smoked mozzarella* In step 1, sauté onion and garlic as directed, but increase garlic to 3 cloves; omit capsicum; substitute 300 g (10 oz) thawed frozen chopped broccoli for the spinach and cook for 5 minutes, or until tender. Sprinkle ½ teaspoon sage over broccoli as it cooks. Substitute 1½ cups (225 g) grated smoked mozzarella for the fontina cheese and regular mozzarella. Add ⅓ cup (40 g) sultanas (golden raisins) to the chicken mixture and omit the basil. Assemble calzones, brush with egg glaze and bake as directed.

Fajitas have come a long way from the original version, which contains strips of barbecued steak. Here, lime-marinated chicken and sweetly spiced onions are barbecued with capsicums and served with tangy goat's cheese.

Chicken fajitas with goat's cheese

500 g (1 lb) boneless, skinless chicken breasts, pounded 1 cm (½ inch) thick (see Basics)

⅓ cup (80 ml) lime juice

¾ teaspoon salt

1 red onion, cut into 4 thick rounds

1½ teaspoons sugar

½ teaspoon ground cinnamon

½ teaspoon ground cumin

¼ teaspoon ground cloves

¼ cup (60 ml) olive oil

2 green capsicums (bell peppers), cut lengthwise into flat pieces

2 red capsicums (bell peppers), cut lengthwise into flat pieces

4 burrito-size flour tortillas (20 cm/ 8 inch diameter)

1 cup (150 g) crumbled mild goat's cheese, or fetta

PREPARATION 15 minutes, plus at least 30 minutes marinating
COOKING 10 minutes
MAKES 4 servings

PER SERVING 2264 kJ, 541 kcal, 39 g protein, 33 g fat (12 g saturated fat), 24 g carbohydrate (9 g sugars), 779 mg sodium, 3 g fibre

1 Place chicken on a plate and sprinkle with ¼ cup (60 ml) of the lime juice and ½ teaspoon of the salt. Cover and refrigerate for 1 hour, or at least 30 minutes.

2 Preheat a barbecue to medium–high. In a bowl, gently toss together onion, sugar, cinnamon, cumin, cloves and ½ teaspoon of salt. Add 1 tablespoon of the oil and toss again.

3 Toss chicken with another 1 tablespoon of the oil. Place on barbecue with the onion and capsicums, 15 cm (6 inches) from the heat. Cook for the following amounts of time: barbecue chicken for 3 minutes per side, or until cooked through; barbecue onion for 4 minutes per side, or until lightly browned and crisp-tender; barbecue capsicums, skin side down, for 10 minutes, or until skin is blackened.

4 When ingredients are cool enough to handle, cut chicken lengthwise into strips; cut onion rounds in half; peel capsicums and cut into strips. Transfer to a bowl, then add remaining oil, lime juice and salt. Toss well.

5 Divide mixture evenly among the tortillas. Sprinkle with goat's cheese, roll each one up like a cone and serve.

Grilled chicken skewers with mango

2 tablespoons green jalapeño chilli sauce, such as green Tabasco

2 tablespoons olive oil

1 tablespoon lime juice

1 tablespoon brown sugar

¾ teaspoon salt

¾ teaspoon ground ginger

¼ teaspoon ground allspice

500 g (1 lb) boneless, skinless chicken breasts, cut into 32 chunks

24 red cherry tomatoes

8 spring onions (scallions), cut into quarters

1 large mango, about 425 g (15 oz), peeled and cut into chunks

1 Preheat a barbecue to medium–high. In a large bowl, whisk together chilli sauce, oil, lime juice, sugar, salt, ginger and allspice. Add chicken, tomatoes, spring onions and mango and toss well to coat. Alternately thread all the ingredients onto eight 25 cm (10 inch) skewers.

2 Barbecue the skewers 15 cm (6 inches) from the heat for 5 minutes, or until chicken is cooked through and tomatoes and mango are piping hot.

LOW FAT, QUICK
PREPARATION 20 minutes
COOKING 5 minutes
MAKES 4 servings

PER SERVING 1490 kJ, 356 kcal, 29 g protein, 17 g fat (3 g saturated fat), 23 g carbohydrate (21 g sugars), 683 mg sodium, 4 g fibre

Chicken, pineapple & bacon skewers

1 cup (250 ml) salt-free tomato sauce (ketchup)

¼ cup (60 ml) unsweetened pineapple juice

3 tablespoons strained apricot jam

2 tablespoons balsamic vinegar

¼ teaspoon salt

½ teaspoon freshly ground black pepper

½ teaspoon dried rosemary

500 g (1 lb) boneless, skinless chicken thighs, cut into 24 pieces

12 slices rindless (regular) bacon (about 200 g/7 oz), halved crosswise

1 large red capsicum (bell pepper), cut into 24 chunks

24 canned pineapple pieces

1 In a bowl, mix together tomato sauce, pineapple juice, jam, vinegar, salt, pepper and rosemary. Add chicken and toss to coat. Lift chicken out of marinade, reserving marinade. Wrap a bacon strip around each chicken piece.

2 Preheat a barbecue to medium. Alternately thread the capsicum, pineapple and bacon-wrapped chicken onto twelve 25 cm (10 inch) skewers. (Be sure to thread skewers through the overlap in the bacon so that it does not unwrap.)

3 Lightly oil the barbecue. Place skewers on barbecue and brush with half the reserved marinade. Cook for 5 to 7 minutes, or until bacon is crisp and chicken is cooked through, turning skewers halfway during cooking and brushing with remaining marinade.

LOW FAT
PREPARATION 25 minutes
COOKING 10 minutes
MAKES 4 servings

PER SERVING 1685 kJ, 403 kcal, 35 g protein, 14 g fat (4 g saturated fat), 36 g carbohydrate (35 g sugars), 1008 mg sodium, 2 g fibre

Grilled chicken skewers with mango

Lemon is such an engaging flavour and its sparkling tartness is particularly welcome in hot weather. Barbecue these colourful skewers on a warm summer evening when turning on the oven is out of the question. Serve them over steamed rice (try adding a little lemon juice to the rice cooking water).

Lemon chicken & vegetable skewers

¼ cup (60 ml) olive oil

½ teaspoon grated lemon zest

¼ cup (60 ml) lemon juice

1 teaspoon salt

½ teaspoon freshly ground black pepper

8 button mushrooms, trimmed

1 yellow capsicum (bell pepper), cut into 12 chunks

1 red capsicum (bell pepper), cut into 12 chunks

½ large red onion, cut into large chunks

500 g (1 lb) boneless, skinless chicken breasts, cut into 24 pieces

LOW FAT, QUICK
PREPARATION 20 minutes
COOKING 5 minutes
MAKES 4 servings

PER SERVING 1325 kJ, 317 kcal, 29 g protein, 21 g fat (4 g saturated fat), 4 g carbohydrate (3 g sugars), 684 mg sodium, 1 g fibre

1 Preheat a barbecue to medium–high. In a large bowl, mix together oil, lemon zest, lemon juice, salt and pepper. Add mushrooms and capsicums and toss well. Add onion and toss gently.

2 Using six 25 cm (10 inch) skewers, thread mushrooms onto one skewer, reserving mixture in bowl. Thread capsicums in alternating colours onto two more skewers, and onion on a fourth skewer.

3 Add chicken to mixture remaining in the bowl and toss well. Thread chicken onto final two skewers.

4 Place all skewers on the barbecue and cook 15 cm (6 inches) from the heat for 5 minutes, turning chicken and vegetables as they colour, until cooked through.

5 Remove chicken and vegetables from skewers and arrange on a serving platter.

Bright, tangy citrus flavours marry beautifully with tender chicken. Here we have a whole rainbow of citrus: orange, lemon and lime, sweetened with honey and spiked with garlic and chilli.

Citrus chicken skewers

500 g (1 lb) boneless, skinless chicken thighs, cut into large chunks

½ cup (125 ml) orange juice

¼ cup (60 ml) lemon juice

2 tablespoons lime juice

¼ cup (60 ml) olive oil

1 teaspoon honey

3 tablespoons chopped fresh coriander (cilantro) leaves

1 red chilli, seeded and chopped

2 cloves garlic, crushed

1 teaspoon salt

½ teaspoon freshly ground black pepper

lemon wedges, to serve

LOW FAT
PREPARATION 20 minutes,
    plus at least 2 hours marinating
COOKING 10 minutes
MAKES 4 servings

PER SERVING 1341 kJ, 320 kcal, 24 g protein, 23 g fat (5 g saturated fat), 5 g carbohydrate (5 g sugars), 721 mg sodium, <1 g fibre

1 Thread chicken onto eight small skewers (if using bamboo skewers, soak them in water for 30 minutes beforehand, so they don't burn). Place in a non-reactive dish.

2 In a large bowl, mix together orange juice, lemon juice, lime juice, oil, honey, coriander, chilli, garlic, salt and pepper. Pour over the skewers, cover and marinate in the refrigerator for up to 8 hours, or at least 2 hours, turning occasionally.

3 Preheat a barbecue to medium–high. Barbecue skewers for 2 minutes on each side, or until chicken is cooked through. Serve with lemon wedges.

As an alternative to wooden skewers you can use long, flat metal skewers with handles (or a loop at one end) —food is less likely to slip off these than round skewers. Have a pot of steamed rice on hand when the barbecued goodies are ready and slide each portion off the skewers, onto a waiting bed of fluffy rice.

Spicy skewered chicken & prawns

2 teaspoons ground paprika

1½ teaspoons dried oregano

1 teaspoon chilli powder

1 teaspoon sugar

¾ teaspoon salt

½ teaspoon cayenne pepper

½ teaspoon garlic powder

350 g (12 oz) boneless, skinless chicken breasts, cut into 32 chunks

16 (about 500 g/1 lb) raw prawns (shrimp), peeled and deveined

1 yellow capsicum (bell pepper), cut into 16 chunks

1 red capsicum (bell pepper), cut into 16 chunks

1 red onion, cut into 16 chunks (optional)

2 tablespoons olive oil

LOW FAT, QUICK
PREPARATION 25 minutes
COOKING 5 minutes
MAKES 4 servings

PER SERVING 1517 kJ, 362 kcal, 45 g protein, 16 g fat (3 g saturated fat), 7 g carbohydrate (4 g sugars), 702 mg sodium, 1 g fibre

1 Preheat a barbecue to medium–high. In a large bowl, mix together paprika, oregano, chilli powder, sugar, salt, cayenne pepper and garlic powder. Add chicken and prawns and toss well to coat.

2 In a separate bowl, gently toss capsicums and onion with the oil.

3 Soak 8 wooden skewers in cold water for at least 30 minutes, to prevent scorching.

4 Alternately thread chicken, prawns, capsicums and onion, if using, onto the skewers.

5 Barbecue the skewers 15 cm (6 inches) from the heat for 5 minutes, or until chicken and prawns are cooked through, turning skewers halfway during cooking.

These delicious wraps are made with lavash (a soft Middle-Eastern bread sold in large rounds or rectangles). The easiest way is to carry the foil-wrapped rolls to the picnic whole, then cut them once you've settled in your picnic spot.

Chicken & basil pinwheels

I clove garlic, peeled

¾ cup (185 g) cream cheese, at room temperature

⅓ cup (80 g) bottled roasted red capsicums (bell peppers), drained

3 tablespoons fresh basil

½ teaspoon salt

2 rounds soft flat bread (30 cm/12 inch diameter), such as lavash

3 cups (450 g) shredded cooked chicken breasts or thighs—leftover or poached (see Basics)

I cup (125 g) grated mild white cheddar (or Monterey Jack cheese)

½ cup (95 g) kalamata olives, pitted and chopped

LOW FAT
PREPARATION 15 minutes, plus
    at least 4 hours chilling
COOKING 5 minutes
MAKES 16 pieces

PER SERVING 539 kJ, 129 kcal, 12 g protein,
8 g fat (4 g saturated fat), 2 g carbohydrate
(<1 g sugars), 305 mg sodium, <1 g fibre

1 In a small pot of boiling water, blanch garlic for 2 minutes; drain and place in a food processor or blender. Add cream cheese, roasted capsicums, basil and salt and process until smooth.

2 Spread mixture onto one side of each bread round. Sprinkle chicken, cheese and olives on top. Tightly roll up each bread round, then wrap in foil and refrigerate for at least 4 hours.

3 To serve, unwrap each roll and cut into 8 pinwheels.

Chicken & green bean frittata

225 g (8 oz) green beans, sliced

2 tablespoons olive oil

1 small onion, finely chopped

¾ teaspoon salt

6 large eggs, lightly beaten

⅓ cup (35 g) grated parmesan

½ teaspoon freshly ground black pepper

1½ cups (225 g) shredded cooked chicken
    breasts or thighs—leftover or poached
    (see Basics)

LOW FAT

PREPARATION 10 minutes
COOKING 25 minutes
MAKES 4 servings

PER SERVING 1529 kJ, 365 kcal, 32 g protein,
26 g fat (7 g saturated fat), 2 g carbohydrate
(1 g sugars), 752 mg sodium, 2 g fibre

1 In a large pot of boiling salted water, blanch green beans for
4 minutes; drain well. Meanwhile, in a large ovenproof frying pan,
heat 1 tablespoon of the oil over low heat. Add onion and sauté
for 7 minutes, or until tender. Add green beans and ¼ teaspoon
of the salt and cook for 3 minutes, or until tender. Cool slightly.

2 In a large bowl, whisk together eggs, all but 1 tablespoon of
the parmesan, the pepper and remaining salt. Stir in chicken and
green bean mixture.

3 Add remaining oil to the frying pan and heat over medium heat.
Pour in the egg mixture, reduce heat to low and cook, without
stirring, for 12 minutes, or until the egg is set around the edges
and almost set in the centre.

4 Preheat a barbecue, with the rack 20 cm (8 inches) from the
heat. Sprinkle remaining parmesan over egg mixture and barbecue
for 1 to 2 minutes, until set and slightly browned. Run a metal
spatula around frittata to loosen it, then slide onto a platter.
Cut into wedges to serve.

The compelling aroma of onions and homemade Italian-style chicken sausages sizzling on the barbecue will draw the whole family outside. These rolls are perfect for an informal backyard barbecue when things heat up in the kitchen and cooking seems a chore.

Chicken sausages on a roll

500 g (1 lb) minced (ground) chicken

½ cup (30 g) chopped fresh parsley

½ cup (75 g) oil-packed sun-dried tomatoes, finely chopped

½ cup (50 g) grated parmesan

1 slice firm-textured white bread, crumbled

1 teaspoon fennel seeds

¼ teaspoon freshly ground black pepper

½ teaspoon salt

2 tablespoons olive oil

1 large red onion, thickly sliced

2 green capsicums (bell peppers), cut into matchsticks

1 red capsicum (bell pepper), cut into matchsticks

2 teaspoons red wine vinegar

4 bread rolls, split

LOW FAT
PREPARATION 25 minutes
COOKING 15 minutes
MAKES 4 servings

PER SERVING 2421 kJ, 578 kcal, 39 g protein, 26 g fat (7 g saturated fat), 47 g carbohydrate (8 g sugars), 1020 mg sodium, 5 g fibre

1 To make chicken sausages, put the chicken, parsley, sun-dried tomatoes, parmesan, bread, fennel seeds, pepper and ¼ teaspoon of the salt in a large bowl. Mix together until well combined. With moistened hands, shape mixture into 8 cigar-shaped sausages. Refrigerate until required.

2 Preheat a barbecue to medium and lightly brush with oil. Barbecue the onion and capsicums for 5 minutes, turning often, until onion is golden brown and capsicums are tender. Transfer to a bowl, then add vinegar and remaining salt. Toss well, cover and keep warm.

3 Barbecue the sausages for 10 minutes, or until cooked through, turning them frequently. Cut in half on the diagonal.

4 Spoon capsicum mixture and sausages over cut rolls and serve.

The pride of New Orleans, the muffaletta is a family-sized sandwich made from a great big round loaf of crusty bread. The loaf is split like a gargantuan hamburger bun and filled with generous portions of ham, salami, provolone and pickled garden vegetables.

Chicken muffaletta

1 large round country bread loaf (20 cm/8 inch diameter), halved horizontally

1 clove garlic, peeled and halved

2 tablespoons olive oil

1 cup (175 g) pimiento-stuffed olives, chopped

1 stalk celery, quartered lengthwise and thinly sliced

1 red capsicum (bell pepper), finely chopped

2 cooked boneless, skinless chicken breast halves, thinly sliced crosswise—leftover or poached (see Basics)

125 g (4 oz) thinly sliced provolone cheese

175 g (6 oz) thinly sliced skinless smoked chicken (or turkey)

125 g (4 oz) thinly sliced, good-quality lean ham

350 g (12 oz) jar of pickled garden vegetables, drained and chopped

LOW FAT

PREPARATION 30 minutes, plus
    at least 6 hours chilling

MAKES 8 servings

PER SERVING 1505 kJ, 360 kcal, 33 g protein, 19 g fat (6 g saturated fat), 8 g carbohydrate (6 g sugars), 1048 mg sodium, 2 g fibre

1 With your fingers, starting 1 cm (½ inch) from edge of loaf, remove and discard 2.5 cm (1 inch) of bread dough from the bottom half of the loaf. Rub cut garlic clove over inside of bottom half; discard garlic. Brush oil over inside of loaf.

2 In a bowl, mix together olives, celery and capsicum, then spoon into bottom of loaf. Layer chicken breast, provolone, smoked chicken and ham on top. Spoon pickled vegetables on top of meats. Replace top of loaf.

3 Wrap loaf in foil. Place on a large plate and set a heavy weight on top. Refrigerate overnight, or for at least 6 hours.

4 To serve, unwrap muffaletta and cut into 8 wedges.

Pita—Middle-Eastern pocket bread—is a convenient container for a take-anywhere meal. For a refreshing change from mayonnaise-dressed salads, try this mixture of diced chicken and fresh herbs in a basil-scented lemon dressing.

Lemon-basil chicken in pita pockets

1 teaspoon grated lemon zest

¼ cup (60 ml) lemon juice

¼ cup (60 ml) olive oil

1 teaspoon dijon mustard

¼ teaspoon salt

¼ teaspoon freshly ground black pepper

¾ cup (45 g) finely chopped fresh basil

3 tablespoons finely chopped fresh parsley

3 spring onions (scallions), thinly sliced

2 tablespoons capers, rinsed and
    squeezed dry

3 cups (450 g) finely diced cooked chicken
    breasts or thighs—leftover or poached
    (see Basics)

4 sandwich-sized pita (15 cm/6 inch
    diameter)

LOW FAT, QUICK
PREPARATION 25 minutes
MAKES 4 servings

PER SERVING 2322 kJ, 555 kcal, 39 g protein,
25 g fat (5 g saturated fat), 44 g carbohydrate
(3 g sugars), 742 mg sodium, 3 g fibre

1 In a large bowl, whisk together lemon zest, lemon juice, oil, mustard, salt and pepper. Add basil, parsley, spring onions and capers and stir to combine. Add chicken and toss to coat.

2 Refrigerate chicken salad until required; pack chicken and pita breads separately.

3 To serve, make a cut in one side of each pita bread and spoon chicken salad into bread. Serve immediately.

The thick, chewy bread called focaccia is traditionally baked with minimal toppings—herbs, sea salt or just a sprinkling of good olive oil. In Italy, a slice of focaccia is a popular snack, but thick slabs of this rustic bread also make wonderfully hearty sandwiches. Look for focaccia at your supermarket or at an Italian bakery.

Pesto chicken on focaccia

PESTO

1 clove garlic, peeled

½ cup (25 g) firmly packed fresh basil

¼ cup (25 g) grated parmesan

1½ tablespoons olive oil

2 tablespoons slivered almonds

¼ teaspoon salt

1 round 225 g (8 oz) focaccia (25 cm/10 inch diameter)

2 cups (80 g) mesclun (mixed salad greens)

2 cooked boneless, skinless chicken breast halves, thinly sliced crosswise on the diagonal—leftover or poached (see Basics)

½ cup (100 g) bottled roasted red capsicums (bell peppers), drained well and cut into thin strips

LOW FAT, QUICK
PREPARATION 15 minutes
MAKES 4 servings

PER SERVING 1242 kJ, 297 kcal, 13 g protein, 15 g fat (3 g saturated fat), 27 g carbohydrate (3 g sugars), 642 mg sodium, 3 g fibre

1 To make the pesto, blanch garlic in a small saucepan of boiling water for 1 minute. Drain and transfer to a food processor or blender. Add basil, parmesan, oil, almonds, salt and 2 tablespoons water and process until smooth.

2 Slice focaccia in half horizontally. Spread pesto evenly on both halves. Top with mesclun, chicken and roasted capsicums, then the other focaccia half.

3 Wrap in foil and refrigerate until required. To serve, cut into 4 wedges.

For this tempting picnic treat, soft flat bread is filled with a spiral of colourful fillings: basil-cheese spread, smoked chicken and roasted red capsicums. Another great combination to try is crumbled fetta mixed with cream cheese, some lemon zest, lemon juice and fresh chopped dill and mint.

Chicken & vegetable wraps

2 tablespoons olive oil

3 cloves garlic, crushed

2 golden zucchini (courgette) or yellow summer squash, about 175 g (6 oz) each, halved crosswise, then thinly sliced lengthwise

225 g (8 oz) reduced-fat cream cheese, at room temperature

½ cup (25 g) fresh basil

¼ cup (25 g) grated parmesan

4 rectangles soft flat bread, such as lavash (28 x 23 cm/11 x 9 inches)

225 g (8 oz) thinly sliced smoked chicken (or turkey)

350 g (12 oz) jar roasted red capsicums (bell peppers), drained well and cut into wide strips

LOW FAT

PREPARATION 25 minutes, plus
    at least 1 hour chilling
COOKING 10 minutes
MAKES 4 servings

PER SERVING 2129 kJ, 509 kcal, 31 g protein, 23 g fat (6 g saturated fat), 44 g carbohydrate (7 g sugars), 795 mg sodium, 4 g fibre

1 In a large frying pan, heat oil over medium–low heat. Add garlic and cook for 1 minute. Add zucchini, sprinkle with salt and cook, tossing occasionally, for 5 minutes, or until very soft. Set aside to cool slightly.

2 In a food processor or blender, combine cream cheese, basil and parmesan, then process until smooth.

3 Dividing evenly, spread cream cheese mixture over flat breads, leaving a 1 cm (½ inch) border all around. Layer chicken slices over cream cheese. Top with capsicum strips and zucchini.

4 Tightly roll flat breads, starting from a short end. Wrap in foil and refrigerate for up to 8 hours, or for at least 1 hour.

5 To serve, unwrap and cut each wrap in half on the diagonal.

Index

Quick & Low Fat recipes

Notes on the recipes

Alternative terms and substitutes

Some ingredients and cooking utensils are known by different names in different countries. Here are some alternative names for ingredients and utensils used in this book.

- **baking tray** baking sheet
- **capsicum (bell pepper)** sweet peppers
- **corn cob** mealie/mielie
- **eggplant** aubergine, brinjal
- **oregano** oreganum
- **papaya** pawpaw
- **rockmelon (cantaloupe)** spanspek
- **fresh shiitake mushrooms** rehydrated dried shiitake mushrooms
- **salt-reduced** low-sodium
- **Swiss brown mushrooms** brown mushrooms
- **thin rice noodles** rice vermicelli

Weights and measures

Sometimes conversions within a recipe are not exact but are the closest conversion that is a suitable measurement for each system. Use either the metric or the imperial measurements; do not mix the two systems.

All cup and spoon measurements are level unless stated otherwise. Australian cup and spoon measurements have been used throughout; 1 cup equals 250 ml, 1 tablespoon equals 20 ml and 1 teaspoon equals 5 ml. Imperial cup and spoon measures are smaller – 1 cup is 235 ml (8 fl oz) and 1 tablespoon is 15 ml (½ fl oz) – so if you are using these measures, some adjustments may need to be made.

Can sizes

Can sizes vary between countries and manufacturers; if the stated size is unavailable, use the nearest equivalent.

Here are the metric and imperial measurements for can sizes used in this book: 225 g = 8 oz; 300 g = 10 oz; 350 g = 12 oz; 400/410 g = 14 oz; 400 ml = 400 fl oz.

The Great Chicken Cookbook

PROJECT EDITOR Katri Hilden
DESIGNER Kylie Mulquin
COPY EDITOR Kirsten Colvin
NUTRITIONAL ANALYSIS Toni Gumley
PROOFREADER Susan McCreery
INDEXER Diane Harriman
SENIOR PRODUCTION CONTROLLER Monique Tesoriero
EDITORIAL PROJECT MANAGER GENERAL BOOKS Deborah Nixon

READER'S DIGEST GENERAL BOOKS
EDITORIAL DIRECTOR Elaine Russell
MANAGING EDITOR Rosemary McDonald
ART DIRECTOR Carole Orbell

The Great Chicken Cookbook is published by Reader's Digest (Australia) Pty Limited
80 Bay Street, Ultimo NSW 2007
www.readersdigest.com.au
www.readersdigest.co.nz
www.readersdigest.co.za

First published 2010

National Library of Australia Cataloguing-in-Publication entry
Title: The great chicken cookbook: a feast of simple, delicious recipes for every occasion.
   ISBN: 978-1-921743-19-1 (hbk)
   ISBN: 978-1-921743-33-7 (pbk)
   ISBN: 978-1-60652-211-0 (hbk, US and Canada)
   Notes: Includes index.
   Subjects: Cookery (Chicken)
   Other Authors/Contributors: Reader's Digest (Australia)
Dewey Number: 641.665

Prepress by Sinnott Bros, Sydney
Printed and bound by Leo Paper Products, China

We are interested in receiving your comments on the contents of this book. Write to: The Editor, General Books Editorial, Reader's Digest (Australia) Pty Limited, GPO Box 4353, Sydney, NSW 2001, or email us at bookeditors.au@readersdigest.com

To order additional copies of *The Great Chicken Cookbook*, please contact us as follows:
www.readersdigest.com.au, 1300 300 030 (Australia);
www.readersdigest.co.nz, 0800 400 060 (New Zealand);
www.readersdigest.co.za, 0800 980 572 (South Africa)
or email us at customerservice@readersdigest.com.au

PHOTOGRAPHY CREDITS
Cover photograph: Baked chicken with avocado relish, page 266.

Photographs: pages 68, 114, 128, 131, 143, 159, 172, 175, 178, 183, 197, 203, 204, 207, 209, 241, 242, 253, 267, 299, 304, cover: photographer André Martin (stylist Grace Campbell, food preparation Gabrielle Wheatley)

All illustrations are the copyright of Reader's Digest, except for the following.
Background pattern: Shutterstock/Olga Drozdova, page 8: iStockphoto/1Photodiva.

Book code: UK 1226
Product codes:
041-4113 (hbk), 041-4192 (pbk)